Haslam's Valley

HASLAM'S VALLEY

Gerald Haslam

Heyday Books, Berkeley, California
Great Valley Books

Heyday Books, founded in 1974, works to deepen people's understanding and appreciation of the cultural, artistic, historic, and natural resources of California and the American West. It operates under a 501(c)(3) nonprofit educational organization (Heyday Institute) and, in addition to publishing books, sponsors a wide range of programs, outreach, and events.

To help support Heyday or to learn more about us, visit our website at www.heydaybooks.com, or write to us at P.O. Box 9145, Berkeley, CA 94709.

Library of Congress Cataloging-in-Publication Data

Haslam, Gerald W.
  Haslam's valley / Gerald Haslam.
     p. cm.
  "A Great Valley book."
  ISBN 1-59714-018-X (pbk. : alk. paper)
  1. Central Valley (Calif. : Valley)--Fiction. 2. Haslam, Gerald W.-- Homes and haunts--California--Central Valley (Valley) 3. Central Valley (Calif. : Valley) I. Title.
  PS3558.A724H36 2005
  813'.54--dc22
                                          2005019778
Cover Art: Chee Chin S. Cheung Lee, "The Valley," 1943. Watercolor, 14.5 x 21.5 in. Collection of Michael D. Brown.
Cover Design: Rebecca LeGates
Interior Design/Typesetting: Lorraine Rath
Printing and Binding: McNaughton & Gunn, Saline, MI

Orders, inquiries, and correspondence should be addressed to:
      Heyday Books
      P. O. Box 9145, Berkeley, CA 94709
      (510) 549-3564, Fax (510) 549-1889
      www.heydaybooks.com

Printed in the United States of America

10 9 8 7 6 5 4 3 2 1

Contents

Essays

Acknowledgments

Special thanks to William E. Justice, Zak Nelson, Malcolm Margolin, and the rest of the Heyday gang for their help. Also, thanks to earlier editors or mentors: Clark Sturgis, Art Cuelho, Eddie Lopez, Ann Ronald, Kirk Robertson, Tom Radko, Gib Smith, Caroline Shrodes, Dick Bratset, Don Hayakawa, Alexandra Haslam, Max Westbrook, W. H. Hutchinson, Larry Press, Jim Clark, Tom Wittenberg, Margaret Dalrymple, and Nick Cady.

Introduction

AN OLDER BLACK MAN NAMED JOE WASHINGTON used to appear in Oildale periodically, walking door-to-door seeking work. My mother hired him to wash windows or mow the lawn, and always gave him lunch along with whatever small salary he requested. One day he entered the Tejon Club, the nearby pool hall where my dad and other oil workers gathered for beer. Mr. Washington was asking the proprietor if he had any jobs for him when a young rowdy called down the bar, "No niggers allowed in here, Rastus. Hit the road!"

The owner, a slim man named Al, reached under the counter and extracted his attitude adjuster, a sawed-off pool cue covered with friction tape, and Mr. Washington flinched. He needn't have, because Al turned toward the big-mouth and said, "Get your ass outta here, you lazy bastard. This guy come in for a job of work. He's not slurpin' beer in the middle of the day. And don't come back!"

My dad, who told me that story, saw no inconsistency in Oildale's racism and Al's action. "Hell, that guy was lookin' for a job," he said. Work was sacred to those survivors of the Great Depression, and they passed that message on to their children.

A combination of conviviality and bigotry characterized the neighborhood in which I grew up, the latter emerging only occasionally. Oildale, my hometown, was a blue-collar enclave of hardworking white folks, many of them Southwestern migrants, reflecting the de facto racial and class segregation that characterized the Bakersfield area (and much of the state) then. It was enjoyable growing up there and I remain amazed at how many kids who did went on to become successful. At last offered something like equal opportunity in California, they responded with ambition and ability.

On the other hand, the racial and economic barriers in the Bakersfield area—especially in the benign guise of neighborhood boundaries and school districting—created segregation that led to ignorance and distrust of one another, and that in turn inhibited democracy and spawned all sorts of silly stereotypes: Okies were stupid; blacks were lazy; Chinese could sure do laundry; Mexicans excelled at knife fights; Japanese were natural gardeners; Jews were shysters...and on and on. In America of the mid-1950s, racism was rampant and undisguised, social class was often as limiting as race, and women could not aspire to many jobs open to men. If you happened to be nonwhite, lower-class, and female, your options were really limited.

There was even said to have been in Oildale a billboard proclaiming "Nigger, don't let the sun set on you here." There had never been such a sign, of course, but even among many of our otherwise wonderful neighbors that statement reflected a common attitude. There had also never been a synagogue or mosque or "papist" church, but there were plentiful Pentecostal congregations. More than a few neighbors expressed reservations about Jews and Catholics. No one even mentioned Moslems.

My elementary school classes in Oildale were full of kids just like me—white, working-class, many Southwestern migrants, often desperately ambitious. In the seventh grade I was sent to a Catholic school in nearby Bakersfield. On its campus were kids of many races, and all economic levels could be found. At first I found myself the victim of stereotyping—"Oildale Okie"—of the same kind that nonwhites suffered locally, and that made me question all the silly stuff I'd been hearing ("If you fight a spade, kick him in the shins; they can't take it there"). I soon learned how inaccurate such nonsense was as a result of athletics, of dating, of partying, of working, and even of fighting with different kinds and colors of kids—who turned out not to be very different at all. That, in turn, led me to recognize that the America I would soon enter as an adult was no more than a work in progress. I was a student journalist then, and I decided that if good people burdened by negative stereotypes could see the way they were behaving, they'd correct themselves. I began to write about that in the 1950s.

By 1955 I had become a stringer for several newspapers. Contrary to widely accepted legend, the mid-fifties were not necessarily happy days. I was part of a transitional generation about as good or bad as any other, shaped by the events and opportunities of our time, particularly by the dynamics of post–World War II California, then in the midst of a stunning transformation. By the mid-fifties, it was a distinctly different place from what it had been pre-1941, except that in the Great Central Valley agribusiness still required a population poor enough to provide seasonal farm labor.

Most Dust Bowl migrants had moved up and out thanks to the economic acceleration of World War II, but Mexicans and blacks and Filipinos were often stranded in poverty. They would rarely be considered for better jobs in the oil fields or building trades, let alone the professions, so they often ended up surviving (and sometimes not surviving) on seasonal farm labor and welfare in the off-season; the latter was used as an excuse for not offering them better opportunities. I had for many years done part-time farm labor to pick up spending money, and my last season of working in a packing shed— 1958—there were no nonwhites doing the cushy jobs like hand-trucking, but plenty among the spiders and wasps in the parched fields. My last year in the oil fields was 1963; no non-whites or women held jobs there when I did because it was believed to be white-men's work.

I did meet many heroes during those years: a physician who treated poor Mexican families without billing them and did so well after his retirement ("I've been given some mighty good homemade tamales," he once told me); a widowed migrant mother from Missouri who toiled in an elementary school cafeteria to put four kids through school, never complaining or seeking assistance; the white principal of a mostly black school who simply refused to allow anyone to treat his students as second-class citizens. Most of all, I met brave people mired in poverty who wouldn't give up hope, even in the face of systemic barriers to upward mobility.

Despite all the complaints I hear about present-day society, I can't consider the 1950s a better time. Many of us had no television sets at home—and that was positive—but we did attend movies and listen to radios. We responded to new (to us) music: rhythm and blues, rockabilly, rock and roll. Cars and drive-in movies changed dating practices and, to a degree, mores. We were by no means all chaste. Fistfighting was epidemic as the social order churned and young men sought to establish themselves; two of my Oildale schoolmates went to prison for stomping a kid to death in an uneven fight.

A smoldering local resentment about how society was changing was revealed when a former Bakersfield boy named Earl Warren, Chief Justice of the United States Supreme Court, helped end racial segregation in schools; "Impeach Earl Warren" signs soon outnumbered "US Out of UN" placards in Kern County. We were also being assured that some people were poor because they were inferior or lazy; the implication was that it was okay not to offer them opportunities. As for health, many local children were still being crippled by polio, although that was about to stop thanks to Jonas Salk, who as a Jew wouldn't have been welcome in many local social organizations. Nevertheless we thought we were safe because the USA had four thousand nuclear weapons (possibly enough to destroy all life on earth) while the Soviet Union had one thousand (only enough to destroy much life on earth).

My home area had plenty of warts, yet I loved it. Our neighbors really were like extended family. In those days before air conditioners, neighbors would water their lawns and chat most early evenings while kids clattered up and down the block on skates or homemade scooters. The town itself wasn't scenic, but I grew up appreciating the mornings and the smell of crude oil that penetrated everything; I thought the rest of the world suffered from bland air. I also treasured the nearby Kern River and its riparian forest. And, of course, I grew to love the goofy gang of Mexicans, blacks, and Anglos I ran around with…Raymie, Duke, Ernie, Tom, Terry, Tiger, Choosie, Quincy, Manuel, and the rest.

They always offered rough therapy. After suffering a humiliating defeat in a junior-college boxing tournament, I was drinking beer with those guys when the phone rang. Raymie answered and after a minute or so he called, "Haslam! It's my little sister. She wants to know if she can be your next opponent." Before I could respond, Tiger said, "Tell her no. She'll kill him."

After a high school football game, I recall our coach asking, "How'd that guy catch you, Haslam?"

"He had the angle," I replied, only to be trumped by a Chicano teammate who said, "You mean he had the Anglo… slow, white *pendejo.*"

In late 1957, after I lost my first love, then flunked out of college, I felt as though my world had fallen apart. I was moping around the house in Oildale when a car carrying four African American friends, fellow jocks, pulled in front of our house. They proceeded to tease me, buck me up, urge me to get back into the fray. After they departed, several neighbors approached my mother and said with wonder something like, "Well, I've never seen anything like that before." While curious, no one had called the cops or armed themselves. My hometown was changing…however slowly.

By the end of that decade I was a soldier and, from other GIs, I learned that my section of the Golden State wasn't considered very golden. In fact, it wasn't considered at all. Guys from elsewhere, who expressed great interest in California, simply didn't recognize the existence of much beyond Hollywood, beaches, the Golden Gate, and maybe Yosemite. That came as a great shock to me, since the Oildale/Bakersfield area then remained for me the umbilicus of the world.

A couple of years later, discharged and married, I moved to San Francisco, where I was denied admission to the creative writing program at the state college. As a result, I had to teach myself, arising every morning before classes or work to struggle at composing a page or two—perhaps just a paragraph or a sentence—and reading omnivorously during every spare moment. My plan then was to become a teacher so I could find at least some time to continue learning how to write.

As it turned out, I eventually earned enough degrees to be hired at a newly opened state college to the north in Sonoma County. All the while I continued my daily writing routine, discovering that it was too late to be Mark Twain or Flannery O'Connor or Ernest Hemingway: those roles had already been filled.

Finally, in the mid-1960s three events occurred that opened my eyes to what should have been obvious all along. First, I read a book, *The Hawk's Done Gone and Other Stories* by Mildred Hahn, and recognized how she'd employed localized settings and characters and a degree of magic to achieve startling fictions. That led me to reread masters I'd earlier enjoyed but hadn't well understood. They now seemed to me to transcend regional material precisely because they employed it so effectively: William Faulkner, Katherine Anne Porter, William Saroyan, Robinson Jeffers, Jorge Luis Borges, John Steinbeck, and, of course, O'Connor.

Second, I realized that the violent events I saw playing out on news coverage of civil rights demonstrations in the South were the logical products of attitudes still openly expressed in my home area: "If some people don't know their place, we'll just have to teach 'em." After having served with soldiers of all colors from all regions, I didn't see how America could justify its existence if it didn't live up to its creed—Thomas Jefferson's aristocracy of worth, not aristocracy of birth being a particular goal. Everyone deserved an equal chance to rise or fall, and that chance was still being denied whole populations of people who were equal enough to die in our wars.

I had by then become a disciplined and determined writer but not polished or original. In 1967 I showed an imitative story to a colleague at Sonoma State named Dorothy Overly, who knew me and my home area well because she had a decade before been my freshman composition teacher at

Bakersfield Junior College. Dorothy said simply, "You need to write about people and places you really know, and use their voices. That area's interesting...and a little strange. Just like you."

She was right on both counts. How many Californians had ever heard the pusher on a collapsing oil rig shout, "Get your head out of your ass and do somethin'...even if it's wrong"? How many ever saw Holy Rollers literally roll in a tent on a neighborhood vacant lot? How many ever heard an old vaquero tell of seeing La Llorona shimmering across the Carrizo Plain? I'd even forgotten how few folks I'd encountered away from my hometown who had ever fallen into a vat of corrosive sublimate solution while dipping seed potatoes or been physically attacked at a restaurant table for the crime of dining with a black friend. I had plenty of material to write about.

In fact, the cast of potential characters and dramatic situations began to seem endless and heaven-sent. About then I also noticed that Robert Duncan and Buck Owens, Merle Haggard and Frank Bidart, William Rintoul and Mary Austin had found plenty in Kern County to write about. The problem wasn't the area; the problem was me.

I began to look more closely at the physical environment and saw things I should have noticed long before. Just north of where I had grown up, I realized, lay a maimed environment, the bed of the largest freshwater lake in the West, now dried, plowed, and irrigated: what had happened? On the prairie where I had daily dallied, tule elk and pronghorn antelope had once pranced away from grizzlies and wolves. In the foothills to which I biked, Yokuts had built their shelters and raised their families. And of course, the real Dust Bowl migrants of whom John Steinbeck wrote were my neighbors and kin. There was far more to write about than could be accomplished in one lifetime.

I went to work, not interested in local color, but struggling to draw upon local characters and situations to achieve a degree of universality. The first of those efforts was a story about class prejudice called "The Doll." It may have read as though it had been fished from deep in O'Connor's reject bin, but it was an honest effort. I began filling pocket notebooks and assorted scratch paper with observations of events, of folks, even of locutions—a habit I still practice—and to employ those bits in stories. The more I wrote, the more I discovered how much I had to write about.

I finally assembled some early stories into a collection called *Okies* in 1971; it gained an honorable mention in the Joseph Henry Jackson Award competition that year…not much perhaps, but all the encouragement I needed. For more than three decades I wrote stories and essays rather than full-length books. Due to demands of work or study or family— five kids by then—I could usually find time and concentration for only shorter bursts of creativity. Those short pieces allowed me to experiment with styles and voices and perspectives.

Over those years, I tried to never say no to an idea that might be a story or essay, and I tried to imagine as many configurations of reality as I could. My reading of Latin American, African, and American Indian stories as well as European and American tales opened me to stylistic possibilities and perspectives I had not previously considered, allowing me to see California anew.

As a result, my own stories and essays and books have been much shaped by the world of literature as well as by my personal California—inland, rural, working-class, multiethnic. It harbors no movie stars, no beaches, no redwoods, but has an abundance of tenacious people of all colors, as well as miles and miles of farm and ranch land, rich oil fields, and communities churning with desperation, joy, passion, and hope, or the hope of hope. Pretty? Not generally. Rich? For a few. Interesting? Oh yeah.

In my heart, in the deepest part of me where I really live, I remain very much a product of my family and my region. Occasionally well-intended friends have suggested that I write about other places and other people, expand my vistas and perhaps my audience. Well, I tried that and I found that the Great Valley grasped my innards like tree roots wrapping rocks, around and through so that it is difficult for me to tell if one exists independent of the other. I have, moreover, come to believe that consequential art must be particular in order to be true.

As a result, my stories are about individual characters who may suggest larger meanings but who are not generalizations. I want those creations to be faithful to their times and places and to the human condition, and to be distinct. If that is accomplished, I'm satisfied.

In the mid-1980s, I began composing nonfiction books about what I called the "Other California," principally but not exclusively California's Great Central Valley. I'm convinced that anything that can be achieved writing elsewhere can be achieved in the Other California, although my own abilities may not be up to it. The region is sufficient.

Having been born in what was then considered an out-of-the-way section of the state now seems to me to have been my great good fortune. I'm especially grateful to have been raised when and where I was because my life stretches from the Great Depression (and a relationship with great-grand-parents who were born during the Civil War) to what I call the Great Expression, today's electronic explosion (and a rela-tionship with my own grandchildren).

My earliest specific memories, though, are not of a place at all but of a person, my mother, Lorraine, reading to me, and she is almost certainly the person most directly responsible for my literary desires. Another, less specific series of recollections hovers there too. An only child, I was until my teens also an only grandchild, so family attention became the lively back-ground in my life. I don't ever remember having been lonely. I grew up sensing I was an extension of my great-grand-parents, my grandparents, my parents, my aunts, my uncles…a comforting sensation indeed. Today, on the near edge of dotage, living in a three-generation household similar to one in which I was raised, I still feel the support of a large family—now cousins, kids, and grandkids—as well as pals who care far more about my well-being than about my degrees or publica-tions or awards.

Ironically, once my work began to gain a few honors I

learned another lesson about being an author. Suddenly pieces
that had been rejected a decade or two earlier became pub-
lishable. Apparently they had ripened in my file cabinet like
fine cabernet sauvignon and emerged richer. I'm glad they
did, because I certainly haven't. Age has brought me chal-
lenges that, in turn, I've been able to turn into novels and stories. It has also delivered some perspective on how we individuals fit into the continuum of life.

For me the continuum began in 1937, and my family was
well established in the Golden State; it was also by then
already culturally and ethnically blended. As my Uncle Willie
used to chant to bedevil one of his sisters, a card-carrying
member of the Native Daughters of the Golden West,

The miners came in '49,
the whores in '51,
and between the two of them,
they made the native son.

By no means were all those miners or all those whores
white. Nor was my family. My California heritage began
when my great-great-grandparents, Ricardo Terrill and
Ramona Botella, migrated north from Mexico in the 1850s
and settled at Rancho Tejon. My mother, who was raised by
her grandmother, Ricardo and Ramona's daughter Esperanza,
recalled that after that tart-tongued lady scorched her husband, Grandpa Joe, José Castillo, he would histrionically
declare *"Adiós! Voy a volver a Chihuahua!"* and storm away.
He'd usually *voy a* the nearby saloon and creep back home
later and a little the worse for wear.

In a tangle of generations and marriages, Terrills and
Haslams and Martins would encounter Silveiras and Johnsons
and Pettichords, Planks and Castillos and Carrs…an ethnic
stew that reflected this state's growth and heterogeneity.
Despite my own Texas-born father, our tribe is now seven
generations in California, and we have blood relatives with
roots in every continent except Antarctica…no penguins.

In truth, the question of to which ethnic or cultural or

religious group I should be assigned has always seemed silly. What I am as an individual—son, father, husband, pal, or even jerk—seems infinitely more important, just as each individual work I publish must stand on its own or fail without reference to earlier successes, real or imagined.

It's also seemed silly to me that in the Great Central Valley as in the nation, in the twenty-first century, equality of opportunity still doesn't exist. Our nation fights wars abroad for principles we don't necessarily observe at home. As an ex-soldier, that offends me; as an American, it offends me even more. We can do better.

I, on the other hand, have had plenty of chances, but I would never have stretched my thin talent so far had I not married someone who not only tolerated my desire to write but encouraged it, and who also became my editor and my dogged first reader—my co-author to a greater degree than even she understands—and who never made demands that would have interfered with my learning process. Jan remains the best mistake I ever made.

April 2005, Penngrove, California

FICTION

The Doll

MRS. HOLLIS SAW THEM WALKING up her driveway toward the front porch, two ragged boys holding hands, the larger pulling the smaller. Okies, she thought, from the camp in Riverview; I wonder what they want, walking so boldly in a respectable neighborhood. Something really ought to be done about them. A person didn't know what to expect next. Just yesterday a skinny, one-legged man had knocked at her door and tried to sell her a can of salve; before that it had been another scrawny man trying to sell garden seeds. Lord, they were spreading into nice neighborhoods like vermin. They'd be wanting to move in next.

Before the boys reached her front steps Mrs. Hollis walked heavily into the doorway and talked through the screen: "Yes?" she said.

The day was oppressively hot, even in the shade of the porch, but the Okies stopped in full sunlight on the front lawn. The larger boy, lean with dirty-looking yellow hair that contrasted with his deeply sun-browned skin, answered in a flat nasal voice: "Lookin' fer work, lady. Kin we mow yer lawn er anythang?"

Although her lawn was indeed shaggy, she didn't want this drippy-nosed Okie near her any longer than necessary. "Well, I haven't got anything for you boys to do, and I doubt if anyone in this neighborhood does," she replied curtly, feeling an immediate rush of satisfaction at having put them in their place. Turning, she reentered the relative coolness of her house.

"Lady," she heard the boy whine.

3

"What is it?" She returned to the doorway. They don't even know when they're not wanted, she thought; they're like animals.

"Could we have us a drank from yonder hose?" The boy's voice was inflectionless, almost exhausted; he pointed toward a rubber hose curled like a sunning serpent near a metal spigot.

Well that's typical, thought Mrs. Hollis. Next thing you know they'll be asking for a meal. "Be quick about it. I've got my bridge club coming, you know!" She turned away from the door again, but abruptly changed her mind, deciding to watch them; they'll steal anything if a person isn't careful.

The yellow-haired boy ambled toward the hose, saying over his shoulder to the smaller boy, "Come own, Henery."

Mrs. Hollis glanced at the smaller boy, gazed away, then shot her eyes back at him in a huge, swallowing look. He wasn't a boy at all! He was a little man! His flat, pasty face was covered by a filigree of fine wrinkles, and he grinned vacantly at her, his teeth pointed like a shark's, his eyes like two tiny ball bearings set in uncooked dough. She felt something like a soft flower opening in her middle, warming her stomach, filling her with an imprecise sense of foreboding and fascination. The little lined face continued to grin at her, its features immobile. Mrs. Hollis fidgeted, shifting her weight from one thick leg to the other. "Uh, hello," she finally mumbled, her voice less harsh and certain than before.

The face, moon-like with metallic eyes, its contour broken by a thin nose as sharp and curved as an owl's beak, remained unchanged, sharp teeth grinning, reminding her vaguely of a wetting doll she'd owned as a little girl.

Before the spigot holding the hose, the yellow-haired boy knelt and slurped heavily the gushing water. He stood after a moment and called to the little man: "Come own, Henery. Take you a drank." Henry obeyed, shuffling with the undisciplined jerks of a string-tangled marionette.

"What's wrong with him?" Mrs. Hollis asked the boy.

"He's a idyet," the boy answered absently, "born in sin."

"Born in *what*?"

"In sin. His ma warn't mur'd."

My Lord, thought Mrs. Hollis, what's wrong with those people, letting a boy know about such things. Yet her fascination compelled her to look once more at the little man who was drinking now, then asked the boy: "Is he your brother?"

"No'm. He's m' uncle."

The idiot stood up and said to the boy, "Na nwa goo."

"Shore is," the boy replied.

"What did he say?" asked Mrs. Hollis.

"Said the water's good."

After turning the water off and grasping one of Henry's hands, the boy said to his uncle, "What do ya say?"

"Nan nyou," Mrs. Hollis heard the idiot mumble; she noticed how small his hands were as he wiped his glistening mouth, and how perfect, like an exquisite doll's. Her own plump hands were swollen and splotched with glandular middle age, and her attempts to fade them with creme had only bleached them so that she appeared to be wearing pink gloves, with splotches.

The boy feigned a departure, hesitated, then turned to Mrs. Hollis. "You ain't got some little thang we could do fer a sammich, do you lady? We're mighty hongry."

Still transfixed by the idiot's guileless grin, Mrs. Hollis vacillated. "We'll do most anythang," said the boy hopefully. Glancing at him, Mrs. Hollis noticed he too had an owl's beak nose and his gray eyes were rimmed with red and streaked. His face was, save for its grainy tan, colorless and void. Well, she thought, I can't turn away the hungry, but I've got to hurry because my bridge club's coming. "You wait on the porch," she ordered with a hint of her previous curtness. "I'll bring you something."

As she walked back through the house past the card table laden with cookies and little liverwurst (she called it "pâté") sandwiches without crusts, she heard the boy's whining voice talking to his uncle. She supposed the boy to be about twelve years old, large for his age though thin, with a viperine face too wide at the forehead, too narrow at the chin; his eyes were not aligned. He wore faded blue jeans that exposed bony ankles, and a torn T-shirt that was on backward so that it

hugged his throat in front (Mrs. Hollis's own plump throat
had grown a little uncomfortable looking at it) and drooped
in back. His neck was dirty. The little man, whose hair was
mousy gray, wore short bib overalls with no shirt. Neither
wore shoes.

She brought each of them a peanut-butter sandwich
wrapped in wax paper. "You eat these after you've gone, hear,"
she told them. "I've got my bridge club today."

"You ain't told us what work to do, lady."

"Never mind that. Take your sandwiches. I'm expecting my
bridge club any time."

"We can come back after if you want, lady," said the boy,
making no effort to take the sandwiches.

"Oh, all right. You come back tomorrow and I'll have some
job for you."

"Thank you, lady," he said, taking the food. "What do ya
say, Henery?"

"Nan nyou."

Later, at the bridge table, Frances Bryant had brought it up.
"There was an Okie came by my house," she reported
between nibbles at a frosted cookie, nodding slowly and raising one eyebrow, "selling some kind of remedy. He was the
awfulest thing I ever saw, all skinny and with one leg cut off."

"Well," replied Mrs. Tatum, the newest club member,
knowledgeably.

"And," Frances continued, "have you ever noticed their
skin, how it's so dark and blotchy? They've all got colored
blood, you know."

"My Ev says they're part Gypsie, kid," interjected Mary
Cannon.

Frances nodded. "Could be. Lord knows they act like
Gypsies, what with never settling down or taking steady jobs.
All the same, Gypsy or not, they're still part colored."

"They're certainly not much better than niggers," Hope
Cuen added. "They're certainly not."

They sat with corpulent dignity around a small card table,
their soft bodies scented against sweat with strong cologne, their

plump little fingers poised away from their hands—like fat white worms tempting unwary fish—while the ladies nibbled cookies.

"Well, Winnie, you're certainly quiet today," observed Frances. "You and Claude have a fight?" The other ladies giggled.

"Oh, no," Mrs. Hollis hid her welling desire to put Frances in her place, "I've just got a lot on my mind."

"You're always daydreaming, Winnie," Frances said with a laugh, exchanging a knowing look with Mrs. Tatum. "You'd better be careful or you'll have those Okies moving in on you. You have to be alert in this world."

"Amen," added Hope Cuen. "Amen."

"Not much chance of that—them moving in, I mean," Mrs. Hollis sputtered impotently. She was always helpless before Frances and wasn't even sure she liked her; she could only think of things to say to Frances after their one-sided verbal exchanges were long over.

Frances continued, ignoring Mrs. Hollis: "Well, you girls heard about what happened at the First Baptist Church, I guess." She looked about her; they hadn't heard. "Well, last week a whole family of Okies came to the services just as big as you please."

"Oh no, kid."

"What did the congregation do?" asked Mrs. Hollis.

"What could they do, being Christians and all? They left them alone, of course. But right after services Reverend Willis and some men went over to them and, nice as you please, told them they weren't wanted."

"Of course."

"That was a nice way to handle things."

"Well, that's just what I thought when I heard," hissed Frances, "but listen to this: that Okie man got mad and started a fight!"

"Oh no."

"The Sheriff had to come and break it up and take him to jail."

"It's too good for them," Mrs. Tatum observed with finality.

"That's just what I think," Frances said. "Now listen to *this*"—she paused as though to savor their attention—"you know that crazy Durant woman, the one who drinks and whose daughter is so loose, well she got angry at Reverend Willis and caused a scene right in front of everybody."

"What in the world did she do, kid?" drooled Mary Cannon.

"Well, I don't know. *Everything.* Screamed. Shouted. Quoted the Bible incorrectly as usual. She even claimed Jesus said everyone was supposed to love their neighbors, so that means everyone's supposed to love Okies! You know how crazy she is."

"What a shame," said Mrs. Hollis.

"They certainly aren't my neighbors," Mrs. Tatum gasped, "not those Okies."

"We'll I'll tell you one thing"—Frances nodded with certainty—"Jesus didn't mean *them*." She glared triumphantly at the other women for a moment. "He didn't mean them," she said once more.

Later, just as the ladies were readying to leave, Mrs. Hollis thought to ask Frances about her brother who hadn't been right. What had ever happened to him?

Frances looked nervous. "Why in the world do you ask?"

"Oh, I just got to thinking that the last time I saw him was when you had bridge club two years ago and your parents were visiting. Remember? And they'd brought your brother with them. He was such a quiet little man."

"Well, when Mother and Father died so close to one another, Brother didn't have anywhere to stay, so Charles and I arranged for him to live up north." She hurried with her final cookie, but Mrs. Hollis wasn't letting go so easily.

"Where up north, dear?"

"Well, at Sonoma. It's lovely there, not hot," she added glancing around the table.

"At the *state* hospital?" Mary Cannon asked. "Oh, kid."

"Well. Well, he's happier with his own kind."

Mrs. Hollis almost inquired if his sister wasn't his own kind, but she wasn't certain Frances would take too kindly to that in her present agitated state, so she let it pass and the afternoon ended for her on an unusual note of triumph.

★★★

Mrs. Hollis hummed in her too-warm kitchen; only if she could convince Claude to accept a salad for dinner in the summer, only if she could. Still, no mere physical heat could disturb the deep pleasure that softened and sweetened her: Frances put in her place for once. And almost an accident at that, for she hadn't dreamed Frances had done—or even *could* do—such a thing. Imagine, her own brother sent to a lunatic asylum. Her own brother. And all Mrs. Hollis had intended was to ask about the little man; those Okies had reminded her of him.

Dinner was unusually gay and afterward she and Claude walked slowly through the Oildale heat to the ice-cream shop on Woodrow Street and each slurped a double cone. Then she sat on the front porch as usual while he watered the front lawn in thick, dimming twilight, Claude shouting pleasantries across the street into other yards where people whose houses they'd never entered shot sleek, silvery sprays over yellow grass. A clatter of children swept up and down the block on or after a roller-skate scooter. When Claude finished, they went into the house and Mrs. Hollis impulsively suggested a game of Monopoly. It was an unusually happy evening for them, and later, in spite of the heat, they made it even happier.

Mrs. Hollis always slept late—Claude had for years arisen early and taken breakfast at a diner—so she hadn't finished her morning coffee when the doorbell rang. Stealing a clandestine glance at the front porch through a barely drawn side curtain, she was stunned to see a flat, gray eye pressed against the glass opposite hers, staring back; it was the idiot. Mrs. Hollis smiled her embarrassment, then joggled to the door and opened it, keeping the screen locked.

"Mornin' lady," said the straw-haired boy.

"Oh. Why, good morning."

They stood facing one another through the fine mesh for several moments, then the boy spoke again. "We come about that job of work."

"Oh. Why, yes. Just let me finish my coffee and I'll tell you what to do." Out of the corner of her eye she noticed that the little man still stared into the side window.

"Awright lady."

She turned back toward the kitchen only to hear: "Lady?"

"Yes."

"You ain't got no extra coffee do you? Me and Henery ain't had us no breakfast to eat." The boy's voice was flat, with no hint of either demand or plea or even expectation. An automatic "No!" flashed into Mrs. Hollis, and she turned quickly, her jaws tightening; she ought to put that boy in his place. She hesitated, looking from the boy to the man who still stood next to the window, then back to the boy again. "Well, I'll get you something. You can pick up the dog dirt from the lawn—there's a shovel in the garage—and then start mowing. Make sure you rake up the clippings; I don't want them turning brown on the grass. The lawn mower's in the garage too."

Mrs. Hollis put a fresh pot of coffee on to perc and made sandwiches, something they could eat outside. And she watched them working on the lawn through the window over the kitchen sink. The large thin boy pushed the lawn mower, the delicate little man raking industriously, if sloppily, behind him. The boy stopped every now and then and said something to the man, who nodded vigorously, then went on raking.

Why, they really weren't half bad, she mused, not when you knew how to handle them. They worked. And there was that idiot man living right with them, she guessed, right with his own family, working, being taken care of, really happy. Wait until Frances and the bridge club hear about this! It's a shame, though, them coming to California where they're not wanted. They should have stayed in Oklahoma or wherever it was they really belonged. But still, they weren't half bad if you knew how to treat them.

The boy wolfed down the sandwich in an instant and drank the hot, unblown coffee with grimacing gulps. The man ate slowly, nibbling and chewing with rapid grins for a long time before swallowing, his tiny hands squeezing the bread a bit too tight so that catsup and mayonnaise dripped—a pink blot—unnoticed by him onto his overall bib. The boy followed Mrs. Hollis's eyes to the gooey stain and told his uncle to wipe himself, handing him a kerchief that was clearly a ragged square torn from an old sheet.

The boy drank a second cup of coffee, then they returned to work, mowing and raking steadily over the nearly half-acre of lawn, resting occasionally in the hot morning and drinking from Mrs. Hollis's garden hose. She watched them from the cool cavern of her house, sitting in front of the blower much of the time. They're hard-working people, she thought, and not half bad. At least they take care of their own, not like some I know.

By the time they finished the lawn and trimmed the edges it was nearly lunch, so she brought them sandwiches and lemonade. She tried to prompt the boy into telling her about his family; much to her dissatisfaction, he said little, answering her with apparent candor but no enthusiasm. She began to feel there was something *basic* about these people, though she didn't know exactly what. The doll-like little man grinned and ate, ate and grinned. A slightly triumphant, exhilarated mood crept into Mrs. Hollis as she watched them eat. She had tamed them; she had them doing her bidding and acting properly. Mrs. Hollis gave each of them one of her good chocolate-covered cherries after lunch, the ones wrapped in red foil.

She set them to digging up dandelions and crabgrass in the afternoon, telling them it was perfectly all right if they did the patches in shade under trees first in the glaring heat, then she retired to the couch under the blower for her afternoon nap.

She had just fallen asleep—surely she hadn't slept long— when a persistent tapping at the front door roused her roughly from the freedom of empty slumber. She drowsed awake but was unaware for several moments before her mind focused on the sound. Arising heavily, Mrs. Hollis's legs felt thick, and her dress pressed to her with perspiration; her face remained creased where the pillow had been creased.

It was the boy. "What do you want?" she groggily asked.

"Kin we use yer bathroom, lady? We gotta piss."

His final word hit her with a dull jolt of revulsion. "You *what?*"

"We gotta piss," he repeated.

The word even sounded filthy. Mrs. Hollis felt her neck and face swelling with anger. "There are limits, young man," she sputtered, "there are limits. You cannot use my bathroom. You can finish your work and leave!" She slammed the door, her stomach churning, near tears, and hurried into the kitchen to fix a cup of coffee. "Piss" echoed within her, and deep inside her mouth, just where her throat started, she felt the warm discomfort that preceded vomiting, but she caught herself, grasping the sink with both hands until nausea passed; she was finally fully awakened. That nasty word. She went into her bathroom, her pride, with its pink rug and curtains, and washed her puffed face, brushed her hair, then bathed herself lightly with cooling toilet water.

Back in the kitchen her coffee was ready. She looked out the window and saw the Okies under her pepper tree talking. They're not children, she reassured herself, they can hold it. I did the right thing. You don't just invite people you don't know to use your bathroom; after all, there are limits. Besides, there was that nasty word. They can hold it.

In spite of herself, Mrs. Hollis mellowed as she sipped her coffee and watched them work. They do have to go just like anyone else, she thought, but where? Not in her bathroom surely. And not outside where the neighbors could see something so nasty. No solution came to her, so she again decided they could hold it until they got home, or at least to the Golden Bear gas station up on Chester Avenue. She hated that word, but was a little sorry she'd told them to finish work and leave. Okies probably couldn't help it, talking like that. Why, her own brother-in-law sometimes slipped and said it. With all the little jobs around the house that wanted doing, she decided to forgive them and tell them to come back tomorrow to fix the roof.

After taking a dollar from her purse, she walked onto the porch and called them from their tasks; they could finish weeding tomorrow in the morning when it wasn't so hot.

They walked to the porch, the little man bent forward a bit as though he'd stiffened up while weeding, and for an instant she wondered how old he really was. The Okies stood below her on the walk side by side.

"You can quit for today. Here's a dollar for your work"— the boy quickly snatched it—"and I'll want you back tomorrow morning to finish the weeds and do another little job I have for you." She heard the boy cackle with a high, hollow sound. "What's so funny young man?"

The boy, who had been looking at his uncle, turned smirking toward her and said: "Looky. He pissed hisself."

A growing wetness darkened the little man's faded overalls, spreading shapelessly on his lap and his legs, urine running in thin yellow rivulets down his dusty ankles and feet, cutting faintly muddy paths, and puddling on Mrs. Hollis's cement walkway. His little doll face grinned stiffly.

A wave of nausea instantly overcame Mrs. Hollis; she slammed through the front door and lurched toward the bathroom, vomiting first in the hall, then in the bathroom on her pink rug. Again and again her body purged itself while she, like a suffering spectator, knelt before the toilet and her uncluttered brain vomited too, drawing deep from a reservoir within her. "Jesus didn't mean them," raced through her mind. "He didn't. He wouldn't. He didn't."

That Constant Coyote

AGREED, WATER OUZELS DANCE through the mad music of mountain streams…

Agreed, quaking aspens disintegrate in wind…

Agreed, I never was what I used to be…

Agreed. Agreed. Agreed.

But don't tell me what's done's done. I've lived too long and held the sticky hands of too many grandchildren, stood watching day slide into earth like a sharpened shovel while our generations clasped. I've gazed ahead into a past as jagged as the crazed castrato calls of evening coyotes. My own coyote, the very one whose song had haunted my sleep as well as my stock—only days after a state hunter had poisoned him and buzzards had disrobed his bones—appeared this morning in triplicate, gloriously alive, from a den above our high pasture on Brekenridge Mountain: the same flesh multiplied, pups probably wiser because of their father's recent fatal mistake. Despairing for my feathers and my wool, I welcomed the old scamp back, even tripled. State hunter be damned. Age teaches you to appreciate characters as much as character. I'd missed the quality of our continuing contest. In fact, I'd been missing a lot of things recently.

I watched my multiplied nemesis pounce on bugs and, one third of him anyway, trap then lose a mouse. You're young again, old-timer, I thought, you'll learn. You'll nail the next one. I observed him wrestle himself down an embankment, snapping and yipping while young momma coyote—the old scamp always did favor youthful consorts—trotted heedlessly ahead past a stand of aspen, scanning for breakfast.

Finally the quartet—momma in the lead—bounded out of sight into an arroyo near Bear Creek, and I hiked back to my pickup, swigged a shot of painkiller, and headed home, satisfied that in this remote region, at least, the eternal struggle would be renewed. Bouncing back toward breakfast, I couldn't help but chuckle at the irony of it all, my genuine joy at seeing the old lamb stealer after all the cartridges I'd wasted trying to plug him.

Damn his old carcass, but every spring it seemed he'd lose his taste for mesquite berries and mice and garter snakes, and commence cropping my sheep. Every spring, about two lambs in, I'd lose my patience and whistle a few 30-30 protests toward him. In fact, I don't know if I ever really wanted to ventilate the pirate, and it was my son who had called the state hunter. After a few seasons I'd finally figured out that the old boy had to be feeding his own youngsters that lamb, the same way I was feeding mine. He needed a better food source for those fuzzy bundles than the spring rodent crop provided. I became more tolerant then, a tad more.

Most of all, I've come to admit that I liked the mangy old coyote, with his desire for young sheep and young lovers. Once, long before this damned disease got me, my son and I were visiting the redwood grove where we've kept our family camp for nearly a century; I was reading, my boots propped up on an ancient stump, while the horses blew and my kid cooked coffee. All of a sudden I sensed eyes on me. I figured it had to be the mystery story I was enjoying, and chuckled at myself. A minute later Len, my son, whispered, "Would you look at that."

I looked. Not fifty yards away on the edge of a clearing sat the old boy staring in my direction. "He probably checked at the ranch to make sure we left our rifles home," I told Len.

"Then trailed us," he added.

"He probably just figured this was a stag party and followed us all the way up here. After all, he *is* a senior partner in this outfit."

Len laughed and finished the coffee. I kept reading, but every time I looked up, there he sat, although once or twice I caught him snapping up grasshoppers like a bum snitching hors d'oeuvres: what a character.

The grove, with its ferns and creek and giant trees, sat in a canyon on the far edge of our property, fully ten miles from the ranch house. My grandfather had bought that corridor of land specifically so we could own it before some renegade loggers cleared those beautiful trees the way they wanted to harvest every other accessible redwood in the Sierra. At one point, he'd even posted a man there—a hard case, I'm told—to protect our timber. Over the years, several chairs had been carved out of small stumps, and one large table had been made by smoothing a large one, the remains of a titan felled by lightning. Two hollowed trees—both still living—took the place of tents; we'd been sleeping in them as far back as I can remember. We had also over the years hammered a few cabinets and boxes on snags, constructed a corral, and built a large fire ring.

There was something enduring about that place. On the stumps I could read carvings made by my grandfather and his pals eighty-some years ago, and I could imagine a lively Texan who had come to California with guts and ambition and built a small empire. He and his pals had slugged down whiskey and told lies and roughhoused in this very place when Cleveland was president, and now my grandkids and their friends were adding their carving to the stumps, their lies to the echoes.

Last month, when I returned from San Francisco after hearing that my cancer was inoperable and enduring three weeks of chemotherapy and counseling, I lit out for the grove. I had enough platinum floating through my system by then to start a jewelry store, a strange fate for a guy who even refused to wear a class ring. Moreover, although my oncologist had assured me that I withstood the effects of the toxin remarkably well, I was feeling punk. My gray locks were evacuating in clumps, and eating was no longer a pleasure. Hell of a note.

At least I was over the initial shock and depression. When the local doc had given me the bad news and urged that I travel north so that specialists at the University Medical

Center could treat me, I had slipped into a sump of self-pity. Brandy hadn't helped, nor had my wife's deep concern. We hadn't told the family I was dying, of course, and didn't intend to until death was just around the corner. But I had remained low until I got things into perspective.

On the day after I returned home from the Med Center, Doris and I had saddled up our horses, loaded Molly, our favorite pack mule, then we'd ridden to the grove for a weekend. It had been a good journey, with trout working the creek along which we traveled, aspen groves shimmering in the breeze, and—a real rarity—a pine marten humping along a deadfall across the water. By the time we'd arrived, we were in good spirits. That's when Doris told me, casually yet tentatively, that the state hunter had killed the old coyote.

"He *what?*" My fuse was short after all that chemotherapy.

"He poisoned that old nemesis of yours."

"Well, *that's* just great," I replied sarcastically.

She stopped and stared at me. "Clint," she said, "you've been after him for years."

"*I've* been after him. It was between us, not some damned state hunter."

"Men!" Doris shook her head and began brewing coffee.

That night I'd sat at the fire after Doris turned in. Sipping brandy, I'd looked carefully at those trees and stumps, their shadows and shapes, thinking that my grandfather, my father, my son and grandson, all of them had known or did know this place. I had never met my dad, and hadn't ever seen my granddad either—both were killed young—but we had all three shared knowledge of this grove, of that bedding place within the hollowed goliath where my dad was built who built me on a feather bed who built Len in the backseat of an aging car who built Timmy and Karen God knows where, all of us products of the same lightning that emptied the tree. Strong stuff, brandy, my personal chemotherapy. I turned in, snuggling next to Doris in the redwood's hollow.

She was snoring. I didn't blame her. This whole damned thing had been harder for her than me, I'm sure. I only had to die. She had to live with it and with the uncertain future. My future was certain. They told me at the Med Center that I had only a matter of months, and they put me in contact with the folks at the local hospice—most of them old friends—so I was downing, along with my brandy, a concoction they gave me to dull the pain that was already invading my middle.

I snuggled there next to my best pal, but my eyes, booze and drugs dimming them or not, would not close. I gazed through the frayed branches of redwoods at more stars than generations of my kin had a right to expect. Then I heard voices…

I started, jerking my head to the side, and saw two figures plop on the stump next to the fire ring. Well, if trespassers wanted trouble they had it. I wasn't in any mood to reason with anyone, nor was I too keen on avoiding trouble any-more. Deciding not to awaken Doris, I crawled out of my bag, pulled on jeans and boots, then slipped on my down vest.

"What do you two think you're doing here?" I demanded in a tense hiss soon as I approached the stump. Both men smiled at me in the dark. "I asked you a question," I said.

The larger of the two turned toward the other and said, "You tell him. He's got your personality."

I heard the other one reply, "The wages of sin." They both laughed.

"I'm waiting," I pointed out, in no mood to play.

"Clint," said the smaller man, "you always did have more guts than good sense."

I looked hard then but couldn't recognize either of them, not exactly anyway. They were kids, maybe friends of Len's, but his pals would know better than to sneak up here without permission. Still, they were vaguely familiar even in the dark and they didn't seem intent on mayhem, so I said, "You boys should've told us you were coming up. A midnight visit might buy you a 30-30 greeting."

I could see them smiling, then the smaller man said pleas-antly, "Why don't you sit a spell and talk. We can't stay long."

"I didn't hear your horses," I said. "Did you hike in?" I remained a little irritated but their manner relaxed me. Besides, I figured I had enough juice left in me to take them if they got frisky.

"We didn't ride in," the larger man said.

"Hell of a hike," I said, still trying to see them clearly in the darkness.

"It's all of that," the larger man replied.

Away, far to the north, I heard a coyote cry.

"This place doesn't change much, does it, Dad?" the smaller man said to the larger.

Dad? Hell, they both looked less than thirty in that light, or lack of it.

"Did Len put you up to this?" I asked.

"Oh, in a way," responded the smaller man.

"That kid," I said.

"He's a good one," the smaller man said. "Like you."

"Like me?" This was getting silly. "Look, boys, I'm tired. Why don't you roll out your sacks and we'll talk in the morning."

"We'd like to," replied the larger man, "but we've only got a little while. We just came to tell you that we're with you in this, and that everything'll be all right. Play out your hand."

"Play out my hand?"

The coyote yipped once more.

"The years don't mean one hell of a lot, but how you live does," the larger man continued. "Lenny here didn't get much of a stake, but he did his damndest."

Before I could speak, the smaller man added, "Dad did the same. You've done a job and you're leaving good stock in that boy of yours, and his kids. We're proud of you, aren't we, Dad?"

I squatted next to the fire ring. "Let's start this all over again," I suggested, wondering whether mixing brandy with painkiller was such a good idea. I felt okay, but this conversation had me befuddled.

"You don't recognize us, do you?" asked the smaller man.

"No."

"And you invited us to stay anyway?"

"Why not?" I asked. "I learned a long time ago to trust my instincts. You two're all right, but I don't remember where we met or your names. I figured we'd shake all that out over coffee in the morning."

"We met in your blood," the larger man said.

"In my blood?"

"Did you expect us to wear sheets and rattle chains?" the larger man asked.

I said nothing, but searched—really searched—them with my eyes in the gentle darkness. The smaller man wore a uniform and not a recent one. As near as I could tell, it was a doughboy's outfit from World War I. The larger man wore jeans, a rough flannel shirt, and a Mexican sombrero; he had a pistol strapped high on his waist, I realized. In the breathless night, their faces finally coalesced, finally became those in the fading photos on the mantel at home.

My granddad had been killed at twenty-nine, victim of a badger hole up on Tejon Ranch that broke his mount's leg and collapsed the big bay onto Grandpa's chest. He spit bloody froth for two days before dying in a line cabin, Grandma said. Three other vaqueros buried him in an oak grove near the cabin. Grandma outlived two more husbands.

My father was vaporized by a German artillery round in France when he was twenty-one. He had lived with my mother, his high school sweetheart, for only a week before shipping overseas to make the world safe for democracy. Momma never remarried.

Which leaves me. Somehow I survived both horses and wars, further building the cattle business Grandpa had started, Grandma had built, and Momma had managed. I'm almost three times as old as my dad and granddad, and have lived to see two further generations of us raise old Ned. And now I've got this cancer, or rather it's got me.

"We figured you'd come back here just like we did. It's the center," Dad added.

Feeling suddenly relaxed with my hallucination, I nodded. "You two want a drink?" I asked. They did—my kind of ghosts.

Sunshine warmed my face when Doris poked me. "Hey, night owl," she said, "I thought we were going fishing."

"Huh? Yeah, oh yeah. My kingdom for a cup of coffee." I smacked my brandy-befouled lips—ugh!—then leaned on one elbow.

She brought me a metal cup full of strong brew. "You must've really been dreaming last night. You were talking to yourself, carrying on."

"I was?"

"You sure were." Her face suddenly turned grave. "Clint, were you in pain?" Her eyes glistened.

"No, not at all." I sat up fully. "Hey, don't let it get you down, hon'. I know it's the shits. I sure as hell don't like it either, but it's out of our hands, so we can't let it ruin what we've got left."

Her hand was on my face and, with the morning sun behind her, she appeared as young as that first morning when we'd awakened in the midst of these same massive trees. "I know," she said. "I know we'll both die and so will everyone else. But it's just that we'll be separated." She did not blink, that good, brave woman who has made my life so, so... so desirable. Thank God for Doris. Leaving her was what I really hated.

"You know what I feel like doing?" I asked.

For a second a startled look crossed her face, then she smiled. "I thought you were sick."

"Sick, not dead."

Her smile broadened. "You know what *I* feel like doing?" she asked, unsnapping her denim shirt.

Far off, beyond our grove, above on a ridge somewhere, that coyote sang. I caught it through our pounding breath and, for an instant, a flash, I realized that I'd never before heard one call this late in the morning, then I sensed our breath, our breath, felt it.

Agreed, we hover in time like sparrow hawks in wind...

Agreed, our lives have passed through redwood exclamations...

Agreed, we never were what we used to be...

Agreed. Agreed. Agreed.

Mal de Ojo

MY GRANDMOTHER really didn't want me hanging around Mr. Samuelian's yard, but I did anyways. He was the old poet who lived next-door to Abuelita and me, and for some reason she didn't like him; she said he was crazy, but us guys all loved him. He was the only grown-up in the neighborhood who treated us like friends, not kids. That week me and Flaco Perez and Mando Padilla we were working with him on a big birdhouse—"a hotel for our little friends," he called it.

"Friends!" huffed Grandma when I told her. "Those birds eat my garden. They leave the nasty white spots! First that mad Armenian *feeds* them, and now he *houses* them. He is *loco!*" She sounded genuinely agitated.

"They're just birds, Abuelita," I pointed out.

"You have no idea the damage they do. Like that crazy Armenian, they are a menace."

What could I say? "Okay."

"I warn you, *mijito*. Avoid that Armenian. He is *peligroso*."

"Dangerous?"

"He reads all those books."

"Oh," I said.

Abuelita prided herself in being plainspoken. My father had once said to me, "Your grandmother not only calls a spade a spade, she calls a lot of other things spades too."

She had not liked the poet much since that first day when he'd moved into the neighborhood and she'd asked if he wasn't an Armenian. He said no, his parents had been Armenians but he was an American, born and raised in Fresno. That answer displeased Abuelita, who always identified people by nationalities…or her version of nationalities anyways.

Mr. Samuelian, in response, asked what nationality she was and, like always, my grandma said "Spanish."

"Spanish," he grinned. "What part of Spain are you from?"

Abuelita really didn't like that—the words or the grin—since she, like me, had been born in Bakersfield. "My *people* were from Spain," she spat. What's funny is that my mom told me our family came from Mexico, not Spain.

"Voy a pagarlo en la misma moneda," Abuelita had mumbled after that encounter, but I didn't understand what she meant, something about paying him the same money. My father was a gringo and he hadn't let my momma use much Spanish around me—before they got divorced, I mean—and I had come to live with my grandma so Momma could go to LA and find a good job.

Anyways, me and Flaco and Mando were working on the hotel that next afternoon while Mr. Samuelian was at the library. We were finishing it up, really, when a big shiny car swooped into the dirt driveway of the yard. Since our neighbor owned only a bicycle, I had rarely seen an automobile here.

A husky man who favored Mr. Samuelian, but real suntanned like he worked outside all the time, he swung from the door. He had the same burst of white hair, the same hook of a nose; his eyebrows were black and he had a ferocious black mustache. One of his eyes was covered by a dark patch. "Hello, my lads!" he called "Where is Sarkis Samuelian?"

"He went to the library," I answered.

"Always reading. He will destroy his vision yet. And who are you young men?"

"I'm Gilbert. I live next door. This is Flaco and Mando."

"Well, young gentlemen, I am Haig Samuelian, brother of Sarkis Samuelian. And what do you work on?"

"It's just this birdhouse," Mando answered.

"Be careful with those tools, my lads. See this?" he tugged at the patch that covered his eye. "A stray screwdriver can put your eye out!"

"Oh!" I said involuntarily. I'd heard all my life about the variety of implements that might put an eye out, but this was my first contact with someone to whom it had actually happened.

Before I could inquire further, the poet returned toting a load of books. "Ahhh!" he called. "My little brother visits! Why aren't you in Fresno counting your raisins?"

"Only a fool counts his raisins and ignores his grapes!" responded the one-eyed man, and he hugged Mr. Samuelian. "I've just been commiserating with your associates here."

"Oh," grinned our neighbor, "these young scamps. They're doing a fine job on the new birdhouse, though. Come in, Haig, we must have coffee. How's Aram? Where is Malik's son now? And Dorothy, still a dancer?" They disappeared into the house.

As soon as they were gone, Flaco said, "That guy, I think he got his you-know-what poked out."

We enlivened the remainder of the afternoon discussing his poked eye. "I wonder what's left. I wonder is it just a hole there?" said Mando.

"Maybe it's all dried up like Mrs. Lopez's dried-up old hand," Flaco suggested.

"Grossissimo!" It was a word we'd invented, so we giggled together.

"Maybe it's like that place where there use to be a boil on your brother Bruno's neck," I told Mando.

"Grossissimo!" he said.

Before we went home that night, Haig Samuelian handed each of us a small bag of pomegranates. "Those are from Fresno, my lads. They are the finest in the world."

"Gee, thanks."

I took mine to Grandma, but she would not touch them. "You got these from that Armenian *pirata*? Him with his *mal de ojo*?"

"Bad of eye?" A lot of the stuff she said in Spanish wasn't clear to me.

"The *evil* eye, *mijito*, the *evil* eye."

"Evil eye? Abuelita, that's just Mr. Samuelian's brother..."

"Another of those Armenians!" she hissed.

"...and he got that eye poked out by a screwdriver."

"You are young," she told me. "You haven't seen behind that mask. You do not understand the realm of evil."

"The realm of evil?"

She stopped then and gazed directly at me. "If you ever look deeply into *un mal de ojo* you will see Hell itself."

"Hell itself?" I didn't have a clue what she was talking about.

"Pray your rosary," she cautioned.

"Okay."

"And don't be working outside in the sun with those two *malcriados*," she added.

"Why?"

"It will make you dark like a *cholo*. You must wear a hat, *mijito*."

Like a *cholo*? That's the name the guys at school called all the kids—mostly Indians—who'd just come from Mexico. Hey, I *wanted* to be dark like them so I wouldn't look different from the other kids in my class. At Our Lady of Guadalupe School, I was the only Ryan amidst Martinezes and Gonzalezes and Jimenezes. I'll tell you a secret: One day, when Abuelita wasn't home, I even put black shoe polish on my hair, but it looked real dopey. I had a heck of a time washing it out before she got back.

Anyways, the morning after our *cholo* talk I couldn't wait to dash outside into the sunlight and slip over to our neighbor's yard, maybe steal a glance behind that patch. The large car was still there, but its owner wasn't in sight, so I helped Mr. Samuelian water his weeds. Then he busied himself reciting his latest verse—"Great unconquered wilderness is calling, calling me! Its crystal peaks and wooded glens all yearn to set me free!"—while staking up peas. Before long, the man with a hole in his face emerged from the small house and began picking and sampling ripe plums from a tree in the overgrown yard. "These are wonderful," he said. "Almost as good as the ones in Fresno."

After a moment, his tone deepened: "You see those sharp stakes Sarkis carves. Beware of them! My eye..." he said heavily, pulling at his patch.

I gulped.

Later that day, me and Mando and Flaco we were erecting the bird hotel when this big mean kid named David Avila, who had chased us home from school more than once, he swaggered up and stood on the dirt border between the yard and the pitted street. A week before he'd caught me and given me a Dutch rub and a pink belly too; he especially liked to pound my pale skin because it turned red so easily. Avila he looked like a large brown toad and he was almost that smart, but he had real biceps and the beginnings of a mustache. Only a year ahead of us at Our Lady of Guadalupe School, he was already a teenager.

Anyways, the big toad he kind of studied us, sneered, then hollered, "Hey, leettle *pendejos*, I can't wait for them birds. I got me a BB gun and I'll keell 'em all. Maybe I'll shoot you three leettle *pendejos* too. You just wait!"

"No, *you* just wait, young criminal!" I heard a shout, and Mr. Samuelian's brother dashed from the plum tree's foliage—I don't think Avila had noticed him there. In a moment, he had the bully by the neck and was shaking him with one hand while he thrust an open wallet into his face with the other. "Do you see this badge?" he demanded. "I'll have you in jail for *years* if you bring a BB gun around here! Do you understand? Do you see this patch? A BB gun!" He shook Avila again.

The bully had wilted quickly under Haig Samuelian's storm, and once released, he scurried away.

"Scalawag!" the one-eyed man shouted after him. "Scoundrel," he continued fuming as he returned, his fierce mustache twitching. "I can have him jailed!" He thrust his wallet toward us and displayed a small badge that said "Friend of the Fresno County Sheriff's Department."

"Ah, Haig! Haig!" called Mr. Samuelian, emerging from his pea patch to pound his brother's back. "Ever the crusader!"

"BB guns!" said Haig Samuelian, and he spat vehemently on the ground and jerked his patch momentarily.

"Come," urged Mr. Samuelian, "let me give you a glass of tea, Haig," and they entered the small house.

"I bet it's a glass eye under that patch is what," said Mando. "I tried to look under when he was pickin' plums, but I couldn't see nothin'."

"I think it's a big ol' bloody hole," suggested Flaco.

"With worms, maybe," I added. "I'll bet there's big worms in it."

"Grossissimo!" chorused my pals.

I joined my grandma talking to our other neighbor, Mrs. Alcala, when I arrived home for dinner. "Esperanza, you didn't actually *eat* the pomegranates that *brujo* gave you?" Abuelita demanded.

"Of course," smiled old Mrs. Alcala, who was Flaco's grandmother. "They were delicious. And he's not a *brujo*, Lupe, he's just another Samuelian, a gentleman but… ah…*very* enthusiastic."

"Enthusiastic?"

"And very friendly," added Mrs. Alcala.

"*Two* of those Armenians now," my grandma said. "Both of them *loco*."

Mrs. Alcala was smirking when she added, "The Samuelians aren't the only *locos* in this neighborhood."

"And what is *that* supposed to mean, Esperanza?"

"Oh, nothing," replied the old woman, grinning as she hobbled away on two canes. "*Hasta la vista,* Lupe."

That long, warm evening the Samuelian brothers sat in wooden lawn chairs talking, and after Grandma freed me from chores I wandered over to listen. "That was the day I fought Dikran Nizibian, the terror. Remember, Sarkis? I fought him for an hour and fifteen minutes nonstop, the longest and fiercest battle in the history of Fresno. We fought all the way up Van Ness Avenue to Blackstone, and then we fought for a mile down Blackstone. Our sweat flowed through the gutters. The police stood back in awe to watch such a battle. Businesses closed. Priests held crosses to their hearts. Doctors averted their eyes. Strong women prayed. Strong men fainted."

"Who won? Who won?" I asked, breathless.

"Who won?" he paused. Mr. Samuelian's brother twitched his mustache and tugged his patch. "I'll tell you who won. Do you see this eye?" he pointed at the cloth covering his empty socket. "The evil Dikran Nizibian tried to *gouge* it out in the middle of Blackstone Avenue in Fresno forty years ago, but…" another pause, another twitch, another tug…"he regrets it to this day because I knew a secret: Never use more when less will do! Never use two when one will do! I had saved my final strength. With it, I threw the ruthless Nizibian from me and broke everything on him that could be broken. I broke several things that *couldn't* be broken. He never fought again, did he, Sarkis?"

"Not that I remember," replied Mr. Samuelian.

"He never bullied anyone again."

"Not that I remember."

"Nizibian the terror was finished," Haig Samuelian nodded with finality, pulling absently at his patch.

"*Gouged* his eye out," I mumbled as I wandered home.

I told my pals the story of the great Fresno fight the next day at school. We were all eager to hurry back that afternoon and hear more from Mr. Samuelian's brother. On our way, however, while discussing the vast pit that had been gouged in Haig Samuelian's face by the evil Nizibian, and hoping at last to catch a glimpse of its depths, we spied David Avila striding toward us. Oh, no! We immediately began sprinting, each in a different direction, in the hope the bully might be confused.

Unfortunately for me, he wasn't. I was the only blond at Guadalupe School, so when Avila selected a target, I was usually his first choice. I didn't feel honored by that. I didn't have time to feel anything but scared because I was too busy sprinting. The bully was after me at a dead run. Although I was carrying my slingshot, it never occurred to me to use it because I was too busy trying to escape.

I was pretty fast for a little kid, and I got even faster with David Avila on my tail, so at first I kept him way behind me. I was sprinting and glancing back, sprinting and glancing back, juggling my book bag. Before long, though, I realized that Avila the terror was closing the gap between us, his toad eyes slits of rage. I worked even harder to escape, but my breath was growing hot and shallow and my thighs were beginning to tighten and burn.

I shot another look behind me, and he was so close that I saw the shadow of a mustache on his upper lip and the pink pimples decorating his bronze chin. My breath was searing me and my knees couldn't seem to lift anymore; my book bag swung wildly from side to side.

Just as I turned the corner of my block, I lost control of my book bag and it dropped, spilling its contents. I was nearly safe, but if I didn't pick up my things, I'd never see them again—and I knew the evil Avila had to be reaching for me.

Hesitating over my books and papers, I glanced back despondently, ready for the twisted arm, the Dutch rub, or the pink belly that was certain, and to my astonishment I realized that Avila had halted. He thrust his hands into his pockets and turned away. When I spun around, I saw the one-eyed Samuelian standing in front of his brother's yard, hands on hips, glaring at David Avila. When I peered once more at the bully, he was retreating rapidly.

I was so relieved that I almost forgot to pick up my books and papers. When I finally did, though, I hurried to our neighbor's house. The large car was being loaded with a suit-case, and Haig Samuelian said to me, "Remember, never use more when less will do, and that young hoodlum will soon learn to leave you alone."

Then the two older men returned to what seemed to be a conversation in progress. "No matter, Sarkis," the younger brother said. "I'll pass the message on to Aram. He will under-stand." The men hugged, then Haig Samuelian noticed what I carried and said, "Don't let this young man play with that slingshot. You remember my eye, don't you?" He pointed toward his empty socket as he swung into the driver's seat.

His brother smiled, "I remember."

"Well, I must be on my way. I have grapes to tend in Fresno." The two brothers shook hands. The larger man tugged his patch and smiled out the window as he started the engine. "Farewell, young man," he said to me.

I didn't reply because I'd noticed something a moment before when Haig Samuelian had tugged at his small mask while sitting there, his face level with mine. I noticed that there was no fair, untanned skin beneath the patch or the string that tied it.

No fair skin.

Beneath the wristwatch Abuelita had given me last Christmas my own surface was pale as a baby's. Then I realized what that had to mean: "You been changin' eyes!" I thought aloud.

"What is that?" the driver inquired.

"Your patch, it's on the other eye. You been changin' eyes," I spoke as I began to realize what had to have been happening: "You been changin' every day."

Haig Samuelian lifted his patch and winked with a twinkling eye I thought I'd never seen before, and said to his brother, "Beware of *this* one, Sarkis. He will go places."

Then he drove north toward Fresno.

Death of a Star-Nosed Mole

HE'D BEEN DRINKING when I arrived that evening, not that he was drunk or anything, but you know a thick old guy like Hal always seems to lurch more, to gasp more, to fumble more with his thick fingers, so I knew he was feeling it. I'd been trying to drop by regularly after work in the weeks since Carrie, his wife, had passed away, and I'd often find him in that dim kitchen sipping beer, gazing at the fading wallpaper.

His solitary drinking worried me. I tried to talk him into getting out of his empty house, but usually he wouldn't. That particular evening, to my suprise and pleasure, he agreed to accompany me to a softball game, so I followed him to the hall closet where he was going to grab a sweater. Just as he started to close the door, I heard him murmur, "Would you look at that."

I glanced in, seeing nothing at first, then noticed in the closet's darkness what appeared to be a dense lump of shadow in one corner. Looking more closely, I realized that it was the form of a small beast. Snapping on the light, we both examined the strange little animal—thick gray fur that shuddered irregularly and a rosy, splayed nose protruding from a bald face. "I'll be damned," Hal said, "Is it a gopher?"

On either side of the face projected thick, fleshy forefeet that looked like plump hands. They were held there almost like a fighter's mitts, high and ready. I thought for a moment before answering him. "No," I finally replied, "I think it's a mole, a star-nosed mole. I saw a picture of one in *National Geographic* once. They're blind, I think."

"I'll be…"

"You ever try to dig one up, a mole I mean? We had one in our garden and I dug damn near to China and never did get him. You never know how deep the earth can be, or how dark. How'd it get in here, I wonder?"

Hal shrugged, "Maybe old Jay the tomcat brought it in. He brings things in sometimes, but never anything like this before."

"Well, unless you want the cat to kill it, we'd better catch it and…well, do something."

Hal walked into the kitchen and returned with a large plastic pitcher, into which he scooped the unresisting animal. We both examined it up close, and Hal finally said, after a deep sigh, "I think I'll keep him awhile. I'll damn sure never get another chance to see one."

"I don't think these guys do too good in captivity," I told him.

He shrugged. "I'll put some dirt in this old terrarium," he explained as he pulled a rectangular glass container from one of the closet's shelves. It had belonged to his son but, like the trophies and scrapbooks and everything else connected with Timmy, it had been buried in that obscurity for years.

We trooped outside and he shoveled garden soil into the terrarium, then carefully dug for earthworms to add as I'd suggested. "These little guys can really burrow with those front feet," I commented because the mole did just that as soon as it was placed in the terrarium, virtually disappearing as soon as it hit that earth. "That article I read said they locate food with that funny nose," I added.

"Huh," nodded Hal, dropping several worms onto the soil in the glass container. For a moment neither of us said anything, then he suggested, "Let's skip the ball game. Come on, I've got some beer in the fridge."

I wasn't too keen on him drinking any more, but I knew it was important for him to talk, so I agreed. We seated ourselves in the kitchen and he opened two cans, remarking, "I still can't understand why Tim couldn't even come home for his mother's funeral." It was Tim, not Carrie, who dominated his thoughts. Tim was their only child.

"Are you sure he knew?" This was a litany we'd recited many times since the services for Carrie, and I could have recited Hal's response.

"If he didn't, it was his own fault." The voice hardened and lowered, became almost a growl. "No one forced him to leave."

I said nothing because I didn't remember it quite the way Hal did. I *did* recall the very morning he'd come to work looking haggard and I'd asked what was wrong. "I don't want to talk about it," he'd snapped, so I'd let it go, but at lunch that afternoon, leaning against a truck's shady side, he'd turned toward me and choked, "I'm sorry about this morning, Dutch. It's just that Timmy's quit the team. He's left school and moved in with some hippies." Looking at his ravaged eyes, I knew there was nothing I could say.

His son had been a starter and a good student at San Francisco State, just as he had at our local high school. He was one of those small boys who tries so hard that he can't be kept out of the lineup. He seemed to retire all the schools Most Inspirational awards. But his dad had never been completely satisfied. I remember him saying to me when Tim was a high school star, "He never gives a 110 percent. Never."

"Hal," I'd replied, "nobody can do that. 100 percent's the limit."

"Not in *my* family," he had replied without smiling.

After the boy had left college and drifted into the drug scene or music scene or whatever scene was around the Haight-Ashbury in the late sixties, his father had been convinced that he'd been too easy on him. "He's soft," Hal'd asserted, "they all are, Tim and the rest of 'em." There had still been a little communication between them at that time, but after his son moved to Canada to avoid the draft, Hal had been outraged and all contact had ceased. No one in town— including his parents—knew where Tim lived or what he was doing; he was, in a real sense, missing in action, and if his mother had mourned, his father had assumed a chrome veneer—refusing to mention his son's name while he grew increasingly intolerant of the antiwar movement, so much so that all of his friends, including me, went to great lengths to avoid talking about it.

When the US finally pulled out of Vietnam, Hal had insisted not only that we'd lost but that we'd lost because the younger generation was in some mysterious manner flawed. "They can't give 110 percent like we did against the Japs," he claimed. I changed the subject.

The funny thing is that for years Hal and Tim had seemed models for the rest of us. They went everywhere together, and Hal never missed one of his son's games. The father had been a good natural athlete himself, but the Depression had denied him the opportunity to compete, so he became his boy's greatest supporter, working to buy him the best of everything, but worried that he might give him too much.

If there was a clue to what finally happened, I think it was that Hal, one of the best guys I've ever known, never talked harshly to anyone except his son. He wasn't mean and it wasn't common for him to chew on Tim, but he just seemed to care so much that at times he couldn't control his…what?…his *passion,* or even understand it. I don't know what else to call it but passion. I guess he was just too involved with his boy.

The closest I ever saw the man come to tears was that time Timmy got lost up at Hobo Hot Springs. A bunch of us who worked for Shell Oil had met up there for a picnic and we were having a big time. Timmy and some other kids wandered down to the river to play and we just forgot them. When the women called everyone to eat, no Timmy.

The funny thing is that Hal and a bunch of us were just talking about his son at the time we realized he was missing. The boy was a standout then in Little League baseball, and we were kidding his dad, saying that Tim must've gotten those good genes from his mother's side of the family. He'd chuckled and said, "Or from the milkman." Then Hal had uncharacteristically darkened and added, "I don't know if Tim'll ever get anywhere in baseball, though. He just doesn't *want* it enough. He doesn't really sacrifice for it." Mind you, we were talking about a twelve-year-old kid.

Anyway, at that very moment, Timmy was missing. We weren't too worried at first, but after looking in all the nearby areas, you could feel everyone thicken; too many people, and not just kids, drowned in the Kern River every summer for us not to consider that possibility. I recall that Carrie had assumed the worst, collapsing in a clutch of women while the rest of us searched ever more frantically.

Just about dusk, a ranger drove his pickup into the parking area where we had assembled to decide what to do next, and out jumped Timmy. He had been out hiking, missed a trail junction, and ended up hiking a couple of miles upstream looking for us. The boy was frightened and exhausted, and he ran directly to his father, who hugged him for a moment, then slapped him hard across the face. "Don't you *ever* do that to us again!" a shaken Hal had sobbed.

The boy'd been stunned, and he staggered back a step, then flew to Carrie while his father, his cheeks streaked with tears, continued raging: "Do you *know* what you've done? Do you *know?*"

But I don't think he was angry at all. I think he was so relieved that he just didn't know how to act. Tim was his everything and he wasn't prepared for those feelings. He was embarrassed at work for the next several days and apologized over and over for the trouble his boy had caused me, although he knew it was no trouble at all. What really bothered him, I think, was his own outburst.

Not that Hal was ever one of those jerks who beats on his wife or kids. I don't recall ever hearing Tim express any resentment or dislike for his dad the way so many teenagers do. Even though he was an only child Timmy never acted spoiled. He was polite without being, you know, sullen—a bright, funny kid who laughed as much at himself as at others. We all liked him and he seemed to idolize his dad.

In fact, it always seemed as though he'd do just about anything for his father. Why, when he was tiny, just a year and a half, two years old, Hal used to bring him to work, as proud as he could be of the little guy. He was always rubbing Tim's curly blond hair, squeezing his fat little hands.

But there was something else he did that always stayed with me. In the course of a visit, Timmy would touch something he wasn't supposed to, nothing of any consequence, just some little baby thing, and Hal wouldn't screech or threaten the way you hear some parents. No, instead he did something curious: He'd say simply, "Bend over, Tim," and that baby would, I swear, right on the spot. His dad would give him a little spank on that upturned bottom, nothing hard ever, then Timmy would cloud up, his little hands rubbing his eyes, and Hal would pat his back, crooning, "Now, now, that didn't hurt." Then he'd turn to us and say, "He's gotta learn."

That baby had to know what would happen when he bent over, but he never hesitated, never failed to do it when his father ordered him to, and Hal never failed to give him a spank. "You gotta be consistent," he once told me. "They're never too young to learn." We were young ourselves then, little more than kids, newly married and just starting our families. I know I felt pretty savvy at the time, but now I know I had plenty left to learn, we all did.

That was years ago, another lifetime it seems like, and we were other people.

Now I sit here with Hal—both of us heavy old men with bare skin shining where hair used to grow, wearing trousers with several more inches around the waist than along the inseams—sipping beer, trying to make sense of all that's gone by so fast. We're hashing and rehashing: Carrie's death, good times at work, the sad state of the nation, the fate of old buddies, and Tim, always Tim. I try to use my family in the conversation to kind of lighten Hal's burden because he keeps returning to old, old business.

Every once in a while, he brightens: "Remember when Tim stole home against North High and won the championship? That pitcher never had a chance." But mostly it was the repeated questions, "Where did he go wrong? What'd those professors up at San Francisco State do to him?"

My old friend seems so shaken that, when he finally falls asleep at the table, I call my wife and tell her that I'm going to spend the night, see that he gets a decent breakfast, and bring him to our house the next day. I help him into bed, then curl myself up on the living room couch rather than Tim's old bed because I want to be alert in case Hal awakens and decides to raid the beer locker.

I was suddenly alert just before six, Hal lurching through the living room. "Hey," I call, and he stops and blinks, swaying there like some heavy beast just out of hibernation.

I roll off the couch—my back aching—"Let me get us some coffee started," I suggest.

"Coffee?" he blinks again, then he seems to focus on me. "Sure. That sounds good."

I put water on to boil, then sneak into the bathroom for a necessary stop. When I return, Hal is standing over Tim's old terrarium, staring into it. "It died," he says to me.

I join him and see on top of the soil the body of the star-nosed mole, its pale hands still, its rosy nose unmoving. Neither of us says anything, but Hal reaches into the glass box and strokes the animal's thick gray coat and touches a plump forefoot. He shudders, withdraws his hand, and gazes away toward the kitchen window where early sunlight is just showing. After a moment, he turns toward me and, out of the blue, he implores, "Why didn't I ever kiss him?"

Ace Low

WHENEVER I SEEN OLD ACE THOMAS sashay up Chester
Avenue, I'd damn near laugh. I mean Ace, he's a little bitty
guy and old, maybe forty or fifty, and all scarred up with a
crooked nose and thick eyebrows and knotted knuckles; if you
didn't know him you'd swear he was half on his ass. He always
dressed like it was still the Depression: tired brown-and-white
oxfords with white sox, and these here seersucker shirts you
could see through, and a beat-up old ten-gallon. He looked
about like he just carried a bindle in from Highway 99.

Sometimes you'd find him down by the bus stop talkin' to
old-timers about back home, Ace squattin' on his heels just
like my granddaddy, suckin' on a quid of Mail Pouch and
rollin' a toothpick around his mouth. And he liked to set on
the bench over by the library too, his legs crossed funny, right
next to each other, not ankle-to-knee. He was always talkin'
to the old guys, always lookin' sad, like he didn't belong in
California at all and wasn't gonna give California a inch. He
was about as down-home as a guy could be.

The funny thing is that Ace he was married and had him a
nice house over on Linda Vista. He had him three boys too—
one just my age—and he sent them boys through college
ever' one. He owned a big '56 Cadillac car then that his wife
drove mostly, and he owned him Ace's Place.

Before they made it legal, Ace had him a card room in
back of his little beer bar down in Riverview. It wasn't hid or
nothin'. Hell, you could see right into it from the shuffleboard. Folks said he paid off the sheriff. Anyways, it was just

this old storage room converted to hold a poker table, but it stayed purty crowded.

I heard Ace made his living from cards, and that the beer and shuffleboard and pool table didn't do more than pay rent. I can't say for sure about that, but I'll tell you old Ace was damn serious about cards. He just didn't fart around where cards was concerned. Usual, he didn't even go down to his place till the middle of the afternoon when he could raise a game. He just let this here fat gal, Olive, open up and run things most of the day.

Olive she was nice. She let us young bucks hang around and play pool and shuffleboard, but she wouldn't sell us no beer. Old Ace he put up with us most of the time, long as we didn't bother the cash customers, but he wouldn't take no shit off any of us guys, like the time Merle Duncan went after the nigger man.

Merle he was the roughest old boy in high school, no question about it: he could really fight. Not that he was mean, but there was times when it seemed like he couldn't help his-self. And, of course, back in them days wasn't no niggers lived in Oildale or Riverview; folks used to say any nigger in Oildale after dark was dead.

Anyways, it was a summer mornin', hotter than a bygosh, and I didn't drive nothin' better than a '40 Chevy. Us guys was nursing soda pops and playin' free games of shuffleboard. Olive's husband he'd hurt hisself out on a rig, and she had to stay home to nurse him, so Ace he was workin' behind the bar, playing Bob Wills's songs for us on the jukebox, and we was teasin' him about how he ought to get some good stuff on it like the Platters or Nat "King" Cole. Ace just laughed. All of a sudden, in the front door walks this sad-lookin' nigger man and his little boy. We was shocked; nobody said nothin' for a minute. This nigger man he took his hat off and held it and he asked Ace: "Mister, is they some little job of work my boy here and me could do for you? Anything at all?" Ace didn't answer right off, he just rolled that toothpick around his mouth like he was studyin' up on what the man asked.

The big propeller fan on the ceiling turned for half a minute, then Merle he couldn't resist. I seen him kindly

puffin' up like he always did before a fight. He growled:
"Niggers ain't allowed in here!" His fists were doubled up, his
neck swole, and he looked about ready to jump the black guy.

"Out!" It was Ace, and the nigger man he turned to leave,
his hand on his little boy's shoulder. "Not you," Ace said.
"Him!" He was lookin' at Merle.

"Wait a fuckin' minute!" Merle hollered real loud.

Ace kept lookin' right at him: "This man come in here
lookin' for work. He never hurt nobody. You lazy bastard, you
ain't got nothin' to say to him. Out!"

I don't know if Merle was fixin' to whup Ace or the nigger, 'cause he never got to either one of 'em. He just moved
toward the front; old Ace come over the bar with this here
sawed-off pool cue he kept, and Whap! He caught Merle
right on the shoulder, then he hit him twice more on the rear
while he's on the floor. "Out!" he said.

Merle was cryin' "My daddy's a-gonna kick your ass" as he
staggered out. Ace never even answered. But Merle's daddy
never bothered Ace, and Ace he put the nigger man and his
boy to work washin' windows.

Us guys never went back to Ace's for a long time after that,
but there wasn't a hell of a lot to do in Oildale back then, or
now either. After a month of hangin' around Standard School,
we kindly moseyed back to Ace's, and he never said nothin',
not even to Merle. My granddaddy told me: "Hell, that little
deal warn't even a pimple on Ace's butt," and I s'pose he was
right. But when that big-time badass from West Texas come to
town, by God, that was a boil!

I recollect it good, 'cause it was my first year in the oil
fields right after I quit high school and I was feelin' flat rich. I
had me a brand new '58 Studebaker—"Stud Wacker" I called
it—and my shit didn't stink. All the guys treated me mighty
special that year. I'd hit old Ace's right after work and hang
around there till about seven or eight ever' evenin', just playin'
pool or listenin' to Lefty Frizzell on the jukebox, or maybe
watchin' the Cousin Herb TV show.

But one night—not really night since it was still light and
hot—in strutted this badass and two of his boys. The West
Texan he was a driller on a wildcat rig workin' out by

Buttonwillow, and he'd heard of the game Ace run. So he
blew into Ace's with two roughnecks from his crew just as the
afternoon crowd was leaving. As luck would have it, there
wasn't a game yet that night, so Ace he was behind the bar
with Olive.

"Where's the big-shot card player?" this West Texan he
demanded.

Ace never batted a eye. "What'll she be?" he asked real
friendly.

Me, I decided I'd stick around awhile longer.

"I'm Clyde Milsap from Lubbock," this big driller
announced, "and I got me twenty-five hundred bucks cash
money in my pocket. I heard there's a old boy hangs out here
ain't afraid to play a little cards. Ain't you got no Ernest Tubbs
on that jukebox?"

Ace drew all three of them boys brews. "What kinda stakes
you figger on playin'?"

"Ten bucks minimum. No limit," grunted Milsap, and I
could see he'd caught on to who Ace was.

"Sounds reasonable," Ace said. "You boys bring your beers
in back." He led them into the card room, then turned on the
light. Two old-timers, this guy called Lucky and another guy
named Floyd, they joined the table. Me, I just stood by the
door and watched while Milsap took off his jacket, and I seen
the two biggest arms in the world; his tattoos just rippled.

"Low ball?" Ace asked.

"Name your fate," said Milsap.

Well, low ball was Ace's game. Period. It was Ace's. But old
Milsap didn't look like nothin' wasn't his game. And when the
cards started, it seemed thataway too. He took the first two
hands when Ace threw his in without callin'. Them other
guys was just fillin' chairs. They didn't do shit otherwise.
Wasn't more than a hundred hit the table them hands anyhow.

Third hand, though, the poker commenced. Ace must have
drew low, 'cause he only asked for one card, then smiled. Milsap
he needed three, then Ace quick pushed a crisp hundred-dollar
bill out, and the other four boys threw their cards in. Milsap
seen him and called with a extra fifty. Ace took him seven-
five-four-three-ace low, and both of 'em was hot after it.

Next hand Ace stood pat, kindly smilin' again. Milsap drew three. Ace pushed $250 out onto the table and ever' one but Milsap folded. The big West Texan he licked his lips and seen Ace. Ace picked up another hundred like he was fixin' to toss it into the pot, and Milsap crawfished. I was standing behind Ace, and I'll tell you, he didn't have no hand a-tall.

I come back about midnight after a date, and they's still at the table. Floyd was long gone, and Lucky he was suckin' wind with his ass. I believe old Milsap was helpin' his two pals out and maybe in the long run that's what whupped him. 'Cause about two a.m. he was stoney broke. Didn't have a pot to pee in or a window to throw her out of. And he was sore.

"You been cheatin', you little prick!" he menaced. His two boys both jumped up and so did he. "You cheatin' son of a bitch!" he went on, red-faced and twitchin' them tattoos on his arms. Them other two looked about ready to lynch old Ace.

"Nobody has to cheat when they play roustabouts," Ace told 'em. "You boys oughta stick to your own jobs. Cards is mine. I don't go out to your rig and tell you how to find oil."

That's when Milsap swung. He threw that big right fist of his at Ace and I figgered he'd kill him, but old Ace ducked under easy as you please. "If you boys're fixing to play rough," he said, reachin' under the table, "then I'll have to."

The three of 'em really got a kick out of that. "Yeah," old Milsap spat, his face as tight as a baby's britches, "we're fixin' to play damn rough." He no sooner'n got that last word out than old Ace he stood up and reached across the table with his big old .44 he'd took from a slot built into the table where he always sat.

Before Milsap could duck or run, Ace squeezed off a round right next to that Texan's ear: POW! Them other two rough-necks was already gone, sparks flying from their feet they run so fast. Milsap he just kindly stood there across the table rockin' on his heels, his eyes lookin' like Little Orphan Annie's; he figgered he's dead, I believe.

"Get your ass outta here!" Ace told him. He leveled that big Oklahoma hogleg right at Milsap's gizzard. All of a sudden, Milsap he reached up and grabbed his head, then his eyes bugged out and he took off like a fresh-cut calf.

Me, I's standin' right by the door, and I swear Milsap never even looked pissed; he looked happy to be alive. He never stopped for his '48 Lincoln either, he just kept a-sprintin' and a good thing he did. Ace kindly strolled to the front door, made sure there wasn't no traffic, then squeezed off a couple more shots at Milsap's feet, and that big old Texan, ever'time one a them bullets busted up dirt, he just let her out another notch. Two-thirds of the way down the block, damned if Milsap didn't pass old Snake Werts, this drunk that was always around. Well, Snake he kindly blinked when he seen that big bastard run by him, and he didn't wait. I guess he figured if there was somethin' up the street mean enough to make a guy big as Milsap run, he didn't need none of it.

Just as they reached the end of the block, Snake caught up to Milsap and commenced passin' him, then they hit a street repair project and the two of 'em lost traction in the loose gravel. Milsap was tryin' to turn the corner and Snake was in his way. They clawed and crawled one another, both of 'em gettin' nowheres, when old Ace he squeezed off another round and busted the gravel up around their feet. That done her! Milsap liked to paved the road with Snake, runnin' clean out of his suede boots and over Werts, who was flat by then.

Lucky went and fetched Snake and brought him, and Milsap's boots too, back to Ace's place. Old Snake he never missed a chance for a free drink. Soon as he seen it was Ace that was doin' the shootin', he brightened up. "I liked to caught him fer ya, Ace," he said. "I had him good down by the corner whenever I slipped." Ace laughed, then told Snake beer was on the house.

But that wasn't the end of it a-tall. Milsap he let word get out he was fixin' to kill Ace. He wasn't used to bein' humiliated, I reckon, and it must've really burned him. Grandaddy said: "Me, if I's simple enough to go after Ace, I sure as hell wouldn't let *him* know about it. He never lasted this long bein' soft." But Milsap spread the word all over Kern County that he's fixin' to plug Ace.

So Ace never waited. He took his big hogleg, climbed into Milsap's Lincoln, and off he sped for Buttonwillow where the

Texan's crew was drillin'. "I believe I'll return that big gambler's car and boots," was all he said.

Well, we waited all day, and Ace he never come back. Olive she was so worried she forgot herself and sold me and Merle each a draft, and I bought old Snake a couple too. Lucky was there, and he finally told Olive to turn on the radio and see if there'd been a shootin' out at Buttonwillow, but we didn't hear a thing. Come supper time, it seemed like half of Oildale was waitin' at Ace's, even his oldest boy, Doyle, had showed up and I never had seen him there before. Ace he never let his family near barrooms.

Pretty soon we seen Milsap's '48 Lincoln chuggin' down Chester Avenue. Up it pulled and old Ace was behind the wheel. Chee-rist on a crutch did he look beat! He looked like he'd been shot at and missed, and shit at and hit. Ace he just set there in the car kindly suckin' his breath, us all around him wantin' to know what'd happened.

"Well," Ace finally grunted, "that old boy's on his way back to West Texas. He ain't a-gonna bother us no more."

"Goddamn, Ace," I busted out, "he beat piss outta you. It looks like your nose is busted."

Ace turned his head in my direction. "It might be at that," he conceded, then showed us his shootin' hand and it was all swole and purple; "I believe this hand is busted too, and couple short ribs on the other side. Sure as hell made drivin' hard. But Milsap got him a few bruises."

"God, I sure hope so," said old Lucky. "Scoot over, partner, and I'll drive you over to Mercy Hospital."

Very slowly, Ace scooted, groanin' a little and having to squint his eyes a bit. Then he seen Doyle: "What're you doin' down here, son?" he asked kindly sharp.

"I just heard about what was happenin', Daddy, and I was worried."

"I 'preciate that," Ace answered, "but this ain't no place for a boy. Go home and tell Momma I'm okey, but I'll be a little late." When Doyle turned to go, Ace smiled. "He's a good boy," he said. "Got all A's on his last report."

Lucky started the car, and old Ace's eyes caught mine, then Merle's. "You two orta be back in school where you belong, not hangin' around no beer joints, or you'll end up like us, scratchin' out a livin' all your lives."

I felt embarrassed and didn't answer, but old Merle never had sense, and he started a "Yeah, but…"

Ace never let him finish. "Reach in my pocket on this side," he ordered. "There's a little souvenir there to show you boys how much fun it is to be a barroom hero."

Merle reached in and pulled out one of Milsap's ears.

Sally Let Her Bangs Hang Down

ME AND LAVERNE HORN we taken our savings out from the bank and had these fancy shirts made up, the kind with different-colored sequins all over 'em. We had the lady put big green cactuses on the fronts with blue and red kinda stars around, and our names on the backs. And that ain't all. We went and bought us new Levi's, and bright red bandanas. Only thing is we didn't have enough money left for boots, so we just polished up our loafers the best we could. And, praise Jesus, we looked pretty damned slick if I do say so myself.

See, me and Laverne we entered this talent contest at the Kern Theatre. They was givin' the winner a tryout with a real Hollywood talent scout, plus twenty bucks, and me and Laverne we wanted to win pretty bad. We was roustabouts then at the Golden Bear tank farm out by Oildale, and we'd been playin' our guitars and singin' for the boys at work, and they said we was real good. We was, too. We knew all the old Bob Wills songs, and Lefty Frizzell's, Maddox Brothers and Rose's, Hank Williams's, Ernest Tubb's, Hank Snow's, Jimmie Rodgers's, all of 'em; we knew their songs.

We knew we wasn't goin' nowhere in the oil business too, us not even finishin' junior high school, and we sure as hell didn't want to end up like the old guys out to the tank farm, all stove up, choppin' weeds when we's fifty or sixty year old, livin' on bacon gravy. No sir.

That night me and Laverne we dressed up and slicked our hair down and went to the Kern Theatre to win. But we had to sit clean through a Buster Crabbe movie before this pimply usher come and got us and took us behind the stage. I'll tell you, my belly was just tight like it is when I'm fixin' to fight. Goddamnit! We *needed* to win.

There was this here old guy that whistled like birds, and this here young guy—a fairy I think—that wore patent leather shoes and tap-danced, grinnin' all the time. After him come a fat gal who played the High-whine steel guitar and sweated. After her a real pretty gal come on and she sang one of them Eye-talian opera songs that nobody can understand so it must be good; she had great big tits.

Well, me and Laverne we went on last. We sang "Sally Let Your Bangs Hang Down," me lead and Laverne harmony, and we done a hell of a job too. When we come to that part of the song:

> I seen Sally changin' clothes,
> She was in a perfect pose,
> *Sally let your bangs ha-ang down!*

folks just liked to raise the roof, a-whoopin' and a-hollerin'. They was really took with us.

When everybody's done, the audience got to clap for each act, it was about even between the gal with the big tits and us. This fat guy that was a Hollywood talent scout he was the announcer. He kindly bounced around the stage, touchin' that pretty gal ever' chance he got and gabbin' away in the microphone. Well, he had the folks clap just for the gal and us, and it come out even again. He done it about three more times, him brushin' up on that gal as much as he could, her givin' him the come on. He looked like he's gettin' hot to me.

Finally the fat guy he hollered: "Well, it was close, ladies and gentlemen, but I believe the little lady is your choice." Lots of folks cheered, but some others booed.

"Well, I'll be go to hell," Laverne grunted to me.

Me, I turned to Laverne and told him: "I'll whup that fat bastard directly!"

"He just wants to get him a piece of tail, I believe," Laverne said to me.

"I'll tell the son of a bitch off," I said, and I meant it too. We'd come to win, and the son of a bitch robbed us.

Meanwhile, ol' fat ass he's prancing around the stage doin' his best to feel up the winner right there. He shooed all the others offstage, then he comes up to me and Laverne and announced we's second place, as if everybody in the picture show didn't know it. He commenced shakin' Laverne's hand, then mine; his hand felt like fish guts. I pulled him up close and hissed in his ear: "Eat shit!" while he's shakin' my hand.

"You're quite welcome," he said, pushin' me and Laverne offstage, me gettin' sorer all the time. Hell, he even knocked some sequins off my shirt shovin' me offstage, so Laverne commenced gigglin' like a damn fool. "What the hell's wrong with you?" I snapped at him, and he told me my shirt it said "Tessie" on the back now instead of "Jessie." Damn but I was sore. "That ain't funny, Laverne!"

We had to leave backstage while the announcer carried on about the pretty gal, and how Hollywood was callin', and shit like that. He was one hell of a windbag, that guy. Laverne he said let's go get us a beer, but I said no, I was a-gonna wait in the lobby for ol' fat ass and really tell him off. So Laverne he went over and set on this fancy couch by the popcorn machine while I stood by the door.

Directly here come ol' fatso, making like a big shot with a cee-gar stuck in his puss, and he's just a huggin' the little gal and carryin' on. With 'em is this weasley guy, the manager of the picture show, and he looked to me like he figured he's a-gonna get some tail too, his face all red and wet. I started to go right up to 'em, then I heard this voice call my name real loud, so I turned and saw Weldon Magee, this ol' boy that's a gauger out to the tank farm. Damnit, by the time I turned back around, fatso and everyone disappeared into the manager's office, so then I's sore at Weldon.

But ol' Weldon sure made me forget in a hurry. He come over and said: "You boys done real good. Real good. I have to say you surprised me. You was a hell of a lot better than that gal, but just her bad luck she was purty."

Laverne he kinda squinted. "What do ya mean *bad* luck?" he asked.

"Hell," Weldon told us, "everyone knows this here contest is phony. That fat bastard is a local yokel. He's a-gonna give that gal twenty bucks, bed down with her, maybe even take some dirty pictures of her, then charge her the twenty dollars back to be her agent. Closest to Hollywood she'll get with him is a Hollywood bed."

"Well, I'll be got to hell!" I said. "How you know all that?"

"That's what I come over to tell you. You know the Wagon Wheel Inn out on Porterville Highway? Well my brother-in-law, Arvell, manages it, and he told me about ol' fat ass. And he asked me to come by here ever' week to keep an eye out for local talent that could sing country songs. I believe he'd give you two a weekend job, good as you sang tonight."

"Good deal!" Laverne barked. "Good deal!"

I couldn't answer. We hardly knew Weldon, so him having kin runnin' the Wagon Wheel never occurred to us. In fact I about half-figured Weldon was bullshittin', but he took us out to the Wagon Wheel that very evenin' and introduced us to his brother-in-law. And by God ol' Arvell was a good guy; he told us to practice up and come back on Friday and he'd give us a try. Then he give us a glass of draft on the house.

Well, we had two days to practice, and we got hot after it. Here was our chance to break out of them oil fields, and we wasn't gonna blow it. We figured to learn some newer songs, so we tried "There Stands the Glass" the way Webb Pierce sang it but, Jesus, I like to lost a nut tryin' to hit the high notes. Laverne he broke out laughin' when he heard me try them high notes. "Damn," he said, "you better put one foot up on a high box next time you do that song, or you'll suck somethin' right up into your belly." Then he liked to fell over gigglin'.

"Oh, to hell with you!" I told him, but I could see how comical it was.

Laverne he just couldn't quit laughin'. "You reckon ol' Webb has to wear a truss?" he asked, tears runnin' down his face, and I couldn't hold out no longer and busted out laughin' myownself. "Give that number a couple more tries," he told me, "and you gonna be singin' them Eye-talian opera songs." Damn that Laverne was a funny guy.

Come Friday night and we's both pretty worried we'd mess up some way and wreck things, even after all our practice. I liked to puked while we's waitin' to go onstage, and ol' Weldon he didn't help none, sneakin' up with a silly grin on his face and askin', "You ain't a-scared are you?"

"Hell no!" I told him, the simple bastard; how would he feel?

But we done real good, and Arvell he hired us on the spot.

Let me tell you that changed things considerable. It was like me and Laverne could see a future in what we was doin', and it even made diggin' ditches and swampin' barrels out to the tank farm a little easier, us knowin' we'd be away from it one day. Better still, folks all of a sudden knowed us. Fellers at work that had ignored us started talkin', and folks on the streets even stopped us to say they enjoyed our singin'. And the gals! Boy, howdy! We just took our pick of the cute girls, and older women too, that hung out at the Wagon Wheel. It was like horny-toad heaven, I'll tell you. If there was any sin-gles come out to the Wagon Wheel that didn't like it, me and Laverne never met 'em. We diddled ourselves cross-eyed on them beautiful things, and even snapped naked pictures of some. I'd never even dreamed of nothin' so good.

In fact, me and Laverne done so good at the Wagon Wheel that after about two months Arvell he hired us to sing ever' night. And, you know, Jesus He was in on the plan. The very day after we got the full-time job singin', we drove out to the Wagon Wheel early while the after-work crowd was still sip-pin' suds before goin' home. Well, me and Laverne just set there nursin' a draft when this ol' boy in a hard hat and oil-stained overalls come in the door and marched right up to the bar. He kindly looked ever'one over, then he announced real loud: "Twelve year own the job, boys, and I just got far'd! Dranks're own me!"

He looked flat pitiful standing there about to spend his sev-erance pay on other guys' beer; he looked exactly like what me and Laverne just escaped. So me, I went over to him and told him Golden Bear was a-needin' a couple boys. He perked right up. "Hell, yeah," he said. "I'll go down there first thang tomorra, by God. That's a good deal!"

Then he commenced tellin' me what a good guy I was, me bein' a big star and all, and him wantin' to buy me a beer. He told me about his boy, and his wife that hated him, and his ol' momma that drove out here from Oklahoma near forty year ago after his daddy got killed by a twister. Boy, howdy, could that guy talk. Still, you can see how Jesus made the plan, because when me and Laverne went out to visit our pals at Golden Bear, there was that same ol' boy on the business end of a hoe.

And that ain't all. It wasn't but a couple months after we went full time at the Wagon Wheel that me and Laverne got a chance on the Kousin Ken TV show in Bakersfield, and ol' Kousin Ken he hired us reg'lar. I went out and bought me a big, shiny Harley-Davidson soon as I got my first paycheck. We's eatin' beefsteak stead of beans by then, wearin' tailor-mades 'stead of hand-me-downs. Yessir, we had us plenty fancy duds, sequin shirts and jackets too. And we had this here Filipino barber that cut our hair to look like Porter Wagoner's and even used hair spray.

By that time I's writing some of the songs we sung, and ol' Kousin Ken he said he'd try to get us a record contract. We hired this kid named Faron Epps to play lead guitar with us so we could have more variety in our numbers. Then we decided to find a girl singer for harmony, so we had tryouts at the Wagon Wheel one Saturday mornin'. Me and Laverne and Arvell and Faron was there to decide if any of the girls would fit in.

And the gals did parade through, most of 'em needin' a decongestant pill, a-singin' all up in their noses, and making big wet eyes. I reckon they figgered they's Kitty Wells, but damned if most of 'em didn't sound like cats in heat. There was some pretty ones, but after a dozen run through, I didn't think we's gonna have no luck.

Then damned if a surprise didn't come. Ol' Laverne he poked me in the ribs and whispered, "Lookee yonder," just after the front door opened and another girl come in. I looked, and there stood the same pretty gal that had whupped us in the talent contest at the picture show. And ol' fat ass was with her. He right away blustered around and demanded "Who's in charge here?!" pokin' at the air with a cee-gar.

"I am," Arvell answered.

"Good," said ol' fatso, "I'm John J. Fergerberger, Hollywood talent scout and theatrical agent. I'm prepared to offer the services of Miss Sally Rolph, the well-known starlet and singer, to your establishment if you can make a satisfactory offer."

Arvell he looked at us, and I looked at the gal; damned if she didn't look like she's about to bawl.

Arvell, he stood up and walked over to the big-shot-dot-the-oh, and he said: "I'll make ye a little offer. I *won't* kick yer ass if ye git outta here right now. But if ye don't, I'm a-gonna kick it right up between yer shoulder blades. Is that satisfactory?"

John J. Fergerberger liked to swallowed his cee-gar. "Huh?" he said.

Arvell just reached over and grabbed fat ass by the collar and goosed him out of the door. "And now for you, ma'am," he said to the girl, and she busted out bawlin', so Arvell he held up.

I went over and put my arms around the girl, and she snuggled right up, little and a-whimperin', her big soft tits warm against my chest. I winked at Laverne. "Take 'er easy ma'am," I said. "Arvell didn't mean it, did you Arvell?"

Arvell he looked pissed.

"Oh," the gal sobbed, "that man hasn't helped me a bit. He even took my prize money, and I just want to sing." Laverne winked at me, and I knowed he was a-thinkin' money wasn't all ol' John J. Fergerberger got off her; Laverne made me sore, him thinkin' the same thing I was a-thinkin' what with me protectin' her and all.

"Out!" hollered Arvell.

"Now wait a minute," I said. "This gal didn't do nothin'." I felt my face gettin' cold and somethin' in my belly tightenin' up.

Arvell he just looked at me. "We don't need her. Maybe old Furburger does."

That pissed me, him sayin' "furburger" right in front of the poor gal. "Watch your mouth, Arvell," I warned him, and I wasn't kiddin' none.

"You get out too," he said, "and take your whore with you..."

I reckon Arvell had more to say, but I caught him with a hell of a lick, knocked him on his butt. I'd of kicked a few of his rotten teeth out too if that damn Laverne hadn't grabbed me and roughed me up some, the son of a bitch. "You ain't messin' this job up for me," Laverne spit, but if I'd a been on top of him, I'd a messed up more than his job.

All the time, Sally she just screamed and howled. I guess opera folks don't see too many fights where they sing. There wasn't nothin' for me to do but take her out into the parkin' lot. Then's when I realized what I'd done, standin' there next to the "Appearing Tonight: Jessie & Laverne no cov. no min. dancing nightly" sign, and all of a sudden I felt like bawlin' myownself. That's when Sally she calmed down and put her head on my shoulder and thanked me. Pissed as I was, I couldn't help but think of how hard me and Laverne had worked for that job, ever since we's in juvie up at Camp Owens years before. And it was gone that quick for a gal I didn't even know.

Well, I had the gal not the job by that time, and there wasn't no use cryin' about it. At least I could try and get me a little piece. I knew that if I'd a crawled back into the Wagon Wheel and begged Arvell to let things slide and take me back again, he'd probably do it, since his audience come to see me much as Laverne, but there's no way in hell I's gonna apologize to that bastard. Naw, I just snuggled up to Sally and took her home with me.

Next day me and her worked on some duets—singin' I mean—and Sally she really could. I figured what with me bein' known and all, I could get us a job at one of the honky-tonks out on Edison Highway or over in Oildale or maybe out to Taft. We worked on half a dozen songs, easy ones, me showin' her how to yodel a little, and how to get that catch in her voice on ballads. She caught on real quick.

While we's practicin', Laverne called up and said that Arvell
would take me back if I come and apologized. I told him
Arvell could kiss my ass. He didn't say nothin' for a while,
then he told me he was sorry we'd got into it, 'specially over
some silly woman. Well, ol' Laverne's a good guy, but him saying that made me sore, so I told him he could kiss off too. He
kindly spit over the phone that Arvell would blackball me if I
didn't come back, and I told him Arvell'd have some black
balls if I ever got ahold of him again.

Me and Sally practiced for a couple days, workin' on songs
a feller and gal could sing that me and Laverne couldn't. Then
on Wednesday the phone rang, and it's Larry Rose who managed the Kousin Ken TV show; he said I was canned. So I
give him a little advice too. Ol' Arvell sure hadn't wasted no
time.

It took one hell of a lot of work to find any job at all, even
though lots of guys wanted to hire us. I could tell. We drove
by the Wagon Wheel and seen how the sign had been
changed to read "Laverne and Faron." Finally, this little beer
bar in Lamont, Okie Ed's, took us on for a small percentage of
the nightly net. We liked to starved for a while, but pretty
soon we's packin' 'em in ever' night. Sally could really sing.

We lived in a little house over in Arvin by then. She's quite
a gal, Sally; we hit it off real good, workin' and playin'.

The only thing that spoiled it was me wonderin' about the
other guys that had had her, especially that raunchy ol'
Fergerberger. It really eat on me.

One night, just before we left Okie Ed's and moved up in
the world with a job at Woody Wright's Corral in Bakersfield,
we finished a set and Sally said she needed to nap before we
went on again. I felt fresh, so I snuck out to the bar for a beer
and seen these two guys a–lookin' at somethin' over in a corner booth near me. They's gigglin' and carryin' on like queers,
and I heard pieces of what they's sayin': "Look at them tits!
You wouldn't think they's real!" one ol' boy said. Then I heard
the other one: "Hell, let's talk to her after the show. She done
it before; I bet we can get her to do it again. She likes it, you
can tell."

Somethin' in me commenced tightenin' 'cause I just knew they's talkin' about Sally, the sons of bitches. I walked right up to 'em, and said: "What're you boys lookin' at?"

Maybe they's drunk, but they never even looked nervous; one ol' boy stared at me bold as a gopher snake and showed me two snapshots; "Your partner," he sneered. It was Sally all right, naked and broke open and hot lookin' in one photo, and worse in the other, a lot worse.

The tightness in me busted and I pushed their table hard up against 'em, pinnin' them two bastards against the back of the booth, and really worked on 'em while they tried to get away. Okie Ed he said it was the worst beatin' he ever seen one man give two, but it wasn't half of what I woulda done. While they carted them two guys out, I picked up the photos and stuck 'em in my pocket. I's a-gonna show 'em to Sally and kick her ass out. I didn't need her, by God, and I didn't need my guts a-churnin' up the way they were just a-thinkin' of her and them pictures and things.

When we finally finished up that night and was drivin' home, Sally asked me what was wrong; she said I'd been actin' real cold toward her ever since that fight. I said me actin' cold oughta be a relief, but she didn't get it. She asked me what I'd fought about, and I wanted to tell her right then, but the words wouldn't come out; my goddamned lower lip kept quiverin' on me, and my eyes felt all warm. But I was a-gonna throw her out, by God.

Then she said there was somethin' she had to tell me and now was as good a time as any. She was pregnant with my baby and she wanted me to either marry her or let her have an abortion. That was all I needed. That really fucked things up. I just felt like a sack a turtle turds. What the hell could I do? No baby a mine was gettin' abortioned if I could help it, and no baby a mine was growin' up a bastard. But how the hell could Sally've got pregnant? I mean, if she's whorin' around like the pictures showed, and she didn't, why now?

I burned them pictures and pissed on the ashes. Soon as our contract with Woody Wright run out, I got us an even better bookin' up in Fresno. I didn't wanta be around Bakersfield no more, 'cause ever' time I looked at the guys in the audience, I didn't know which ones had banged Sally and which hadn't. I didn't know who had copies of them pictures—and others, maybe—and who didn't. I just couldn't stand thinkin' about it, with her carryin' my baby and all. My belly got to hurtin', and I had to give up beer and commence drinkin' milk all the time.

One evenin' before we moved to Fresno, somethin' happened that showed me again how much Jesus works in our lives. Who should come in the Corral but John J. Fergerberger. Sally was in back, and the band was tunin' up while I was puttin' a new string on my guitar, sittin' on the edge of the stage. The front door busted open, and I heard the voice demand, "Where's the manager?!"

"Right here," I hollered.

He come over, then said I wasn't no manager, but I'd do for now. I felt myself gettin' tight while he blabbed about how he was Sally's manager and wantin' his cut and how he'd get a lawyer on me and that's when I ruined a good acoustic guitar on his fat head. But I couldn't stop. I stomped him so bad that Heavy, the bouncer, had to pull me off. It was Jesus put Heavy there when He did, and I'm grateful 'cause I believe I'd a killed Fergerberger. He had to go to the hospital as it was, but for some reason he never pressed charges or sued either.

Finally, after we moved to Fresno, and was married and everything, Sally she brought things to a head. I guess I'd been actin' funny or some such, but I just couldn't forgive her, or even tell her why I was sore. I couldn't stand to get close to her after seein' those pictures to kiss her or even touch her. She come to me and said I'd changed and was makin' life mighty rough on her, her bein' pregnant and all, and that if I didn't love her she'd rather have our baby in a gutter. She said she'd conceived the baby with love, but now she knew I was just playactin' and she wasn't goin' to lead that kind of life. I almost told her off right then, but somethin' in me got all warm and soft.

I didn't know what to say. A man can't love a woman that done what Sally had, but I couldn't stand to lose her either, not to mention the baby. Maybe if I told what I knew about her she'd be humbled and beg me to forgive her, but then I couldn't forgive her because she'd know I knew. Oh Lord.

Sally had commenced packin', a-cryin' to herself, and I just stood there like a cow in quicksand, not knowin' what to do but sink. I closed my eyes and just prayed, my belly a-boilin', and Jesus he reminded me of Mary Magdalene; Jesus never let me down yet.

"Sally," I finally was able to say, "I need you, honey. Don't leave. I'll make things right again." I put my arms around her and kissed her, and pretty soon my belly didn't hurt. But I couldn't lie and say I loved her, 'cause a man just can't love a woman who's whored. I sure as hell wasn't lyin' when I told her I couldn't live without her, though; I really couldn't. And that shows how clever Jesus works too, 'cause He had me apologizin' when she was the guilty one.

It wasn't long after that night we commenced singin' sacred songs at the Full Gospel Tabernacle, just before our first son, Laverne Jessie, was born. Then we quit singin' in barrooms altogether. And it was right after Laverne Jessie's birth that we got discovered and made our first golden record in Nashville. Maybe you heard it. It's called "What a Friend We Have in Jesus."

The Great Kern County Gator Hunt

YOU SHOULDA HEARD US BOYS roar whenever ol' Wylie Hillis busted into the Tejon Club that evenin' just a-frothin' at the mouth. We all liked to fell off our bar stools. See, Wylie, he's a retired driller us young guys like to tease—you know, play jokes on—so whenever he showed up so agitated we just figgered on givin' him a rough time as usual, 'specially since he claimed he seen a alligator.

"Oh Lord!" he gasped. "There it was right smack in the Kern River where I's fixin' to catch me a mess a cats. Damndest thang ever!"

"Bartender," I hollered, "gimme some of what ol' Wylie's been a-drinkin', 'cause it's sure worked good on him." That give the boys a kick.

"Your ass!" was all the ol' man said, and I have to admit he did look scared, his eyes all bugged out.

"Sheee-it, Wylie," sang out Big Duncan that was a derrick man for Shell, "you sure it wadn't no lizard out for a swim?"

"Goddamnit, Dunc, I'm from East Texas and I know me a gator whenever I see one!" the old man snapped.

Bob Don Bundy had graduated Bakersfield Junior College and he's a smart bastard, that's why he worked in a office. Well Bob Don he kinda laughed. "Hell, Wylie, gators are warm-water animals. That damn Kern River'd freeze a gator's nuts off."

That never stopped Wylie, "Then there's a nutless gator cruisin' around over yonder."

Earl that owned the joint, he was tending bar with another guy, and he chimed in: "Well, he oughta be mean, what with his nut problem and all."

"You go fartin' around the Kern River," warned Wylie, "and you might have a little nut problem of your own."

"Hell," said Bob Don real fast, "ol' Earl's always had a *little* nut problem. Just ask his ol' lady."

"Ask *your* ol' lady!" barked Earl over the laughter.

Well Earl he stood Wylie a beer while the rest of us was waitin' on the ol' poop to calm down so's we could figger out what he really *had* seen. But Wylie stuck to his guns, swearin' up and down he seen a gator sure as hell. When we told him there was no way a gator could live in that cold water, he just shrugged: "Go tell the gator that."

We'd been pullin' purty good on brew all afternoon, and we liked to rag ol' Wylie, so Bob Don he right away suggested we could all drive out there and check on Wylie, winkin' at me. I caught right on. "Why not?" I added.

Much to my surprise, Wylie took the bait. He jumped right off his stool. "Come own, boys," he barked. "I'll run ye out there myownself." We all piled into Wylie's pickup, him and Big Dunc fillin' the cab while me and Earl and Bob Don worked on fresh beer in the back. Out we bounded past Standard School toward the Golden Bear Refinery and through on a service road where we sometimes went rabbit huntin', then along a dirt track, dust boilin' up behind us as we headed toward the bluffs and river below 'em.

Nowadays they got a freeway and side roads and canals and even houses out there, but back in them days—the 1940s—before they went and built Isabella Dam and dried things up, it was a regular swamp with big ol' trees and vines a-hangin' like in the Tarzan movies. The Kern River it split up into side channels in there so that it looked more like a southern bass crik than a California trout stream.

Maybe it's that beer gettin' bounced around in my belly, or maybe it's that long, warm, kind blue-orange evenin' we usta get in Kern County before the smog, but I never felt so cocky whenever Wylie he finally stopped the truck. *Sheee-it,* that place looked flat spooky.

To make matters worse, ol' Wylie had been fishin' way to hell and gone in the big middle of the thickets, so we had to walk through them trees and bushes for about a mile, it getting darker and darker, animal sounds all around us: bullfrogs, a coyote singin' real lonesome, then half the dogs in Oildale cuttin' loose givin' him hell, and even some birds screechin'. Then come a roar wasn't none of us could identify, half like a diesel horn, half like a horny cow. Hell of a noise.

"A bull gator," proclaimed ol' Wylie with this I-told-ya-so tone in his voice.

"Bullshit!" my own voice louder than I expected 'cause I's gettin' a little edgy. "Ain't no damn gators in California!"

"That's a gator for damn sure," Wylie went on.

"No way," said Earl.

"Hah!" snorted Wylie. The ol' poop's gettin' cocky out there in the woods. Then he commenced marchin' deeper and deeper into 'em, us guys followin' but not too happy about it. To make matters worse, the moon it went and slipped behind the only damn cloud in Kern County and ever'thing turned even darker.

"He-he," cackled Bob Don and I knew right away he's gettin' good and scared. Reckon we all was.

Directly we come to this little pond that was part of the river's overflow. We usta gig frogs there sometimes. Big Dunc he spoken right up: "Don't see no gator. Let's get outta here."

"Hell," said Wylie, "I never said the gator was here. It's in the river." Then he snapped on the big ol' flashlight he'd been carryin'. "Lemme show you boys how we hunt gators back home." He sent the beam searchin' over that frog pond. "Ya look for the reflection of their eyes, little and red, mean," he lectured.

Behind us some kinda animal busted through the bushes and I liked to lost my beer right there. Me, I really wished I's back at the Tejon Club, I even wished I's *home,* that's how shook I was. Bob Don he taken off but stopped real quick; in the dark he couldn't remember which way to go. "Shit, Wylie," gasped Big Dunc, "we believe ya, so let's get outta here."

Before Wylie could answer, Earl said: "Hell we do, at least I don't. You boys ain't gonna crawfish, are ya?"

As a matter of fact I *was* gonna crawfish, so I cinched up my butt and acted real indignant: "Hell no!" I couldn't let no sumbitch think I's scared, 'specially since I was.

That's what took us another fifty yards farther, into hangin' vines and suckin' water and fallen limbs, darker all the time, nobody talkin' or hardly breathin'. Then Bob Don let out a war whoop: "Snake! Snake!" Him dancin' some steps ol' Fred Astaire never done.

Wylie flashed his light and I kinda spit at Bob Don—my own heart thumpin' like a runaway freight train—"That ain't nothin' but a damn piece a rope!" But it was all coiled up next to the trail like a big rattler, which surprised me, and it did look like a snake. Folks don't hardly leave coils of rope out in the middle of nowhere. That vexed me some.

Thirty or forty yards farther and Earl howled—"It's got me! Oh Lord, it's got me!"—his voice turned soprano. He was a-whoopin' and a-jerkin', bouncin' all over hell. Whenever we got aholt to him he's whiter'n a accountant's legs, so we calmed him down some—us a little shook ourselves 'cause of all the ruckus—and we untangled his trousers from the barbed wire some fool had went and strung across the trail. Earl he's shakin' like a preacher after meetin'. "Dunc's right," is all he said, "let's get outta here."

"Yeah," shot Bob Don, "I need a beer."

Big Dunc, he just give a tight grunt.

Me, I's fixin' to agree, then ol' Wylie he tossed in his two bits' worth: "Fixin' to twist off, boys?"

That done 'er. "Hell no!" I spit at him. "Let's find that big bad gator!" I wasn't gonna let no ol' fool like him think he had me scared.

Not five strides up the trail Big Dunc fell in that hole. He never give a peep, but just climbed out and commenced hoofin' it back toward Oildale. We never seen no more of him that night. "Oh Lord," gasped Earl, "that's a gator hole sure as hell." Well, it looked to me like somebody had just gone and dug a pit, so I just snorted, "Come on."

We crept a bit farther till we come to a spot where the river widened real flat so it looked like a bayou. "This here's the place, boys," Wylie announced.

"All right," I demanded, "where's it at?"

"I don' know, rightly," the ol' man admitted. "Anywheres around here, I reckon."

"You mean you brung us clean out here and you don't even know where that gator is. Just what I figgered. A damn lie." What with being shook and all, I got hot right away. "You're apt to get your butt kicked pullin' this little stunt."

"Here," said Wylie, handin' me his flashlight. "You find it. They *do* move around. They got legs and they swim, ya know."

That remark liked to cost Wylie what was left of his teeth, but I grabbed his flashlight and moved its beam around the water. Nothin'. Just when I's fixin' to crown Wylie with it, somethin' did glint close to shore, so I flashed the light toward it and—Lord have mercy!—two red eyes shone back at me.

I knocked Bob Don ass over teakettle whenever I spun around and exploded back up the trail. Wasn't nothin' short of a giant redwood coulda slowed me down, boys, 'cause I's pickin' 'em up and layin' 'em down. Then damned if Earl he didn't pass me. But not for long. I cut in the afterburner and flew right on by him and Wylie's broke-down ol' pickup too. I wasn't waitin' for that ol' boy! I wasn't waitin' for nobody! I's headed *O-U-T* out, and fast!

Me and Earl we's on our third beers, inhaling them bastards, whenever ol' Wylie's truck it pulled up in front of the Tejon Club. He dumped Bob Don off—Bob Don lookin' flat sick, eyes like broke eggs—then waved and pulled away. I never waved back. I just drank me another beer.

Next day after work me and Earl we took our shotguns out there, but we never seen no gator. "Prob'ly swum off lookin' for warmer water," Earl suggested. I only nodded, 'cause I'd saw a couple bicycle reflectors tacked on a log stuck in the bushes. I'd saw and thought about it too. Thought hard.

"Okay, Wylie," I said to myself, already layin' a plan. "Okey-dokey."

The Call of the Great Frog King

HE'S A SMART SUCKER, Bob Don Bundy, that's how come us boys took him serious whenever he told us his plan. See, it wasn't but a couple weeks since that lamebrained Wylie Hillis had went and tricked us with a fake alligator in the Kern River. Well, ol' Wylie never knew the kinda guys he's a-messin' with, I'll tell ya that much. He's a playin' with big-leaguers when he played with us, by damn.

Us boys we's settin' around havin' us a serious discussion that afternoon whenever I realized Big Dunc and Earl, that ran the Tejon Club where we hung out, they still hadn't figgered out the trick. Me, I'd seen them bicycle reflectors tacked on a log and I'd told Bob Don all about 'em. Course, you can't expect Dunc and Earl to figger things as good as Bob Don. They never graduated Bakersfield Junior College like him.

Anyways, that afternoon we's all sippin' suds in the Club and a-watchin' *Roller Derby*. We's discussin' who's the dirtiest team we ever seen—the Bay Bombers, we decided—when Earl he ups and says real thoughtful, "Why do ya suppose there ain't more gators in the river? I mean, if there's one, there oughta be a mess of 'em."

"Well," answered Bob Don, a-winkin' at me, "that cold water freezes their nuts off so they can't breed."

Earl narrowed his eyes. "Is that a fact?" he asked.

"Yessir," Bob Don went on, soundin' mighty solemn, like maybe he's a personal friend of the nutless gator, "it's kinda like nature's birth control, otherwise there'd be gators (all of the river) just snapping up all the tubers from Los Angeles."

"Is that a fact?"

I couldn't help but laugh, 'special whenever Big Dunc he said, "Hell, if they'd do that I might just buy 'em all nut warmers so they *can* breed."

"Get one for yourself," snapped Earl, who'd just caught on to the joke.

"One's all he'd need," said Bob Don.

"Screw you," Big Dunc growled.

"See there," I stuck in, "Dunc *does* have a sex life."

"A couple a you peckerheads are a-fixin' to get your asses kicked," warned the big man, puttin' down his beer, so I right away changed the subject, tellin' him and Earl how ol' Wylie'd fooled us. Whenever I finished, Big Dunc growled, "Why that ol' farmer! How's come him to pull that crap?"

"I believe he resented it the time he brought that widder woman in here to show off and us boys commenced that unofficial fartin' contest," I suggested.

"He did look a tad pissed that time, didn't he," Earl agreed.

"Thin-skinned, ain't he?" growled Dunc.

"And his lady friend looked flat embarrassed," Earl pointed out.

Bob Don grinned. "She looked just plain flat to me," he said.

"A lotta difference that'd make to ol' Wylie," I added. "He couldn't remember what to do with a woman anyways. His horse has been dead so long he don't even have to lock the barn no more."

That give the boys a kick. "What can't get up can't get out," Earl tossed in.

But Big Dunc, like he sometimes done, was still grindin' at bein' tricked. "You wait till that ol' Arkie comes in here. I'm a-gonna kick his ass for him is what, trickin' me."

"Cool off, Dunc," advised Bob Don. "I've got a better idea. Why don't we just give Mr. Wylie Hillis a taste of his own medicine?"

Me and Earl right away agreed—hell, it sounded like fun— but Big Dunc he never looked too sure till Bob Don pulled that newspaper clippin' from his pocket. "Listen to this," he ordered. "Officials of the Department of Fish and Game are seeking means to combat the spread of the African Swamp Frog. This large, aggressive exotic is spreading into California from Mexico. It devours native bullfrogs and displaces them in the ecosystem. A full-size adult male may be three times the size of the largest bullfrog.

"Well, there's more," said Bob Don, "but that's the important part."

We all looked at him. "So what?" grumbled Big Dunc that wasn't the brightest bastard to come down the pike.

"You guys get it don't you?" asked Bob Don.

We never.

Bob Don he made this clickin' sound with his mouth, then he said real slow, "Who likes to gig frogs better than anyone we know?"

"Why, Wylie Hillis!" I snapped.

"That's right," said Bob Don, "Wylie Hillis. And who can we trick out into the swamp and scare the shit out of if we do it right?"

"Wylie Hillis!" I snapped again, then I added, "and I got a idea how." I may not've graduated Bakersfield Junior College, but I'm half smart myownself, and that's why I recollected this guy I'd knew in high school. His real name was Albert but none of us called him that. Nope, to us he was the Great Frog King.

He could make the best fart sounds in Oildale, with his armpit I mean, croak them devils out like frogs after a rain. The Frog King he'd stick his left hand under his shirt and cup it in his right pit, crook his right arm, then pump that sucker like a one-winged goose tryin' to fly. And lord, the sounds he could make.

I'll tell you somethin' else, the Great Frog King wasn't just talented, he's a smart sucker hisself. He won the damn spellin' bee at North High and liked to made the honor roll to boot. And he's a athlete too. Hell, he could shoot snooker as good as anybody in our class. But even in the pool hall it's them poop sounds made him famous. I recollect how he played "Peg o' My Heart" with his armpit that time in study hall. He even tried to enter the North High talent contest but this teacher she wouldn't let him.

It's only natural I'd thinka the King whenever Bob Don come up with that plan. And Bob Don he was real impressed with my idea. "He sounds perfect," he said. "We can get him to lure Wylie into the heart of the swamp, then dump the old-timer. That'd teach him a lesson he wouldn't forget."

"I'd rather stomp the bastard," complained Dunc.

"No, Dunc," said Bob Don real persuasive, "we're all agreed that we'll trick him back. There'll be no *need* to kick his ass when we're done with him. Now here's how we'll do it…"

Ever'time ol' Wylie come in the Tejon Club for a beer, us boys we commenced talkin' about these great big huge frogs we'd been seein' in the Kern River. We never talked to him, a course, we just gabbed real loud to each other, and I could see his big ol' leathery ears kinda flap, him a-takin' the bait slow but sure just like Bob Don'd said.

"Yessir," I announced to Big Dunc, "the size of a badger it was. If a guy could gig one a them suckers, he'd have frog legs enough for Thanksgivin' dinner."

"Is that a fact?" Earl answered before Big Dunc could say anything, and I'm not sure he hadn't forgot we was just a-trickin' Wylie.

"Yeah," Dunc said.

Bob Don had went and posted that there frog article from the newspaper on the bulletin board near the door, and I seen Wylie look it over real good. Then Bob Don, clever like always, he made up this official-lookin' announcement in the office where he worked and he posted it. What it said was that them African frogs had been seen in the Kern River. Ol' Wylie give that a good look-see too.

Meanwhile, I'd got in touch with the King and he was hot as could be to go along with the joke. In fact, what he done was stick his hand in his armpit and pump out a couple sounds that coulda been sea lions a-barkin'. "How're those for African frogs?" he asked.

"Perfect," I said, just a-rubbin' my hands at the thought of Wylie Hillis gettin' his comeuppance. Boy, ol' Albert hadn't lost none of his talent, even if he was a bookkeeper.

When ever'thing was set, we sprung the trap. Wylie he come slouchin' into the Tejon Club that afternoon and ordered him a beer, settin' at the other end of the bar from us boys like always, not unfriendly, just wary. We'd all showed up early that day and poured down even more beer than usual waitin' for the ol' fart, so I can tell ya that I at least was pretty loose by the time he showed up.

Once Hillis'd settled down, Bob Don announced just loud enough, "Well, fellas, it looks like a perfect night for frogging."

"Yeah," I answered just like we'd planned, "but we better bring heavy-duty stuff if we're going after them big suckers."

"That's a fact," added Earl.

Wylie eyed Big Dunc, who never said nothin', then asked, "Goin' froggin' boys?"

"Yeah, we thought we just might kill the night that way," replied Bob Don as casual as could be.

Easy does it, I thought, since we'd already drove ol' Albert out to the river and fortified him with a pint a Four Roses to fight the chill. "We ain't had no frog legs to eat for a while," I added, winkin' at Bob Don, "and a few of them suckers'd sure taste good."

"That's a fact," agreed Earl.

Wylie kinda looked at his beer, then said, "I hope you boys ain't sore over that little alligator deal I pulled on ye."

"Us? Sore?" replied Bob Don as innocent as a newborn babe. "Why, we appreciate a joke as much as anybody. Naw, we forgot that a long time ago, didn't we, Dunc?"

Dunc stared straight ahead at the big dill pickle bottle on the bar, his eyes lookin' like a taxidermist just inserted 'em.

"Dunc?" Bob Don repeated.

"Yeah," the big man finally croaked, the veins on his thick forearms knottin' beneath his tattoos. He wasn't too good a actor.

"Well, I'm happy to hear it," said Wylie. "I'd sure like to join y'all for a little froggin'," he added, "'specially if you're a-goin' after them big bastards."

"Sure ya can," snapped Earl, and I give him the high sign. Hell, he was a-gonna give the damn plan away, what with him bein' so obvious.

71

But Wylie never caught on, the simple bastard, and before long us boys had him out on the sidewalk talkin' frogs. But he was stubborn, insistin' on takin' his own pickup. Sayin' he had to go home and fetch his waders and gig. Well, that was just his tough luck 'cause we took a bag a beer with us, killing a few more brown bottles a-waitin' on him, then made for the Kern River. We had that ol' boy right where we wanted him.

It had gone and turned dark by the time we got there, us parkin' in almost exactly the same place we had that time he'd made trouble for hisself by trickin' us. In fact, that's the same place we always went. Well, by damn, the worm was fixin' to turn and us boys had had us a good laugh all the way out there in Bob Don's truck, talkin' about them giant frogs and tossin' brown bottles off into the bushes.

We all trooped through them trees and vines for a damn mile, a-carryin' our lights and gigs and sacks to put the giant frogs in, and a-totin' a pretty good beer supply in us, me havin' to stop and water the trees a couple a times just like the other boys till we reached that little swampy pond that was part of the river's overflow.

"Where's them giant frogs?" asked Wylie.

"They're off in the bog," explained Bob Don. "We're going to have to wade a little."

"Good enough," replied the ol' fart.

To me and Earl, Bob Don whispered, "Where the hell's your pal the Frog King? He's supposed to give us a concert."

A little stung, I said, "He *will*." But I's wonderin' myownself.

Earl, he damn near hollered, "Sure hope we *hear* some frogs directly," tryin' to let Albert know we's there. He's a subtle bastard, Earl. In fact, we's hearin' nothin' *but* frogs all around us, but only the usual Kern River croakers.

We hit the water then, Bob Don warnin' us not to use our flashlights till we was right next to them Giant African suckers. "Giant African?" said Big Dunc that was also a big chickenshit when it come to the woods. I poked him in the ribs. Still no sound from the Great Frog King, that peckerhead.

Well, we sloshed through them creepy reeds and weeds, up to our ankles in water, up to our asses in beer, ever'thing darker'n a preacher's soul, us boys actin' like we's all hot to gig them African giants, but gettin' hotter'n to gig the Great Frog King that let us down. "I told you a pint was too much to give him," I whispered to Bob Don, but he only shushed me.

"I surely don't see no big frogs," pronounced Wylie, beginnin' to sound dubious.

"They're right up there ahead," Bob Don cracked, his voice turned a tad ragged. That damn Albert he was a-wreckin' our plan.

Then Wylie kinda veered off to the left in the dark and I couldn't see him no more. "Hey!" I called, but he never answered. That tore things! There we was wet, our beer turnin' sour and our plan about shot, and now the victim had took off just when we coulda had him. I stopped, but Bob Don hissed, "Keep going, boys. Maybe we can strand the old bird out on the island."

That's when the Great Frog King finally come through, right after Bob Don'd told us that. From off in the distance come this kinda metallic "Oo-gah! Oo-gah!"—the call of the Great Frog King—and it wasn't like no frog I ever heard before. Leave it to ol' Albert to come up with a new one. Me and Bob Don grinned at each other in the dark.

"Oh boy!" said Earl.

"What's that?" asked Big Dunc, his voice a-quiverin'. Nobody answered.

No way Wylie coulda missed that there sound. Now we had him. We was in muck halfway up to our knees by then, almost to this little island surrounded by cattails, a place we'd frogged before. There was a low, smoky mist comin' up from the wet around it. That's where we'd left the Frog King, but it sounded like he'd moved to a better place. I told you he was smart. "Oo-gah! Oo-gah!" come that sound again.

"I'm sure glad that's ol' Albert," chuckled Earl real tight.

"That's it, Frog King," crooned Bob Don, "lure the old squirrel."

Whenever we hit that high ground, it come clear to me that Albert had moved into the swampy area in front of us. He's hidin' in the high reeds and his "Oo-gah! Oo-gah!" sounded real mysterious in the dark. I picked up the pace a-hopin' to spot Wylie—we still hadn't flipped on our flash-lights, although Big Dunc and Earl had their fingers on the switches I could tell. That's when I stumbled. "Key-rist!" I spit.

"What's wrong?" asked Bob Don that was right next to me.

"This damn log tripped..." I stopped 'cause I realized it wasn't no log. It was Albert, the Great Frog King, all curled up around that empty Four Roses bottle. While I's lookin' down at that fartknocker, I heard "Oo-gah! Oo-gah!" comin' from the swamp.

"What the hell?" asked Bob Don.

"Then who's...?" groaned Earl.

"Oh shit!" gasped Big Dunc, and four flashlight beams popped on at once.

I swung mine toward where I thought I heard that sound comin' from and I noticed somethin' pushin' toward us through the cattails, a kinda blunt thing movin' real slow like a gopher snake after a mouse. Even with my light I couldn't make it out too good. "What's that?" I asked.

"What?" asked Bob Don, his voice a octave higher.

"Oh-h-h shit!" moaned Big Dunc.

"Oo-gah!" come that sound and it come directly from that blunt thing. "Oo-gah!" I squinted real hard tryin' to see what it was, ready by then to spin and run if I had to. Then I seen them eyes, huge white eyes a-gapin' at us through the low fog and the reeds. That blunt thing had eyes.

Big Dunc seen 'em too. "Oh-h-h shit!" he cried. "It's the Giant African Frog!"

Before he got the last word out I'd already made my move, turnin' full stride to get the hell outta there, but damned if I didn't trip over that damned Albert again and sprawl ass over teakettle.

Big Dunc, meanwhile, was just gettin' unlimbered. He bowled over Bob Don so fast that they both flew twenty foot before they landed. Poor Earl had took to spinnin' his wheels, spirit willin' but feet not cooperatin'. Bob Don was howlin' that the giant frog had bit his tail and he was climbin' all over Dunc tryin' to get a-goin'.

I was back on my feet by then and I wasn't waitin' around
for nobody, 'special not no Giant African Frog. I whizzed by
Dunc and Bob Don, them lookin' like mud wrestlers except
that the latter had somehow gigged his own butt in the spill
so he had a pole hangin' from it. Earl got goin' about then
and he give me a good race back to the truck but he never
beat me.

We's puffin' there, our gigs and flashlights back in the bog,
me holdin' a tire iron I'd took from the tool box to fight that
devil off with if it'd followed us, when we heard what sounded
like a elephant stampede. We ducked behind the cab, but it's
only Bob Don and Dunc, covered with mud so's they looked
like they was in a minstrel show, a-sprintin' in their waders.
Bob Don had shed his spear. Each was pissed at the other.

"What *was* that thing?" asked Earl.

Safe back at the pickup, my breath startin' to come regular,
I had me the same question. "Well," I said, "if it really is a
Giant African Frog, the King's been et by now and good rid-
dance."

"Let's get outta here," urged Big Dunc.

"Oh-h-h," Bob Don moaned, rubbin' his ass where he'd
gigged hisself.

"Well, what's the plan now?" I asked him real sarcastic.

Earl he was lookin' down the path we'd just run up. "We
can talk about that back at the club," he suggested. "Let's go."

"I'm gettin' outta here," Big Dunc said.

"Oh, hell," Earl sang out, "it's comin'. It's followed us."

Dunc took off, a-plop-ploppin' back toward Oildale as fast
as his waders'd take him. Earl he stood there with his head
turnin' like a owl's, not sure whether to run or stay. Me, I
clutched that tire iron and squatted down behind the cab
again. I's fixin' to put a dent in that sucker if it come for me.
And that brave Bob Don started to climb into the truck,
dropped his keys, then scrambled all over the ground tryin' to
find 'em. We never had no flashlights.

Then we heard that voice: "Get any frogs, boys?" That ol'
fart Wylie Hillis. He never waited for no answer. "I got me
eight big bullfrogs but I never seen no giant Afercans." He
held up his gunnysack and I could see a big lump in its

bottom. "What happened to you, Bob Don?" he asked real concerned.

Our leader looked up from the ground, halfway under his truck. "Nothing!" he snapped. "Let's go." He wasn't talkin' to no Wylie Hillis.

"What about Albert?" asked Earl that had calmed down just a tad.

"Screw him," spit Bob Don, who'd finally found his keys, opened the truck's door, and was sittin' down as gentle as he could.

"Albert?" asked the old-timer.

While they talked, I wandered to Wylie's pickup to look at the frogs in his sack that he'd thrown into the bed and I noticed this small box. Wrote on it was *United States Government Surplus Inflatable Two-Man Raft, One Each*. Next to it sat this little can a white paint. Well, I never told the boys what I seen, but I thought about it, thought hard, and while we's drivin' back to the Tejon Club I said to myself, "Okay, Wylie," already layin' me a scheme. "Okey-dokey."

He's in real trouble now, by damn.

The Great Vast-ectomy Escapade

I COME IN THE TEJON CLUB that afternoon and there set the boys, all but 'cept Bob Don anyways, havin' this real serious discussion. "Shit, yeah," said Earl that run the place, "she had the biggest damn rack in our class. You shoulda seen them devils. Like mushmelons."

"Still, they wadn't no bigger'n ol' Mary Sue Rampetti's," insisted Dunc. "Yessir, she sure as hell was fun to stand in front of in the cafeteria line, them big, soft jugs a-pushin' into my back. I liked to creamed my jeans ever'time she done that."

I believed him. Hell, Big Dunc used to lose his load ever'-time a gal *looked* at him, which wasn't all that often.

"She was hot for my body," added Big Dunc that had a lotta body to be hot for, most of it lard, and that was famous for not gettin' laid in high school. Half the band was diddlin' this one galfriend of his, but he was stuck playin' pocket pool.

Bob Don come in about then, draggin' his anchor a bit it looked like, and he ordered hisself a brew. I knowed he's tired because he never said nothin', no jokes even, just set there drawin' pitchers in the sweat on his beer glass while us guys kept on bullshittin'.

Wylie Hillis, this ol' retired driller that was there, he piped up, "Why is it so many gals with big tits're so damn ugly?"

That was a good question, and we all took to thinkin' about it and, after Bob Don that graduated Bakersfield Junior College and was a expert on most stuff never spoke up, I said, "Hell, that's nature's way to sorta even things out. A purty face don't *need* no big boobs."

Wylie he nodded real thoughtful.

"Just look at Dunc," I went on. "He's got that big ol' body and no plumbin' to speak of. Me, half his size, and they call me tripod."

It went clean over Dunc's head. "Huh?" he said, but the boys was laughin' to beat hell.

After we quieted down some, ol' Earl he asked, "Y'all remember Mary Sue's older sister, Jennie?"

"Jennie," I gasped, "you talkin' *serious* ugly now!"

That's when Bob Don finally spoke up, soundin' grouchy, "Can't you guys talk about anything but women?" he said. "That's all I ever hear around here anymore."

I started to tease him some, since he usually does his fair share of jawin' when it comes to gals, but before I could Earl responded real indignant: "Why, hell yeah! We was talkin' politics just awhile back, 'member Dunc? You was saying how much you'd like to get in that lady senator's pants?"

"Damn rights!" agreed Dunc.

"What's eatin' on your liver, perfesser?" demanded Wylie that was jealous of Bob Don's education.

Bob Don he just smiled. Hearin' about politics seemed like it cheered him up some.

"Anyways," Earl went on, lookin' at me again instead of Bob Don, "I seen ol' Jennie Rampetti on the damn TV the other day just sure as hell, and she's a lawyer. A gen–u–ine lawyer! And she ain't fat no more. And she ain't ugly."

"It wadn't her," Big Dunc said flat out. "No way in hell. Ol' Jennie's prob'ly a circus fat lady nowadays."

"You never even seen the show," insisted Earl.

"Yeah, but I seen Jennie more'n once," Dunc snapped back.

"Well, mister smart-ass, I seen her and that lady that was interviewin' her she said she graduated Bakersfield High in '54, so it had to be Jennie."

"Be damned," said Dunc, a-blinkin' his eyes.

Me, I's semi–stunned. "I'll be go to hell," I said. "And you say she never looked too bad?"

"She looked like good nooky to me."

"And a lawyer to boot."

"Damn rights."

Nobody said nothin' for a minute, then Earl he piped up: "Any of you guys ever take ol' Mary Sue out?"

None of us had.

"Well, I did whenever we's seniors." His voice it sounded downright triumphant.

"Git anything?" asked Dunc, real anxious.

"Yeah," grinned Earl, "I got the worst case a blue balls I ever had. Looked like a damn bowlin' ball. Boy, howdy, was them suckers sore!"

Well, I liked to fell off my bar stool laughin' whenever ol' Earl he added, "I had to soak them suckers for a solid hour before I could to go to bed." Ever'body was hee-hawing and a-slappin' the bar, ever'body but 'cept Bob Don. That's whenever I figured somethin' was serious wrong, so I sidled next to him and asked, "What's up, pard?"

He looked at me and I could see his face was all pale. "I gotta go in the damn hospital."

"The damn hospital?!" I said. "Why?"

"To get my balls carved," he said, his voice tighter'n a banjo string.

"Your balls?"

"Skeeter wants me to have a vasectomy."

"Your wife wants you to have one a them deals, how come?"

"Well," he explained, "she can't have any kids, so she says it'll make life easier on her."

"Relax," advised Earl that'd been listenin', "I had me one and it wasn't nothin'."

"Nothin' to it," Dunc agreed.

"Me too," I told him. "I had me one. Didn't you know that? Right after our fourth was born. Course in my case, they called it a vast-ectomy."

Even Bob Don laughed. Then he said, "I just don't like the idea of someone cuttin' that area."

"Hey, that's a disaster area anyways," I said, and ever'body laughed again.

"Nothin' to it," Big Dunc repeated.

"Me, I don't cotton to doctors none," Wylie Hillis told us. "Back in Arkansas where I come from don't nobody go to one. Don't need to."

"Bullshit," said Dunc that don't exactly admire Wylie.

About then ol' Shoat Whilhite that don't belong to Big Dunc's fan club moseyed in and give us a howdy. I filled him in on Bob Don's vast-ectomy. Things was quiet for a minute, what with so many don't-likes sittin' together and all, then Earl he volunteered, "Hell, I'll save you the money and do 'er myself, just as a favor. I got my fishin' knife out in the pickup. Wait a minute and I'll go fetch that sucker."

"Fat chance," exhaled Bob Don. "I've seen you clean fish."

"Ain't no fish ever complained."

"That's because they all died," added Shoat, and we laughed again.

Wylie took his old straw cowboy hat off and scratched his spotted dome. "What the hell is a *vast-ectomy* anyways?"

"You ever castrate a calf?" asked Dunc.

Bob Don give him a sour look.

"Don't be a chickenshit," Dunc sneered.

It looked like to me Bob Don was gettin' semi-tired of Dunc's big mouth, but he'd have no chance if he took a swing at that big sucker, so I said to Wylie, a-hopin' to break the tension, "It's whenever the doc he cuts them little tubes in your sack so's you can't make no more babies."

"He cuts on you *there*?"

"Nothin' to it," said Dunc. "You ain't got nothin' to lose anyways."

"Not me," Wylie puffed. "Nosir, not this ol' boy."

"It really ain't all that bad," said Shoat.

Wylie said he wondered did it hurt, and I said naw, but I's sore for a week or so after.

"Nothin' to it," advised Dunc.

"All you guys had it done?" asked Bob Don, soundin' relieved.

Me and Earl and Shoat all nodded. Wylie he put his hand on his fly like he's protectin' somethin'. Dunc said, "Nothin' to it."

Finally, Bob Don he said, "When did you have it done, Dunc?"

"Me? Are you shittin'? I ain't lettin' no sawbones carve on my gear!"

"Hell," I said, "they couldn't find no tools small enough to work on Dunc anyways."

"Your ass," he grunted, givin' me a hard look.

"That's because in his case there's nothin' to it," added Shoat, and Dunc he come off his bar stool with his fists balled.

Shoat, that'd fight a damn gorilla, he hopped right down and went nose-to-nose with the big guy, and us boys we right away separated 'em. Besides, Dunc never looked too anxious to tangle with a guy that'd swarmed him a few years back, so it didn't take much tuggin' to pull him away. He was bluffin', I believe.

That broke up the party. Dunc took off and so did Shoat. D'rectly, Wylie Hillis did too, still a-clutchin' his fly like he'd been wounded. Me, I walked out into the parkin' lot with Bob Don that looked like he's a-feelin' better. "It really ain't that much," I assured him.

"Yeah, I guess," he grinned, "but I've never had any surgery anywhere, let alone *there*, so I'm a little wary."

"Hey," I admitted, "I's scared shitless, but it wasn't bad. And Heddy she felt a lot better about things afterwards, if you know what I mean. It'uz a good move for me."

"Thanks," he said, "that makes me feel better."

"When're you havin' it done?"

"Next week."

"Just hang loose," I advised. "Drink a few medicinal spirits in here at Dr. Earl's and you'll be fine."

"Good enough," he grinned, then climbed into his pickup and started its engine. Just then who should swing back into the parkin' lot but Big Dunc. He come outta his truck and swaggered over to us like we's gonna have a shoot-out, but when he got next to us he said, "That damn Shoat better watch it or I'll have to kick his ass."

"Yeah," I said real dry.

"And besides, Bob Don," he added, "I been to one a them vast-ectomy oriental sessions myownself, that's why I know there ain't nothin' to it."

"Oriental?" I puzzled.

"Orientation," Bob Don corrected.

"Same difference," snorted Big Dunc.

"Hey!" Bob Don added real quick, "if you've been to the orientation, why haven't you had one?"

"You callin' me chickenshit?" snapped the big man.

"I'm asking why."

I chimed in: "Yeah, Dunc, why?"

"Listen here, Bob Don, I'll tell you this much: if a little peckerhead like you gets one, I *sure* as hell will. I'll march down there the minute you get yours."

"Guaranteed?" I said.

"You callin' me a liar?"

Ol' Dunc 'uz really on edge, so I just said, "Nope. But we'll be checkin' with ya."

That whole next week, Dunc kept carryin' on in front of ever'body, insistin' there wasn't nothin' to it. Between him and that damned ol' Wylie Hillis howlin' about how doctors just screw folks up, well they about undid all the good I'd done reassurin' ol' Bob Don. He got tenser and tenser as the big day come closer, and Dunc for some reason kept on runnin' his mouth.

"Yessir," Dunc he told this one drummer that come in, "take a look at Bob Don there. He's about to get nutted." Another time, Dunc called out whenever this colored singer with a real high voice come on a TV show, "He sounds just like Bob Don's a-gonna." About the only time he shut up was when ol' Shoat come in; I guess Dunc never wanted to have to kick his ass.

Anyways, I could tell how much he was a-gettin' under Bob Don's skin, so I finally called him on it. "Why don't you just butt out, Dunc?" I challenged.

"Maybe you want your little ass whupped," he snapped right back.

"Let's go!"

Before the big turd could roll off his bar stool, Earl spoke up: "You start any shit, Duncan, and you'll never drink another beer in this place. So either shut your fuckin' trap or find another place to hang out." Earl sounded hot and Dunc knew he meant what he said, so he cooled it. He also knew Earl kept a sawed-off pool cue and a shotgun under the bar. Besides, Dunc never had no other friends, so we had him by the short hairs. He finished his beer, then said, "I'll come back whenever you guys ain't so touchy," and left.

And that's when I come up with the scheme. "Listen," I said, "it's time we shut that big prick up. He said he'd go in and have a vasectomy if you did, right?"

"Right," agreed Bob Don.

"Okay, and you're a-goin' in on Friday, right?"

"Right."

"Then on Thursday we give Mr. Duncan a little taste of his own medicine."

What made it double good was that Thursday was Big Dunc's day off, so whenever I got off work that afternoon and hit the club, he'd been there a long time pourin' beer down his neck. I slipped onto the stool next to him and said, "Well, I wonder how Bob Don's a-doin' over at the hospital?"

"This the day?" snorted Dunc, that had his nose semi-outta-joint ever since I stood up to him.

"Yep. Fact is, it's prob'ly all done by now. He said he might drop by to have a beer on his way home."

"I cain't wait to hear him talk," said Dunc tryin' to sound smart, but soundin' nervous instead.

Just then in stumbled ol' Wylie Hillis. "Where's the perfesser?" he asked right away.

"Gettin' hisself nutted," answered Dunc real smart-alecky.

I let it slide and Earl, that knew about the plan, he winked at me. I ordered another beer and listened to the jukebox and waited. D'rectly, just like we planned, up drove Bob Don. Dunc he heard the diesel pickup and said, "That must be him." He never sounded too chipper. I guess he'uz remem-berin' his promise.

After a minute, the front door it swung open, and in hob-bled Bob Don on these crutches we'd borrowed, lookin' like the ass end of bad luck. He moaned real loud each step he took and made a face. "Damn," said Dunc.

"I may not have no education," said Wylie Hillis, a-headin' for the door, lookin' like he could lose his beer any second, "but I'm too damn smart to let any sawbones cut on me." Out he went.

I swung down from my stool and helped Bob Don get settled next to Dunc. Immediately—I mean *right now*—Dunc come off his seat and said, "Well, reckon I gotta ramble."

"Wait up," I said. "When're you a-goin' in for your operation, Dunc?"

"I got errands to run for the ol' lady," he said.

"Bob Don's did it," I pointed out, "now it's your turn."

"I'll get around to it," he spit, soundin' semi-pissed and more than semi-scared.

"How was it, Bob Don?" asked Earl, and I could tell that Dunc wanted to hear and never wanted to at the same time. He sorta hovered there right behind where Bob Don set.

"Oh," said Bob Don real weak, "it was rough."

"I'll bet," Earl nodded.

"Well, that vast-ectomy cain't be too bad if you guys all had one. It cain't be too rough a-tall," Dunc said, a little of that fake courage a-creepin' back into his voice. "Don't make such a big deal out of it."

Seein' that Bob Don had survived, Dunc was gettin' flat brave. He climbed back onto his stool to finish the half a glass a beer he'd left. "I might just go and get me one d'rectly. Nothin' to it, anyways."

"Naw," Bob Don agreed, "nothin' to it. And they even let me keep these." He reached into his pocket and pulled out the damn *piece a resistance*, them bloody sheep testicles we'd picked up at Pascal Ansolobehere's ranch that mornin', and he held 'em out to Big Dunc.

Dunc timbered, a-keelin' over stool and all, hollerin', "*Ho-ly shit!* Get them thangs away from me! Get them nasty thangs away!" His face looked like a cue ball. He scuttled toward the door with Bob Don after him, a-holdin' them sheep nuts out and sayin', "Come on, Dunc. There's nothing to it. Let's call the doctor right now."

"No way, you crazy bastard," cried the big guy as he scrambled out the door, "no way in hell!" Dunc jumped in his truck and spun rubber clean up to Chester Avenue a-makin' his getaway. The last thing we seen was two giant eyes a-starin' at us as he fishtailed away.

Bob Don he turned back toward me and Earl, still holdin' them balls in one hand, a big grin on his face. "Well," he said, "let's talk politics. What was that lady senator's name?"

The Great Xmas Controversy

'Twas the week before Christmas and all through the club, us boys we was watchin'...well, a lousy football game is what we was watchin'. That's as much of that poetry deal as I can do, anyways. We had one of them minor bowl games on the tube, the Draino Toilet Bowl, the Copenhagen Snuff Bowl, or some such, two teams from the South with 6-5 records makin' we're-number-one signs into the camera.

The phone rang, and Earl that runs the joint he answered it, then called, "It's for you, Bob Don. Skeeter," he added.

Bob Don he crawled off his stool and took the handset. "Okay, Honey," he said. "All right, Honey. And a quart of milk? Okay, Darling. Soon. I won't be long. All right, Baby."

On the windows facing the street, a single, sorry string of Christmas lights blinked now and then, and a wilted-lookin' cardboard Santa was taped there too. I said to that tightwad proprietor, "You never spared no expense on decorations this year, did you, Earl?"

"You ever *buy* any a them lights?" he demanded. "They're *real* high."

"Them things work about as good as ol' Wylie's gear, see," added Dunc. Wylie, he'd made the mistake of tellin' us he'd been to the doc to see about more plumbin' problems.

"The hell!" snapped that ol' Arkie. "I'll outscrew you, numbnuts."

We all laughed.

Bob Don he finally hung up, and ol' Dunc that was on the prod for some reason he nodded at him, then sneered to me, "Pussy-whipped, see. Bundy sure lets his ol' lady boss him around."

"By God," asserted Hillis, glad for the chance to change the subject. "The missus she don't never call me whenever I'm here at the club. She knows better."

Bob Don he set back on his stool and asked, "What's the score now?"

Southern Mississippi had just scored a touchdown and tied Vanderbilt.

"Who's the hell's a-playin'?" Dunc demanded. He'd been watchin' the whole damn game.

Earl he rolled his toothpick, then told Duncan the score.

"Well, them guys ain't worth a rat's ass, see," said the big guy. "Back when I's playin' army football, that'uz a rough deal. Me, I's the best in my damn outfit."

I looked at Earl, Earl he looked at Bob Don, Bob Don looked at Wylie. I'd played football with Dunc at high school, so I said, "You're still pickin' splinters outta your ass from Bakersfield High. You never got nothin' but pine time because you couldn't play worth a shit."

He couldn't either. Slower'n a damn slug and none too brave, as I recall.

"Oh yeah!" the big guy puffed up. "Well, the coach never liked me, see. He liked them coloreds. But in the army, by God, I's..."

"We know, you'uz a piss-cutter." I shook my head and grinned.

Just then the telephone it rang again, and Earl he answered it. "Dunc," he said, "your little bride."

"The War Department?" The football star cringed for a second, then said, "I just left."

"He just left."

Earl he stood there for a long time, noddin' and grinnin' and suckin' on that toothpick. Then he hung up. "She says you was supposed to bring laundry detergent home a hour ago and you'd better snap to it d'rectly or she's gonna come over here and get you."

"Oh yeah?" snarled Dunc, defiant as hell now that the War Department had hung up. Then he slipped off his stool and hurried to his pickup.

"That's ol' Dunc," I said. "Back in the army, he'uz the best in his outfit at dealin' with women."

That give ever'one a laugh.

A minute later, the door opened slow, and there stood this ragged, skinny Oriental guy and a couple little kids. I don't remember ever seein' a Oriental in the club before. He held a hat in both hands. "You boss?" he asked, his English soundin' real strange to me.

"Who me? Hell no," Wylie replied. "That guy there is," noddin' at Earl.

"You boss?"

"Yeah." Earl's eyes narrowed. I think he could smell something that might cost him a buck or two. His toothpick went still.

"You got wo'k?" The voice was soft, but the man looked directly at Earl.

"Got what?"

"Wo'k."

Earl made a face.

"He means work," Bob Don said.

"Hell no, I cain't pay nobody to do no work."

Bob Don made a face himself...at Earl...then he turned toward that man. "What kind of work do you do?"

"Any. No pay. Food."

"He doesn't want your money, Earl. He just wants somethin' to eat."

"Well, I..."

I reached into my pocket and withdrew a bill; those folks needed food more than I needed another beer. "Give him and his kids each one a them cellophane sandwiches and some chips and a soda pop. On me."

"Well...okay," Earl nodded.

I added, "And give that man a broom to sweep this place so he can feel like he earned it."

"Okay."

He did that and the skinny man carefully swept the Tejon Club. I never seen that floor so clean. His kids stayed with him, not touchin' the food until their daddy he was finished.

"You got mo' wo'k?"

"No, I ain't got no more work."

"Wait a minute," I said. "Me and Heddy can scare up a job or two around the place for this guy. How 'bout you, Bob Don?"

"Sure."

"Wylie?"

"I ain't got nothin' for no Chinaman to do."

I turned toward the man and said, "You come on back tomorrow and we'll have some work for you, okay?"

"Oh," he grinned, "nice. Nice. I come." Then he scooped up them sandwiches and sodas and chips and took off.

"Where'd that Chinaman come from?" asked Wylie.

"I don't know," I said, "but I'm gonna find out." I walked to the door.

"Hey, you're gonna miss the rest a the game," Earl pointed out.

"Big loss. This time Dunc's right. Even *he* could probably play with them two sorry teams. See you guys later."

That man and his kids had just rounded the corner on Chester Avenue, so I strolled along behind as they hurried along south all the way to the Kern River—or its dry bed, anyways. We'd been havin' a damn freeze and it was colder'n a witch's tit outside. My breath was busting white steam. Them three they climbed the levee and disappeared into what was left of the forest that usta line the stream. I followed 'em but kinda lost track, and then I come around a bend and I seen that man with three women and maybe eight or nine little kids, and they was splittin' them three sandwiches and all, lookin' happy but real ragged and cold.

They also looked real familiar. Whenever my folks come out here from Oklahoma, and I wasn't but a little bitty kid, we'd camped right in these same woods. We'd built us a shelter outta whatever we could find, just like these folks done, and me and my brothers and sisters we was hungry a lot, just like these kids. I have to tell you, it grabbed me damn deep to see folks livin' like that in California in the 1990s. And me with a well-fed family, two cars, two TVs, a nice house, a good job. It got me to thinkin'.

Just then two more men, both of 'em, lookin' tired and hungry and sad, they showed up, and some of them kids run up to 'em and laughed. The other guy, he'd saved 'em some chow and give it to 'em and that pepped 'em up some. So it was a whole gang stranded here just like we was whenever we come out lookin' for work way back when.

Whenever I got back to the Tejon Club, Wylie and Earl was into it: "That's X-in' out Christ is what!" insisted Wylie. The ol' Arkie he was pointin' a finger at Earl's face.

"Hell, Wylie, I *got* that deal free at the Church of the Nazarene! Or Mildred did. She brung it home from church." The proprietor had went and taped a fancy "Merry Xmas" sign on the mirror over the bar. I kinda liked it.

"Well, by God, the missus she goes to the Assembly a God and the preacher there he told her that that 'Xmas' deal it was X-in' out Christ! He give her a deal to read up on it." Hillis thrust his unlit pipe forward. "And besides, that Santy deal you got in the window, that's really *Satan!* Just look how it's spelt. That's how come him to wear a red suit. That was in the deal the preacher give the missus too."

"Well, that preacher's fulla shit, see," suggested Duncan that was back on his favorite stool. "If you spell that different, it's still s-h-i-t!"

"You're fulla shit, Duncan!" snapped Wylie, his pipe quiverin'...

Yeah, the Christmas spirit—or maybe the *Xmas* spirit—was in full bloom at the club. "Listen, you peckerheads," I said, "I wanta tell you what I just seen." I did that and, to my surprise, nobody laughed, nobody said nothin' mean.

"You mean that little Chinaman and some others're a-livin' out by the river? Hell, I thought that there kinda stuff 'uz ancient history," Wylie said.

"They're probably Hmongs," suggested Bob Don. "I read where a bunch of them came here from Fresno hoping to find fieldwork, but the freeze this year killed crops, and there's no work around right now. They're probably stranded."

"What's Hmongs?" asked Earl.

"They're from Vietnam...or Cambodia...or Laos..."

"No shit?" Dunc he seemed interested. "I never seen no Viet Nams that they kicked our butts in that war. I figgered them Viet Nams for great big bastards, see."

"Little guys," I said, "with wives and buncha little kids—three families it looked like, tryin' to make do right where that ol' Hooverville camp usta be."

"Little guys and they kicked our butts?" Dunc he seemed amazed. "It's a good thing for them I wasn't still in the army then, see."

"Right," grinned Earl.

"We gotta help them folks out," I announced and I wasn't jokin'.

Wylie he was lookin' real dubious and he said, "I don't know 'bout no *Viet Nams*…"

"You know about *folks*, don't you? You know about bein' cold and hungry, don't you? You know about little kids without no decent clothes, don't you? That's all you need to know," I snapped, probably stronger than I should've, but his silly "Viet Nams" shit got to me.

"Jerry Bill's right, boys," agreed Bob Don. "Let's figure out what we can do for those families."

"But if they was the ones that went and kicked our butts, see, why should we help 'em?" asked Dunc.

"The ones that're here fought on our side, Duncan," explained Bob Don Bundy real slow. He read all the time, and he knew his history real good. "The commies kicked them out for helping us."

"Some of 'em was on *our* side?" marveled Dunc, the foreign affairs expert. "Well, that's diff'rent, see. What do you wanta do, J.B.?" he asked me.

"I still don't like that X-in' out Christ deal," added Wylie, lookin' for a argument.

I give him a glance that'd kill grass. "Forget that crap!" I barked. Seein' them poor folks out there had me on the prod. I got us back to the subject: "I vote for us givin' them folks a early Christmas," I suggested, "and today we need to scare up some grub for all of 'em."

"How much you reckon somethin' like that might run?" moaned the ol' penny-pincher, toothpick droopin'.

"How many more a them cellophane sandwiches you got there, Earl?" Hardly nobody ever bought one.

"Well, those're real expensive," he said.

"Bullshit," I said. "Tally up a dozen of 'em, a dozen cokes, a dozen bags a chips—at *your* cost—and us guys'll split it four ways."

"We will?" croaked Wylie.

"You damn rights," agreed Dunc.

Bob Don said, "Certainly."

"I…I guess we will," Wylie finally nodded. Then he mumbled somethin' about "Viet Nams."

Earl he slunk to the sandwich display and begun baggin' food. That toothpick of his it hung at a tragic angle.

Just then the telephone rang, so I answered it. "Tejon Club," I said.

"Is that you, J.B.?" asked Heddy, my wife.

"It sure is, Babe."

"What time will you be home?"

"Before long. Listen, lemme tell you what I seen today." I explained the whole deal to her.

When I finished, she said, "Oh, Jerry Bill, we can't let them live out there like that."

She's a good gal, so I knew she'd say that. Well, she took over callin' the wives while me and Dunc delivered food out to that camp. It was a sad, sad deal, I'll tell you that much, and them folks was sure happy for them crummy sandwiches. One sorry tent was all they had for the whole gang. It seems like they did have two old cars, but one was broke down and they never had money for gas anyways. The little guy that'd come into the club earlier, he said they'd come here hopin' to find work, and that they had kinfolk in Fresno and wanted to get back there.

Well, ol' Dunc he upped and volunteered to have his oldest boy, Doyle, that he was a fix-it man, work on that car. I told the Vietnamese guy to bring ever'one to the club that next day and we'd have work for 'em all, and that little guy he liked to've bawled he was so happy. "Oh, thank!" he said. "Oh, thank!" and he pumped my hand and Dunc's.

That next day the club it looked like one of them Hollywood-movie Christmases. Heddy and Dunc's bouncy wife, Dee Dee, they'd fixed up a tree; Heddy told me ol' Earl's first words when he seen it was, "How much'd *that* run?"

The gals they set up other decorations too. And they'd helped Earl's frau, Mildred, and Wylie's missus, Olive, cook up a turkey and all the fixin's. Skeeter, that was Mrs. Bob Don Bundy, her and my boy Craig and his pals Junior and Jeffrey, they went out and bought ever' one of them little kids three presents: a toy, some gloves, and a jacket. Me and the boys bought each one of them adults a jacket and gloves and rounded up a big tent from ol' Bo Simmons. Hey, we all got jobs and it's only money.

And you shoulda seen them little Vietnamese kids' faces whenever they come in the front door. Even ol' miser Earl had to grin. It was worth every damn penny, boys. Every damn penny. Pretty soon Craig and junior that they was on North High's football team and wearin' their letter jackets, and Jeffrey too, they was tossin' a football—one of the gifts—with the bigger kids. Most of them Vietnamese kids was wearin' their new jackets and gloves right there in the club.

Directly we all ate turkey and pumkin pie. Then a surprise come: Ol' Cletus Rollins, preacher at the Assembly of God, and B. J. Mayfield, preacher at the Church of the Nazarene, they showed up—the first time they'd ever been in the Tejon Club—and they brung three big boxes of clothes, and some groceries too. That was real good of 'em. I have to admit, I've thought different of them churches ever since. Directly, Heddy and Skeeter took to teachin' the little kids to sing Christmas carols and them kids they caught right on.

Pretty soon I seen Dunc and his dainty little wife, that hadn't been reconciled all that long, lookin' all starry-eyed together, Skeeter and Bob Don they was all cooned-up, and even Wylie and the missus looked like they was about to snuggle. But I was wrong about ol' Wylie.

For whatever reason, he decided to buttonhole Earl again and, like a broke record, start in on him: "I still think you oughta take down that X-in' out Christ deal, Earl," asserted the Arkie, pointin' at the offendin' "Merry Xmas" proclamation. "It's a damn sin is what it is."

Before Earl could say anything, Heddy detached herself from my arm, smiled, and patted Wylie's shoulder. "Don't worry about Christ, Wylie," she smiled. "He's here." And she nodded toward them happy folks with their food and their presents.

Then Heddy M. Hogsett, my wife, she walked right back to me and kissed me in front of God and ever'one. "I'm proud of you, J.B.," she said.

"Me too, Dad," said Craig, and that big lunk that he was first string on the high-school football team, you know what he done? He hugged me right there.

Well, I felt funny, like my throat had went soft and my eyes was warm. But to tell you the truth, I was semi-proud of myownself.

Hey Okie!

WE COULD BUY BETTER EGGS in town at the market than we
could from Mr. Barnhall, clean ones and all white, so I don't
see why we drove clear out to his ranch in the first place. The
ones he sold us looked like clods. So did Barney Barnhall, for
that matter. If he wasn't the sloppiest man in Kern County, he
was certainly a leading contender. My brother, Junior, used to
say Barney was the only man in the world who could get the
inside of an egg dirty.

None of those things fazed my Pop, though. He'd worked
on ranches around Arvin and Lamont and Edison with Mr.
Barnhall way back in the forties before I was born, and he
harbored no doubts about the man's quality: "He sweated seventeen years in other guys' fields, *hijo,* saving a down payment
for that place of his," Pop told me. "If he'd wanted to dress up
like Pedro Infante he'd still be working for wages. In this life,
hijo, you make choices." My father had labored for over twenty
years in California before he could buy our small place, so he
knew something about hard work.

Still, now that we lived in town, most of us kids preferred
the clean white uniformity of store-bought eggs. To tell the
truth, we really didn't mind Mr. Barnhall himself as much as
we disliked having to wash chicken shit and straw and feathers
off the eggs he sold. His stories were great. Hearing him talk
was like reading a book and it always reminded me of the visits back to Texas to my pop's family in McAllen where my *tiás*
and *tiós* would talk into the night telling us about *la llorona*
and *los chisos* and stuff like that.

Anyway, we'd drive out to Barnhall's place and park next to an elephant's graveyard of old Fords and Chevys and Plymouths, at least one usually undergoing autopsy, its innards hanging above it from an A-frame, then we'd climb out and wait for Mr. Barnhall to emerge from one of several sheds that sprouted like a shantytown between his house and corral. Pretty soon, he'd appear, raise a huge hand and grin, then amble toward us.

"Howdy, Manuel," he'd say to my pop, "which un is this?"

I have eight brothers and three sisters, and Mr. Barnhall had never got any further than telling the boys from the girls.

"This *payoso* is Julio, my college student. He's at Cal State."

"College, eh?" Mr. Barnhall would grunt, spitting a stream of tobacco juice and cinching up his jeans under his big belly to slightly reduce the slice of flesh that protruded like a hairy melon between his shirt and trousers. "Don't waste 'er, boy." Then, after a pause: "There was a big ol' long-peckered kid back in Checotah," Mr. Barnhall would muse, "that got sent to college. Well, sir…" and the afternoon would pass, usually in the shade of the huge pepper tree next to his house.

Our greeting was special, though. Many times while we were visiting Barnhall's, other cars would drive up and Mr. Barnhall would amble toward them and all I'd hear him ask was, "Y'all wont iny aigs?"

We'd played this scene—variations of it—regularly from the time I was in junior high school and Mr. Barnhall had returned from Corcoron and bought his spread between Arvin and Edison. Us kids got a kick out of going out there from Lamont where we lived, especially if Pop brought beer with him. That's when it really got good.

The very first time I ever remember visiting Barnhall's my pop took a huge bag of beer with him and the two of them squatted beneath that pepper tree surrounded by the carcasses of dead automobiles, drank from brown bottles, and talked. Finally, the beer working its subtle magic, Mr. Barnhall plunged into his house, then emerged with an ancient windup Victrola, the kind with a speaker that looked like a large, grotesque flower. He put on a record I was to hear over and over again on our visits to his place, a tinny voice wailing:

Hey Okie
If you see Arkie
Tell him Tex has got a job
Out in Californy
Just a-pickin' up prunes
Squeezin' oil outta olives....

The big man commenced dancing, twirling in the dust, shuffling his heavy feet until the song ended and he plopped down next to Pop and drained the last of his beer.

Of course, dancing wasn't Mr. Barnhall's strongest point. Mainly he told tales. It was on that very first visit, as I recall, that he got started on the weather and hard times. "Yessir," said Mr. Barnhall, "the wind it got so bad there around Checotah that it blowed all the topsoil away. Me and my brother Dean we had to work three days a-haulin' post holes and storin' 'em in the barn against whenever we'd need 'em again."

It took me a minute to catch on. "Post holes?" I asked my Pop, who was laughing.

"Hell of a kid you got there, Manuel," Barney observed, grinning at Pop. "Smart as a whip, ain't he?"

Another time Pop and Junior and I brought Mr. Barnhall a mess of doves we'd shot and he began talking about wing shooting he'd done back in Oklahoma when he was a kid. "Course," he pointed out, "ain't never been no birds harder to hit on the fly than ground squirrels."

"Yeah," Junior snorted, "but we're talking about shooting on the fly, not on the ground."

Mr. Barnhall grinned like a fisherman reeling the day's first nibble. "Well, son, back in them days the dust it blew so thick that me and Dean we'd take our scatterguns outside and practice wing shootin', just a-knockin' off squirrels a-burrowin' overhead."

I looked at Pop and he grinned at me. We both grinned at Junior. Then everybody laughed. It was fun going to Mr. Barnhall's.

It just seemed natural to recommend him when Dr. Givens, my social issues teacher at Cal State, told the class about his interest in interviewing "Dust Bowlers." He was initiating a project, he explained, "to give them pride in their heritage, a sense of accomplishment and worth." It seemed like a sensible notion to me, much better than studying child labor in nineteenth-century England or women's suffrage.

Dr. Givens was a tall, thin young man given to expansive hand movements and rapid comments. He used more four-bit words than most of us had ever heard before. "This is part of my ongoing examination of the agricultural proletariat. I'm especially concerned with raising the level of social consciousness among the working class," chattered the prof, nodding all the while. He told the class further that he had received a grant from a national foundation; moreover, the college had empowered him to offer credit to any of us who helped him.

When I told him that I could arrange for him to interview an Okie friend, he nodded, spouting, "Uh-huh! Uh-huh! Uh-huh!" He had the metabolism of a lemming and was always moving when you tried to speak to him, giving the impression that he just couldn't wait for you to finish so he could launch another salvo of speech. "A Dust Bowler? A real Okie?" he asked. Before I could reply he nodded, "Uh-huh! Uh-huh! Uh-huh!"

"Uh-huh," I said.

That evening, I mentioned to Pop that one of my professors was going to interview Mr. Barnhall. Pop looked up from his newspaper, sipped one more time from his can of beer, then asked, "You cleared all this with Barney, did you, *hijo?*"

"Sure. I called him."

"And your teacher, he knows something about working people?"

I grinned. "He's an expert. He's got a PhD from Hahvahd."

"Uhmmm," responded Pop, a funny little half-smile on his face as he snapped his paper back up before his eyes: end of conversation.

Professor Givens drove us out to Barnhall's place that next day, the prof surprising me with the aggressive way he tooled his fancy Datsun sports car. In fact, the car itself surprised me.

He seemed more like a nice, conservative Volvo man, or maybe a Mercedes diesel.

As we roared past the old Weedpatch Camp, me holding tight to the armrest, happy for the seat belt that anchored me, Givens—in the midst of his continuous flow of talk—mentioned how good it would be to meet an Okie "who had risen from starvation and filth and poverty." When he mentioned the names of a prominent grower, a locally famous attorney, and a country music legend, I wondered if Mr. Barnhall was the kind of man he was prepared to meet. I also wondered, though I said nothing about it, why people like the ones he named needed anyone to give them pride in their heritage or a sense of accomplishment and worth. Thinking about it, I couldn't imagine any of our Okie friends who lacked pride or a realistic sense of worth. I began to understand that funny little half-smile Pop had given me. What was I doing in this car with this guy? Well, at least I could answer: one unit of credit toward graduation, with a big, fat A attached, I hoped. Anyway, Barney Barnhall had risen above two of the professor's categories: he wasn't starving and he wasn't really poor.

"You say this man is a poultry farmer?" asked Professor Givens.

"He sells eggs."

"Oh," nodded the prof, then he continued almost absently "I only buy organic eggs from health food stores."

"Barney's are organic," I grinned.

Mr. Barnhall didn't realize I was in the car when we arrived. The prof bounced out first while I unhooked the unfamiliar seat belt, and his embroidered blue work shirt and hundred-dollar cowboy boots—not to mention his pale skin and thin wrists—caused Barney to give a double take, then amble from the cadaver of an ancient Ford where he had apparently been performing a post-mortem, and ask, "Y'all wont iny aigs?"

"Mr. Barnhall," I said, finally climbing from the car's cockpit, "it's me, Julio."

He squinted. "Oh yeah. How're you a-doin', son?"

"And this is Doctor Givens, who'd like to interview you."

The two shook hands and Barney, ever the gracious host, grinned his gap-toothed best, then extended his left hand. "Here's a little present I just found yonder," he said. The prof, hesitating momentarily while he examined his crushed paw, finally thrust it forward and received a brown egg flecked with chicken shit, feathers, and grass, all organic of course. "One of them hens went and laid 'er under that there Ford," Barney explained. Givens quickly passed the egg to me, then wiped his hand vigorously on his trouser leg. I dropped it into my jacket pocket.

"You a doctor?" asked Mr. Barnhall.

The professor was amused. He stifled a little laugh, "No, not a *medical* doctor. I'm a doctor of philosophy."

"You ain't no real doctor, then?"

Professor Givens began to frame an answer, then glanced toward me with a bemused expression on his face. "No," he replied.

Barney grunted as he turned and headed for the pepper tree where he usually entertained guests. Givens scurried along behind him, chattering, while I lugged the professor's briefcase. When Mr. Barnhall stopped next to the tree, the prof whispered to me, "Isn't he going to ask us in?"

I shrugged as though ignorant. In truth, I had never been in the house, and I doubt if my Pop had either. Even when we drank beer there and had to drain our radiators, we just moseyed over and washed a tire on one of his old cars. It never even dawned on me to want to go inside.

It did dawn on Professor Givens, however, who whined as he set up his tape recorder: "This would be so much simpler indoors." Once his machine was adjusted and he had extracted a sheath of notes—his questions, I assumed—from his case, he glanced around for somewhere to sit. Barney had squatted, and I plopped cross-legged on the scraggly grass. "Fetch me a lawn chair, won't you, Gonzalez?" the prof ordered. I patrolled around and finally came up with a stout-looking old crate, which I delivered with a flourish. "Thanks," sniffed the prof, dusting the crate with his handkerchief before gingerly sitting on it.

"What was it that brought you out to California, Mr. Barnhall, handbills?" he asked in a brusque, irritated tone.

"Handbills?" The interview was off at a roaring start. Barney obviously hadn't a hint what Givens meant.

"You know," prompted Givens, "fliers. Printed announcements; from California growers urging you to come west."

"Oh hell no, I never seen nothin' like that."

"It was the dust storms, then?"

"Naw. We could live with dust all right. Hell, there was always dust back home. What run me out was the go'ment."

I knew I wasn't supposed to interrupt, but I was studying the New Deal in my American history course, so I asked, "The government? I thought the New Deal set up relief agencies for farmers during the 1930s."

"A major thrust of the Roosevelt administration's recovery programs," began Professor Givens, in a tone alerting me that a lecture would follow, but Barney cut him off.

"Re-covery my ass! The go'ment worked about as good then as it does now." He spat a brown puddle of tobacco juice in front of him. "Hell, this teller from the AAA—it weren't no Alcoholics Anonymous, but it sure as hell drove a bunch of us to drank—this feller he come out and give a big check to Mr. A. R. Cantrell that owned about half the county..." (Givens gasped, "Uh-huh! Uh-huh! Uh-huh!" obviously ready to clarify matters, but Barney wasn't through.) "They went and paid him not to grow so many crops for a while. So Cantrell he ups and buys tractors and gang plows with his money and kicks all his tenants, including me and my brother Dean, off'n his land. Land we was borned on."

"Uh-huh! Uh-huh! Uh-huh! But surely you can't blame the Roosevelt administration for that?" smiled the prof, again on the verge of a lecture.

"The hell I cain't!" growled Barney. "The goddamned go'ment give that money to A. R. Cantrell. Who the hell did they think he's a-gonna spend it on? Us? Hell's far, ol' Roosevelt, he's a rich guy hisself."

"Uh-huh!" sputtered the professor. "You aren't asserting that FDR was in league with established capital, are you?" he demanded, his voice rising.

"Hell no! I don't even know what that means. But I do know his boys went and give that money to A. R. Cantrell and that's why I'm in California."

Professor Givens emitted a long sigh, rolled his eyes at me, then changed the subject. "Uh-huh," he said, "okay. Let's go on. How important were the songs of Woody Guthrie in keeping up the migrants' spirits and in organizing them?"

"Who?"

"Woody Guthrie, the bard of the Dust Bowl migration," explained the prof, once more giving me a strained look.

"Was he any kin to Jack Guthrie?" asked Barney reflectively.

"Who?" Givens was stumped.

"They were cousins," I explained, the prof's eyebrows raising. The subject had entered my turf now. "Woody wrote 'Oklahoma Hills Where I Was Born' and Jack sang it."

"Is that a fact?" marveled Mr. Barnhall.

"He also wrote 'The Philadelphia Lawyer' that the Maddox Brothers and Rose sang."

"I'll be damned. I got both them records."

"Uh-huh! Uh-huh! Uh-huh!" interjected the prof. "But I was referring to his serious work like 'Talking Dust Bowl' or 'We're the Guys' or 'Dust Storm Disaster,' you know, the songs that really stirred the people,"

Barney looked directly at the professor and replied, "Never heard of 'em."

The look on Givens's face made me realize my one unit of credit was blowing away like panhandle topsoil. Voice tight, he tried one more question: "Mr. Barnhall, where exactly did you stand during the farm labor strikes of 1937, '38, and '39?"

"Where'd I stand?"

"Yes, where exactly?"

If I'd have been carrying my rosary beads, I'd have fingered them at that moment and prayed for Barney to deliver one straight answer to Professor Givens. I should have known what to expect.

"Mostly I stood up to my ass in some guy's field a–pickin' or a–choppin' or a–irrigatin'," Barney responded.

Goodbye one unit, I said to myself.

"But the movement!" spouted the professor. "Don't you remember Woody Guthrie's lyrics, 'We're the guys who grow the crops…'?"

"Hell's far, him again?" Barnhall interrupted. "Listen, we's broke and our wives was sick and our kids was starvin' and, by God, we was workin' men, so we worked, worked our damned butts off. We let all them big city fellers strike. We worked."

"Uh-huh! Uh-huh! Uh-huh! But if everyone had shared that attitude there'd be no justice for farmworkers today."

"If'n we hadn't had that attitude there'd be a whole lot more of us dead right now. That wasn't no pitcher show, pard, that was real. I felt sorry for some of them folks a–strikin', but I had my own to feed."

"And it didn't bother you that you were scabbing the jobs of Filipino and Mexican workers?"

Oh shit! I waited for Barney to punch the professor's clock, thinking I'd not only lose my unit, I'd lose my buns in the process. For a moment the big man's eyes narrowed, then he asked, "What kinda car you drivin'?"

Blinking, Professor Givens looked at me and his eyes said non sequitur. "Datsun, why?" he replied.

"How's come you went and bought that instead of a American car?"

"What in the world does Buy American chauvinism have to do with anything?" spat the prof, unaware, I'm sure, how near he was to sudden unconsciousness.

"Is it cheaper than a American car, and does it work better too?"

"Uh-huh, I guess, but…"

"Well, that's what I was," Barney said tightly. "All us guys we worked better and cheaper because we had to. We was hungrier."

The professor's head jerked as though he had just been goosed. "Uh-huh!" he said. "Uh-huh! Uh-huh! Uh-huh! But you took the jobs of third-world people, stole them!"

I ducked, but Barney didn't swing. Instead he replied in that same tight tone, "It ain't stealin' for a Jap to work cheaper and better than some ol' boy in Dee-troit, but it is stealin' for me to work cheaper and better than some other ol' boy in Delano? Damn," snorted Barnhall, "I'll bet you only drive on one-way streets."

The professor stood suddenly, then faced me. "The man's got something there, Gonzalez," he said, sounding as though surprised to hear himself. He began to reload his briefcase, the tops of his ears scarlet where they showed through his thin, shoulder-length hair. "I've got to admit that I've never thought of it like that," admitted the professor. "Mr. Barnhall, you've given me something to think about. Perhaps I've relied too much on the library. My ideas in this area want revision. I need to spend more time in the field. Uh-huh, more time in the field."

"Or the fields," Barney added. I was again afraid he'd pushed too far because I sensed that Givens had given about as much as he could, especially in front of me. In fact, if he'd learned a lot from Barney, I'd learned as much in the last few moments when Givens climbed off his PhD and acknowledged he still had things to learn. It was as though, to me at least, he'd been transformed from an unrealistic egghead into a man. For an instant I even wondered if I knew for certain what it meant to be a man.

"Yes, or the fields," Givens conceded. "I'd like to return when I've had a chance to revise my questions."

"Shore thang," Barnhall replied, and I figured they were parting the best of friends, but when the prof scurried to his car, Barney hissed out of the corner of his mouth, one of his huge paws grasping my bicep: "I'm shore glad that little fart ain't no real doctor."

I had to laugh. "See ya, Barney," I said. "I owe you a beer."

"Or three," he added.

Givens and I had only traveled a mile or so before he turned and said to me, "He wasn't quite what I'd expected."

"He's not what any of us expect, I'll bet," I responded.

"He's cut from a different bolt of cloth than anyone I've known."

"Yeah," I agreed, "and I think I know why. Have you ever been really hungry, Dr. Givens?"

"Except for fasting, no."

"Me either. Not without food, or the hope of food," I explained. "Well, Barney Barnhall, and my folks too, they have. They've got their degrees in hunger, and I'll bet that if the world falls apart tomorrow, they'll survive, because that's what they got their PhDs in." I wasn't challenging him; I just wanted him to understand my sense of Barney.

We arrived at campus and the prof dropped me next to the gym where I'd parked my pickup. "Gonzalez," he said as I popped the door shut after climbing out, "it's been an education." Then he drove away.

Just as I turned to climb into my truck's cab, I felt a lump in my jacket's pocket. I pulled Barney's egg out so I wouldn't break it, thumped my hand on the side mirror, and fumbled. The egg shattered on the State-of-California-Parking-By-Permit-Only pavement below me, leaving the yolk strangely intact. "Damn!" I spat and again started to climb into the cab when something on the yolk caught my eye. I squinted to see it clearly, then dropped to my knees: a greasy fingerprint on one edge of the yellow, smudged, but distinct.

She's My Rock

ME AND SOME OTHER BOYS had stole us a case of Lucky from
this truck that was deliverin' to the Tejon Club, and we was
flat frog-eyed whenever we drove into the Mohawk Serv-U-
Self on Norris Road. I was a-fillin' the tank when old Clyde
Mays he come back from the pisser a-gigglin' and carryin' on:
"There's a gal over in yonder van," he said, "that's hot for your
body." He pointed toward a U-Haul gassin' up at the next
island.

Well, I believed him. Why shouldn't I? I mean, I wasn't
half-bad lookin', and besides that I was drunk, so I wandered
over to that van, unbuttonin' my shirt and pullin' my jeans
down a bit so whoever the gal was could see my built. When
I got to the van, I looked in the side door and seen these
skinny legs bendin' over in a big mess of watermelons. I crin-
kled my eyes up so I'd look like Ferlin Husky, then I said:
"Howdy."

The gal looked up and Lordy! That's the ugliest gal I ever
did see, and a harelip to boot. "Nya wanna buy a wanermelon?"
she asked me, and I guess she was smilin', her lip all pulled up
into her nose like someone mended it on a foot-pedal sewing
machine. That made me laugh, picturing some fat old doctor
puttin' this here ugly baby up on the machine, then whap-
whap-whap! sewin' her mouth up while her skinny legs was
a-kickin' around.

"Whan's vunny?" she asked, her eyes turnin' sad all of a
sudden. Well, ugly or not, I couldn't let Clyde know he'd
tricked me; 'sides, I could always get me a flag to put over her
face and screw for Old Glory. I wasn't gonna crawfish on

screwin' this little old gal any more than I would on a fight, though I believe I'd rather've fought her; who wants to diddle a harelip gal anyways? "I'm just laughin' at you in there with all them watermelons," I told her. "Looks to me like they ain't much room to set."

She smiled again. I think.

"Why don't you come over to my car and we can get comfortable in the back seat." I reached out and touched her hand real gentle, just kind of tickled it the way that drives 'em nuts, and she stayed bent over them watermelons, her eyes gettin' big. That's when I realized she was real young; I wasn't but seventeen myself, and I'll bet she wasn't more than fourteen, but that ugly face surely aged her. Anyways, I don't believe she knew what I wanted.

"Hunh?" she asked.

I stepped closer, then touched her thigh, it all warm and smooth and not harelippy a-tall, and I felt her shudder. I was getting' hot all of a sudden myself, and I started wonderin' if I really did have a flag in my car. Her eyes just sparked over that tore-up excuse for a mouth. Lord, she was one ugly girl! Ewe-gly! Double-ugly! Still, them eyes and the way her thigh felt, I just figured tail's tail.

Then damned if somebody didn't sock me right on the shoulder, and I heard Clyde and the guys laugh. I spun around with my fists cocked, and there stood this good-lookin' gal maybe thirty-five, forty years old; she just spit at me: "You keep your goddamn hands off Nola Sue or I'll kick your pimply butt clean back to Weedpatch!" She meant it. (You know, drunk as I was, I asked myself: How the hell does she know about me having pimples on my butt?)

Smack! She slapped my face. "Nola Sue," she ordered, "you close them doors. I'll deal with this punk," then damned if she didn't bust a watermelon right on my chest, the juice runnin' down into my jeans and all.

What could I do? That lady she had me by the short hairs. I mean, I couldn't sock her. Besides, she's meaner than cat shit, and I didn't know for sure if I could whup her; some of them old honky-tonk gals is mighty rough. So I just hustled back to my '40 Chevy, tryin' to act like I thought it was a big joke, with that watermelon all over me and flies buzzin' 'round, sticky melon juice drippin' down into my drawers; I felt so damned stupid. I climbed into the car and drove us out to Kern County Park as fast as I could. Whenever we got there I kicked the livin' shit out of Clyde Mays.

After we'd been there a hour or so, I barfed up all the beer I'd drunk. What a wasted day. Then a damned deputy he drove up just when Bobby Joe Hurd was pukin', and caught us with what was left of the beer we'd stole. We all got sent to juvie that time.

Next summer I was fishin' in a canal out by Greenfield with a pole I'd swiped from Thrifty's. Geneie Hicks was with me; we wasn't catchin' nothin'. There was one big colored lady up the bank from us, but she wasn't doin' too good either.

Anyways, up drove this beat-lookin' station wagon with old, cracked wood peelin' off the sides. And guess who got out: the lady that busted the watermelon on me, and Nola Sue the harelip. They had these real long poles tied to one side of the wagon, and they commenced loosenin' 'em. I pulled my cowboy hat down over my eyes and just set there a-hopin' they wouldn't see me.

They finally got their poles untied and come walkin' up the bank. The mean lady never even noticed me, but damned if that harelip gal didn't, her eyes lockin' in on me whenever she passed, then glancin' back all the time after they got their rigs in the water up the canal. Geneie Hicks seen her and said: "Damn but that's a ugly girl yonder."

"You ain't shittin'," I answered, not lookin' up.

"Does she know you from somewheres? She's surely lookin' you over."

"Let's get out of here," I told him. "We can drive up Kern Canyon and catch us some trout."

"Sounds good," said Geneie, so we packed up our gear and toted it back to my Chevy. Parked right next to me was the big ol' Caddy that the colored lady drove. It was unlocked, so I swiped some cigarettes and two of them wire seat cooler things and a blanket from it; the glove compartment and the trunk was locked, though. Just as I threw the stuff from the Caddy into my car, I heard a voice say: "NI sneen nya."

I turned around and, ugly as a sinner's soul, there Nola Sue stood. "Mind yer own beeswax," I snapped at her.

"NI won' tnell on nya."

"Thanks a lot," I said real sarcastic, then climbed into my Chevy and got the hell away from there. She give me the creeps, and I didn't want her old lady seein' me either.

We drove out Nile Street, through the last of the orange groves and the open hills, then into the canyon. Up by Richbar we seen a couple cop cars and a ambulance and a fire truck. We stopped and this here fat lady she run right up to my window and stuck her head in: "A Mexcan drownded," she hollered, "right in the river, and skin divers is lookin' for 'im." The lady's eyes was all wide, and she kindly panted. Before I could answer her, another car pulled behind us and she run back to it.

I parked the car and me and Geneie we walked over to where a crowd of folks was watchin' them skin divers. Off to one side of us two Mexcans set on a log with their arms around this here Mexcan girl. None of 'em was cryin'.

"It don't look half bad," I heard one old boy say to his wife. "Hell, I could swim it easy." I poked Geneie in the ribs and whispered: "LA." He laughed. Them bastards from down south thought they could do anything, but me, I knew about the river: pullin' along lookin' smooth and easy, it had one hell of a suck; I liked to got drownded there myownself back when I's fourteen.

Old Geneie he's real comical. He poked me back and whispered out the corner of his mouth: "Well, hell, it looks like the Mexcans cinched the Kern River Sweepstakes for this summer. This here's about the twentieth one that drownded, and ain't but a dozen Okies done 'er. I shore hate losin' to Mexcans. But at least we ain't last. Niggers ain't drownded but five or six, and I don't believe they's been a Chinaman or Jap or Flip done 'er yet." I like to split a gut tryin' not to laugh out loud. Old Geneie he never even grinned: "I shore hate to lose," he said.

They had them one hell of a time findin' that Mexcan's body, so me and Geneie we went back to where the cars was parked and rifled the open ones. Drowndins are pretty good, like wrecks, 'cause folks get excited and don't lock up whenever they park. We got all the junk we could pack into my Chevy's trunk, cameras and ever'thing. And we found a full pint of sloe gin in a '59 Merc. It was a real good haul. We should of took off right then, but Geneie he said he'd never seen a dead Mexcan before, so we pulled two or three long times on the sloe gin and went back to the river.

Just about the time they found that Mexcan, a lady and a man came runnin' up to a sheriff from where the cars was parked and they was yellin' about how someone broke into their car. Me and Geneie just looked at each other, then moseyed back toward my Chevy and got the hell out of there before the cops got too curious.

We buzzed up to Hobo Hot Springs and bought us burgers at the café. Afterward Geneie he went up to the campground to look for this girl he knew, so I broke out my pole and commenced fishin'. When I got upstream I seen a campfire on a sandbar, but didn't think nothin' of it except that it was near dark and the game warden might be out soon lookin' for guys fishin' late. I'd brought what was left of the sloe gin with me, so I reeled in and set myself on a log under this here big tree. It was real quiet up the canyon at night; all you heard was the river a-suckin' past.

Then this voice said real soft-like: "Hni."

I looked up and damned if that Nola Sue wasn't standin' right in front of me in this here bikini, her body all outlined against that bonfire on the sandbar, her face hid in the dark; she'd filled out some. I started to leave, then thought better of it. "Hi," I said, "what're you doin' here?"

"Ny nomma an her bnoyfriend is cnookin' not nogs yonder," she nodded toward the sandbar. "NI sneen ya fishin'."

I'd been pullin' pretty good on that sloe gin, so I didn't think too straight, my head rememberin' that ugly face, my pecker just seein' that good body. "Set a spell," I finally said, and she come over to me, kinda slow and shy. I reached up for her hand, then pulled her down next to me, careful not to see her face. And, as it turned out, I never even had to kiss her.

★★★

After I come out of the county road camp in '65 and got me that job cleanin' burlap sacks at the Sierra Bag Company, I commenced hangin' out at this honky-tonk, The Sad Sack. It was a real dark place out on Edison Highway where the cocktail waitresses went topless and they had this other gal that danced behind the bar stark neked. They charged a buck for a glass of beer.

What kept me goin' there was this waitress named Penny who had the pinkest nipples I ever seen and pointed, and who had a face that liked to took my breath away; her mouth looked like a red flower. She got really friendly with me 'cause I bought her lots of champagne to drink. It got to where I'd come in and she'd just smile at me, and all the other guys looked half sore. They knew I was a-takin' over.

Only thing was that my wages at the bag company couldn't stand them dollar beers and champagne at two-fifty a glass. Besides, I needed to buy Penny some presents, 'cause she wouldn't put out less I did. So I got in touch with some of the boys, and we commenced hittin' gas stations pretty reg'lar, always late at night whenever there wasn't but one old boy workin'. We never hurt nobody, and damned if we didn't scoop us up some money.

Penny she loved it. I told her what I was doin', and she laughed and said she was my gun moll. I bought her a new Dodge and moved us into a nice place over on Flower Street. She quit out at the Sad Sack and I had to step up my service station business, her buyin' clothes and all, hittin' one a week for a long spell, drivin' up above Fresno and clean down to San Diego so's the cops wouldn't know where to expect us guys next. In the back of my head I knew Penny was a hustler, but it wasn't my head I was listenin' to. I even quit my job at the bag company, and maybe that was what really caused me to get caught.

I come home early one day after casin' a gas station over in Arvin and caught Penny and this Mexcan makin' out on the couch; she didn't have nothin' on but her drawers, and she was doin' somethin' for him she hardly ever done for me. Jesus Christ! It was damn lucky I wasn't carryin' my pistol, 'cause

I'd of shot both of 'em. Still, I beat her bloody and stomped that Mexcan.

I left 'em there on the floor and drove over to Oildale and found some of my partners at the Highland Club. There was this big strike of Mexcans goin' on out at the grape fields north then, and most of us guys didn't like it a-tall. I mean, they wasn't just Mexcans, which is bad enough, but they was Commies too. I didn't have no trouble gatherin' up a gang of boys to drive out to McFarland with me to whup us some goddamn Mexcans. I surely wanted to work over a few of them greasy bastards. I wanted to kill 'em and send 'em back to where they come from.

The first couple fields we seen had too many of 'em, and sheriffs too. But over by Cawelo there was a small field with mostly Flips workin' in it and maybe half a dozen Mexcans carryin' signs on a dirt road next to a irrigation ditch. We pulled up, two carloads of us, with some clubs we'd picked up on the way, and we pounded piss out of 'em and run 'em off. Them Filipinos in the fields laughed, and some of the guys started to go after them, but I stopped 'em. "Them ain't Mexcans," I said, "they're on our side." Then this one Flip he come up to me and said there was another bunch of greasers down the dirt road a piece. "You kill kill," he said, and I liked to laughed at how funny he talked. Still, I wasn't through with goddamn Mexcans—the crooked, greasy bastards—not by a long shot. I needed to whup me a few more. I *needed* to, 'cause Penny and that Spic kept flashin' into my head.

Maybe some of them guys we'd beat up earlier had warned 'em, but the Mexcans at the next field was waitin' for us. They fought like white men, and one guy, just when I's fixin' to wallop him, he spun around and hit me across the bridge of my nose with a board. That's all I recollect. When I come to, I's in a hospital room. I could just barely see; my eyes had gone all fuzzy on me. They knocked me out and done a operation, but when they finally took the bandages off, I couldn't see no better; in fact, I believe it's worse. And it got worser.

If that ain't bad enough, Penny pressed charges for assault and rape (ain't *that* a kick in the ass!); that Mexcan was hurt bad and they got me for somethin' called mayhem; one of my boys told about the gas stations; the only thing they didn't charge me with was whuppin' them strikers, even the cops couldn't fault me there. The public defender told me I could get life for all the stuff they had on me what with my record and all. Then he said maybe a judge would go easy since I was *blind*.

When I heard that word I wanted to bawl. Blind! That meant I wasn't goin' to get no better, and the goddamn doc never even told me. Blind, and goin' to jail over that damned woman and her Mexcan. That night I tried to hang myself, but I couldn't even do that right.

The public defender knew what he's talkin' about. I only got five to twenty years at Vacaville because I was blinded. And somethin' funny happened after the judge passed sentence and the court adjourned. I heard the defender say "All right" to someone, then this small hand touched my arm:

"NI'm sorry," said a voice and I knew right then who it was. Ugly gals is hard to forget.

"I don't need nobody's fuckin' sympathy," I kindly spit at her, jerkin' my arm away. I tried to walk away but bumped into the goddamn table.

"Cnan nI wrnite nya?"

"Leave me the hell alone," I said, then, damnit, I busted out cryin'. "Dead people don't need no letters," I sobbed.

"NI'll wrnite," she said, touchin' my arm. "Nyou ain' dead."

Nola Sue did write, by God, and a couple months at Vacaville surely taught me to welcome anythin' I got. My folks was both dead by then, and I never had no mail 'cept from her. After a while, she asked in a letter if she could come up and visit me. That was hard, 'cause there she was just a-sendin' me letters and stuff, and willin' to drive clean up to Vacaville but, to tell the truth, I just didn't want none of the guys up there to see me with a harelip, so I wrote her no.

Then she sent me this here tape recorder so I could send her letters without havin' to dictate to some other guy, and that really helped. She sent me lots of presents—Christmas, birthday, and just of the hell of it too—so I made her a leather wallet and key case, and had this other ol' boy tool it all fancy. Then she wrote and asked again if she could come up; she had vacation, and she'd surely like to visit me.

I couldn't tell her no again, good as she'd been to me. So up she come, me really dreadin' the whole thing. When I heard her talkin' all funny, I just wanted to crawl away, but damned if I didn't forget all about the way she sounded once she was tellin' all about how things was at home. And it felt mighty nice to have a woman's hand reach over and squeeze mine. It felt damned good.

I was all mixed up between being happy and sad whenever I headed back to my job at the hospital laundry. I enjoyed havin' Nola Sue to talk to, but it made me feel sadder bein' inside. Then I heard this one ol' boy kindly whistle through his teeth while I was passin', and he said to whoever was next to him: "I just seen the ugliest woman in the world. Gaw-awd damn but she was enough to gag a maggot." The other guy laughed.

"Shut your fuckin' trap!" I hollered at 'em.

They didn't say nothin' for a second, then the guy doin' all the talkin' he said, "What's wrong with you, pard, you're the lucky one. You didn't have to see her."

I started swingin' but only messed my hands up.

★★★

I spent nearly three years inside that time, and I determined that I'd never go inside again. I just wasn't worth it. On the day they let me go, Nola Sue was there to pick me up. We never discussed it or nothin', but I just naturally moved in with her whenever we got back to Oildale.

She'd helped me find a job sandin' paddles at this here new canoe factory out on North Chester, and I went right to work when I got home. The job wasn't that much, but between the both of us—Nola Sue worked as a beauty operator—we ate regular and even snuck in a little in savins. Three nights a week Nola Sue drove me to school so's I could finish my high school diploma. She helped me avoid the boys, and she seen to it I never missed no meetins with my parole officer either.

One afternoon I stopped after work with some fellers from the factory for a beer. I no sooner'n set, and I heard this familiar voice call out: "Damn if that ain't a squirrely lookin' Okie sittin' yonder!" It was that crazy Clyde Mays, and even if the parole officer wouldn't like it, he surely sounded good to me. "Come over here, you skinny fart," I hollered, and directly he was sittin' next to me a-pumpin' my hand. "You old sack a shit," he said, "damned if you don't look fat and sassy."

Well, we had lots of old times to talk about, and he filled me in on where ever'one was now. We had us a few more beers than I'd planned and I stayed later. Finally, I said to him, "Wait a minute, Clyde. I got to call home so my ol' lady don't get too worried."

"What?" he asked. "You pussy-whipped by a harelip gal? Shit, I can almost see screwin' her and lettin' her donate a little money, but I sure as hell didn't think you'd be pussy-whipped."

That pissed me. "I ain't pussy-whipped!"

"You act like you really give a shit for that ugly harelip gal," he laughed, just eggin' me on.

"Talk sense!" I snapped. "Tail's tail, and blind guys don't get much choice."

"I 'precciate that," Clyde went on, "but don't let no woman get aholt to you, bo, or you'll damn sure take a pussy-whippin'."

"Well I don't give a shit for her, so shut up about it!" He did, and we talked a while longer, but the fun was gone.

Whenever I got home that night, Nola Sue asked if I'd eat and when I said I hadn't she went into the kitchen. Me, I set in the livin' room and turned on the radio so I could listen to some good country music. I didn't feel too hot and it wasn't just the beer I'd drunk. Directly, she come in and put a TV tray in front of me and told me where things was on it. I didn't like the sound of how she talked, all n-sounds, so I just said, "Shut up and leave me be!"

She did, takin' herself back into the kitchen, then I heard her cryin', snortin' in that funny way harelips do. Old Stoney Edwards come on the radio and went to singin' about how his woman was his rock. Well, I set there awhile, that beer a-workin' in me, and I heard Nola Sue had quit cryin' in the kitchen. Somethin' in me wanted to apologize, but I couldn't be pussy-whipped by no harelip, so I rared up and hollered for her to come out from the kitchen, me puffin' like a ol' bull, I's gettin' myself so worked up.

Soon as I heard her shuffle kinda close I raged at her: "I don't need no goddamn harelip!" But I no sooner'n got the words out than somethin' wet and hot salted my cheeks. "I don't need no goddamn harelip," I said again, my lower lip commencin' to shiver so bad I couldn't hardly talk.

I waited for her to bawl some, but she never, and my own face just wouldn't get under control. She never said nothin', and I could only hear my own breath snortin', makin' me wonder in my darkness if the whole thing wasn't just a beer dream, and maybe I's alone, stuck in a cell somewheres, or maybe just inside myself. Then I felt her hand, cool and real, on my face. I wanted to slap it away, but I couldn't move, so I blubbered one more time: "I don't need no goddamn harelip."

She had both hands on my face then, cradlin' it, and she answered: "No, but nyou need a woman."

And she was right.

Walls

AL STOOD A MOMENT in front of the bar's restroom, stood glancing up and down the hall until certain he was alone, then darted in. He hunched into a toilet booth, closed the door, and sat without lowering his trousers. He felt safer.

It was a dim room, dimmer still in the booth, but Al could read most of the wall without his penlight. There was nothing special, not at first anyway.

Cindy does it with flipinos. He paid no attention.

Want nine juicy inches? Meet me at one p.m. Ugh! Some pervert.

Here I sit all broken hearted... That again.

I lade Julie Whitesel. Call for a lay 538-1112. There, there was one. He pulled his notebook from a breast pocket and wrote both the number and name. Then he scanned the rest of the wall, finding only one other good one: *If you want something really hot call 537-4375.* He preferred having a name, but mystery intrigued him too.

The next booth contained nothing interesting, but on the wall behind the urinal there were two numbers. One, all by itself with no explanation: *538-8975.* The other, written in a red marking pen, *Knob Jobs 536-2149.*

Before leaving, he glanced at himself in the mirror, ran his fingers through his hair, then saw another number scribbled lightly near the mirror: *gang bang, 538-2341.*

Casually, Al strolled from the bar, nodding to the waitress as he left, then he hurried up the street to his car, feeling electricity lighten his step, feeling it tingle him as he rushed home. He had calls to make.

An older woman answered, so he asked tentatively, "Julie?"

"Just a moment," the older woman replied, then he heard her call "Julie! It's for you, dear."

A voice almost like a little girl's, high and clear and innocent, said, "Hello?"

"Hi, Julie," he said. "You don't know me, but this friend of mine he said you were nice and maybe I could call you."

"Who?"

"Who? What difference does it make?"

"Who told you?"

He was suddenly uneasy. "Oh, this guy named Steve," he improvised.

"Steve Garcia?"

"Yeah, Steve Garcia."

Her voice lightened. "Steve's nice. What's your name?"

Relieved, he improvised more. "Donnie Rogers. I'm new in town. Just moved from Fresno. I kinda hoped we could make a date and you could show me around. Okay?"

There was a pause. "No, I can't. My folks don't let me date boys they don't know. Maybe if I saw you at school or something we could get to know each other, but I can't go out with you." Her voice, still clear and innocent, was firm.

"Won't you at least think about it?"

"I really can't. I've gotta go now. You can call back sometime if you want. Like I said, maybe if we meet at school we can talk. Tell Steve I said hi."

"But..." The line went dead. Oh damn! He slammed the receiver into the cradle and sat staring at it. It happened every time someone hung up on him, and it was like absorbing a punch in the belly. He gasped and rubbed his eyes. Oh damn, he repeated to himself.

The second number somehow wouldn't dial well. He tried three times before he finally got it. He needed something hot, he needed something right away. After the third ring a hoarse man's voice barked at him: "Do you believe on the Lard Jesus Christ? Are you washed in the blood of Him that went and died to save Mankind? Have you took *Jee*-sus for your personal savior? If you ain't, you're with them vipers and serpents of the

Ee-vil One, you're in the clutches of Satan hisself! *Ree*-pent ye sinner! *Ree*-pent ye rotten sinner! Gasp!" the voice sucked for breath, then snorted on: "Verily I say onto you the Lard *Jee*-sus is Lard of all!..."

This time Al hung up, dropping the phone as if it was indeed hot, then scanning his quivering hands. Why wouldn't they leave him alone? All he wanted was someone to listen to him, someone to touch him.

Five-three-eight-eight-nine-seven-five, and Al waited. Busy signal. He sighed, and hung up.

The next number troubled him. *Knob Jobs* leered back at him as it had in bold red behind the urinal. *Knob Jobs*. He knew what it meant, and the very thought weakened him. But there was a number with it, and numbers were meant to be dialed. Maybe he ought to try that other number again first.

Five-three-eight-eight-nine-seven-five. It rang this time, just twice, then a woman's voice answered: "Uh-huh?"

Al hesitated. "Hi. You don't know me, but a friend gave me your number."

"Who this?" the woman demanded. "That you, Darneal? You *bull*-shittin' again?"

He knew immediately she was colored, and exotic images tickled his loins. "No, my name's not Darneal. My name's Don Rogers. Darneal gave me your number."

"Darneal did? Damn."

"He said you're nice and maybe I could have a date."

"Darneal say that? How you know Darneal? You sound gray."

"Ah, I used to work with Darneal."

"Bullshit! You in the joint with him, right? Bet you a bad honky if you a friend of Darneal's." Her voice warmed. "Whyn't you ease on over, and bring a little taste with you, baby."

Al cleared his throat. "Where do you live?"

"I thought you know Darneal. Didn't he tell? You sure you ain't no pig? You startin' to sound like a pig."

"No, no I'm not. I'm a friend. Just wait and see."

"Don't start some shit," she warned, her voice lower and dangerous. "Don't start some shit now!" Then she hung up and again Al sank back into himself.

Damnit anyway! What had he said wrong?! She was almost ready to let him come over, then she hung up. What was wrong? And now he had to face that *Knob Jobs* call.

A flat, masculine voice answered. "Yeah?"

Al choked on the words, had to clear his throat, then tried again. "About those knob jobs..."

"What? Who the hell is this, some wise guy?"

"You don't know me..."

"I don't wanna know you, buddy, but if you wanna meet me somewhere, I'll kick your ass!"

Al slammed the receiver down, trembling uncontrollably. He had felt that voice's hand thrust up through the telephone's speaker and grasp his throat, grasp and twist and choke. What's wrong with people? Why all the hate? Oh God, he moaned as he sank back on his chair. He rubbed himself where the meaty fingers had grabbed, trying to forget the pain, the sudden choking, gagging horror.

Al gathered himself, calming a bit, and walked to the cupboard where he filled an un-iced glass with bottled daiquiri, then bolted it. He poured another, and drained it somewhat more slowly. After pouring a third glass, he returned to the phone.

He was feeling better, and his pain and fear were beginning to give way to outrage. Who the hell did that big stiff think he was, anyway? Al had half a mind to call him back and tell him off, but the image of that thick hand reaching from the speaker, the tattooed, hairy wrist, prompted him to simply suck angrily at his warm daiquiri. "They oughta put people like that away," he said to himself, and his body shuddered involuntarily.

Well, at least he had another number to call, another chance. He was easing now, relaxing, and he took the time to fill his glass once more. Five-three-six-two-one-four-nine.

Before one full ring someone snapped on the other end: "Harley's." It was a high-pitched man's voice, cracking, sounding ancient.

"I'm calling about gang bang."

"What race he in? Which track? Come on, palsy, we're in business. This ain't no fortune-teller's place."

"Track?"

"Look, palsy, you bettin' or not? They're startin' at Golden Gate in three minutes. I gotta keep this line open for cash customers," groused the old voice.

The daiquiris urged him to tell the aged aggressor off. "Listen," Al snarled, "I'm not gonna let you..." The old bastard clicked off. Well screw you, palsy, Al thought. He was tempted to call back and ream the old bastard, but the daiquiris suggested something else. He looked back at his list; there it was, 538-1112.

He dialed quickly, thrusting his finger into the small plastic holes and zipping the numbers. He'd have his say now, damnit! He'd damn sure have his say. The innocent voice answered. "Hello?"

"Julie?"

"Y-yes," the power of his voice caused her to falter.

"This is Don—I called you a while ago. Now listen, I'm gonna give you a lay you won't forget, and I'm gonna do it now. Where can I meet you?"

The girl's voice lowered until it sounded like a hungry animal's growl. "You know where Burger King is?"

"Sure."

"I'll wait for you on that corner," she growled. "Please hurry."

"I'll hurry." Smelling her musk, her juices from the phone, he reached through the line and touched her, feeling the girl shudder, give. Well, he was gonna take.

Al circled the block once before he saw her standing near the phone booth, small and pretty and young. It was rush hour, so traffic clogged the street, camouflaging him. He circled again. The daiquiris had left him alone in his car watching her, and his stomach began to roll. He circled the block a third time with a copper taste welling in the back of his mouth, for he saw that the girl was really waiting to trap him, waiting to pull him from his car and expose him to the parade of leering cars and hairy-armed drivers.

After his fourth circuit, she was gone, swallowed by the lust of another, swept into the quagmire of thick wrists and tattoos and voices that threatened from all sides. He had to vomit.

In the men's room at Burger King he puked, purged his belly until he stood watery and empty before the toilet and scribbled wall, stood vacant before the threats and promises of a wall he knew so well, a wall that knew him.

"Ahhh," he moaned and extended his arms, leaning forward until he pressed against its cold, glossy finish, until he felt the wall's cool comfort, felt it pull him into itself, soothe him.

Homecoming

NOBODY COULD MISTAKE KEN for a Jap now, he was certain of that, not with his right sleeve pinned neatly to the shoulder of his uniform jacket, not with three rows of ribbons decorating his breast; no, especially not with sleepless nights and shattered dreams, nights spent trying to recapture that terrible instant when his war had ended.

He remembered crawling up that muddy ridge, his throat hurting, his eyes dry as dirt, covering fire snapping over his head; remembered hearing the voices of his buddies around him, the bumps of mortar rounds, the shrill, unmistakable cry of a dying soldier from the German emplacement ahead; he remembered the whirling, whirring action on all sides as he struggled toward the machinegun that had pinned his unit in the gully below. He remembered everything until the dull swirl after he had seen a grenade arcing from the German emplacement toward him. That was where it ended. Everything. His war was over.

Sitting now in the NCO Club at the army terminal in Oakland, he swirled brandy in a snifter—the belligerent bartender had complained about having to search for so exotic a glass—good California brandy. It tasted like home, the grapes his father and grandfather had grown, the grapes he had pruned and packed for as long as he could recall.

Home. Sergeant Ken Tsukeda had hesitated to even think that word in combat when death anticipated his every move, yet it was the right word. He sipped again the rich, brown liquor. *Home* was exactly the right word.

Next day he traveled south over Highway 101 to Los
Angeles on a Greyhound bus, thinking all the while that
his route paralleled Highway 99, only a mountain range
away from the road that passed so near his family's farm. As
slow as the journey was, Ken didn't mind. The bus seemed
to stop at every small town, and each community had its
own unique familiarity to a returning soldier. Two other
uniformed men sat near him on the bus and they soon
began talking; all three had bought their bloody tickets
home near Casino, a place they swore they'd never forget.
They were more concerned with being home than with
horrors they might have seen, have shared, so their conversation quickly drifted away from battle toward more
important topics like women, jobs, and who would win the
World Series.

Since all three faced long waits at the LA terminal before
transferring to other buses to continue their journeys, they
decided to treat themselves to "civilian" hamburgers at a
greasy spoon across the street from the depot. The small place
was jammed with working people buzzing over the chicken-
fried steak and breaded veal cutlets, so the three soldiers had
to wait for a trio of stools to open up at the counter. Once
seated, each looked at a menu—a typed page inserted
between clear plastic sheets—joking that their mess halls had
offered better choices.

When the fat waitress finally approached, she ignored the
other two men and addressed Ken: "What are you?" she asked
in a low, cold tone.

He was startled. "What am I?"

"What are you?"

"What the hell are *you*?" he demanded, and she flinched.

Ken felt an invisible hand begin gripping his throat, and his
eyes were suddenly dust-dry. "I'm an American soldier," he
choked, fighting rage. "But what the hell are *you*?"

His two buddies suddenly awakened to what was happen-
ing. "Hey!" shouted one, a straw-haired boy from Escondido.
"What is this?" demanded the olive-skinned sergeant from
El Centro.

Clearly frightened, the waitress nonetheless persisted, her voice shrill. "Is he a Chinaman or a Jap?"

"I'm an American soldier!"

"I never asked you that!" she screeched, her eyes wide. "I never asked that! I believe you're a Jap, and we don't serve no Japs!"

A dark rage boiled in Ken, the same fury that had led him into the teeth of German and Italian fire more than once. He stood slowly, pushing from the counter with his left arm. "What did you say?"

Leaping to his feet, the straw-haired boy growled: "You fat bitch. One more word out of you and I'll knock you into next week!"

The sergeant from El Centro had risen slowly, his countenance flame-red, and he faced the embarrassed diners. "Did you hear what this slut said? Did you? This guy's got a friggin' Silver Star! His friggin' arm was blown off! And you assholes just sit there! You're a bunch of friggin' Nazis! Maybe we shoulda shot *you* guys in Sicily!"

The diners looked down. None of them challenged the three enraged men, and the waitress cringed against the wall. "Come on," Ken gasped, his eyes scorching the now-terrified waitress. After one last challenging glare at the diners, the three soldiers slammed out the door.

Pale, leaning against the wall with one hand fluttering at her ample breast, the waitress remained speechless for a long moment. Finally she muttered weakly, "I oughta call a cop," followed by "Jap-lovers!" Then, as she noticed several customers leaving with disgusted looks on their faces, she demanded, "Hey! You gotta pay!" But she had lost her force.

The three soldiers pounded back into the depot and plopped onto a wooden bench. Their recent pasts had prepared them for action, not talk, so they said nothing, sitting instead in shared tension until their buses arrived. They exchanged addresses and agreed to remain in touch, then began the last legs of their journeys.

Ken could not relax as the bus zoomed out of LA toward Riverside, then through San Bernardino and finally up Cajon

Pass north into the Mojave Desert. Through the desert night he saw only occasional lights glittering in the distance, them and stars brighter and more numerous than he remembered. He sat back then, finally relaxing, and allowed the bus's drone to slip him into sleep.

"Your stop, soldier." It was still dark when the bus driver awakened him. For a moment Ken strained against disorientation, then he replied, "Thanks."

There was no depot in Independence. Instead Ken found himself standing on a sandy street in front of a drugstore that was closed and dark. His watch read 4:58 a.m. It was chilly, and a cup of java would have hit the spot, but no open cafés were visible so he sat on his duffel bag and lit a smoke.

A moment later, from nowhere it seemed, a sheriff's car materialized, crunching up the street with only its parking lights on. Too weary to care, Ken remained seated on his duffel, coughing in the brisk desert air, smoke exploding from his lungs.

The deputy stopped his car next to Ken. "You need somethin', pardner?" he asked in a noncommittal tone.

"A cup of coffee."

The sheriff chuckled. "That's not on the menu. What are you waitin' for?"

"A ride out to Manzanar."

"You might have a long wait." The sheriff's tone lightened. He had noted Ken's uniform with its empty sleeve and rows of decorations. "Just back from overseas?" he asked.

"Yeah."

"Well," the sheriff suggested, "I might just swing by the camp this morning on my patrol. Toss your bag in and I'll run out there."

"Thanks."

Waiting in the visitor's room, Ken pondered the nails on his left hand; they were dirty. What a nuisance not being able to clean them without an act of congress. He did rub two spots from his trousers and comb his hair just before the door opened and his mother burst in, engulfing him with kisses and tears. They clutched one another for a long minute, Ken fighting his own tears, then she pushed gently away and surveyed her son. "You look tired," she said.

"I'm pooped," he acknowledged, only then noticing the uncomfortable-looking man who stood just inside the door. "What do you want?" Ken asked him.

The man looked at his shoes. "I'm sorry, Sergeant Tsukeda, but it's the rules."

"They have to monitor visits," his mother explained.

Glaring at the man, Ken felt his throat tightening. "I'd like to visit my mother alone," he said.

"Look, I don't like this either," the man said.

"Please," croaked Ken.

"Oh hell!" shot the man. "I'll wait just outside the door."

"Thanks."

There was so much to tell her, but his mother didn't give him a chance. "Your father is going back," she told him, her voice breaking. "They moved him to Tule Lake. And Tommy."

"Tommy?"

"He went no-no."

Ken sat back down. "How can they go back where they've never been?"

"Your father says it's better than staying where they've never been wanted."

He could not control tears now and wasn't certain whether they were tears of rage or despair, or at whom they were directed. "How can they? What about the farm? What about us?"

"He wants to talk with you."

Ken rested his face in his left hand, and his mother stepped forward and cradled his head. "You've been hurt terribly," she sighed.

"I've been hurt," he agreed.

"Does the arm bother you?"

"I can still work," he replied almost absently. "Why didn't someone write and tell me?"

"What could you have done?" she asked.

He hesitated. "The same thing I did in combat, I guess. Nothing."

"You did something."

"Not enough," he whispered. "Not enough," then he kissed his mother once more.

Near the main gate he waited for the jitney that would carry him back to Independence where he would catch the Greyhound for the long haul to Tule Lake. Two young soldiers on guard duty smiled and tried to spark a conversation. "It musta been rough, huh, Sarge?" volunteered one.

"Yeah," Ken replied.

"You see a lot of action?" asked the other.

"Some." His throat began to tighten.

"Boy," the guard puffed, "that's where I'd like to be, overseas where the real war is."

"Yeah," said Ken, snuffing out what was left of his cigarette. Beyond the guard box and the camp, the Sierra Nevada loomed, and beyond them, in the Great Central Valley, was the farm on which he and his father had been born. Ken reached up awkwardly with his left hand and began tearing decorations from his jacket and throwing them onto the dusty earth.

"Hey!" called one guard, "You can't do that!"

"Watch me," responded Sergeant Ken Tsukeda.

"Don't!" said the other guard just as Ken threw his Combat Infantryman's Badge onto the ground and grasped the small purple ribbon his arm had cost him.

"You shouldn't, Sarge," urged the guard as Ken tossed the Purple Heart onto the ground.

With one last, awkward, left-handed movement, Ken tore the Silver Star from his breast and threw it.

Happily Ever After

YOU REMEMBER THEM ON QUIET EVENINGS when you've consumed one more drink than you need: the kids you grew up
with who didn't live into maturity. The all-league end, killed in
a jeep accident at Camp Pendleton; the good-natured gal who
banged us all, drowned in the Kern River; the student body
president who bled to death after a car crash; the first girl you
ever really kissed, crushed when a train breached her parents'
car. And the girl you loved, you loved, O God you loved (the
liquor has you now), a red smear on the lake after she fell from
her water skis and was cracked by a following boat. You
remember them with an eerie belly, with little pockets soften-
ing and bursting within you.

Your senior year in high school and you had to defend against
Leroy Davis in the play-off game. Together you felt old, for you'd
known each other since kindergarten, and a high school title-
game seemed life's ultimate. Scared? he asked just before you
went into different dressing rooms to prepare for battle. You hesitated then answered honestly: Yeah. Me too, he grinned. Ten
months later he was dead. Gone forever.

But are they really gone, any of them? You still half expect to
bump into them as you round a corner while visiting your old
neighborhood; you can hear their shouts or moans or giggles
echoing the winds of your memories and, it seems, in the very
breath of home. Where are they? Where are you?

Everyone scurried to find a date for Rena Cobb's funeral.
It was the social event of your junior year. And she laid there,
colorless yet painted, in a fluffy dress, her poor old skinny father

sobbing. The guys who claimed they'd got her exchanged knowing looks, while those who really had—if they came to the funeral at all—looked at the floor in pained confusion. Rena's death broke the chain of being: she had given you life, she had given you masculinity, now both were in jeopardy. Some essential balance was upset and you never fully righted it.

And Julio, the president: Mr. Everything. Driving home from the winter prom, in the back seat of Bob Truston's car with his date, a drunk sideswiped them and Julio was thrown into a ditch where a group of scavengers stole his wallet and watch and studs but didn't report the accident. He bled to death before an ambulance finally arrived.

Memories merge and emerge like a magician's endless chain of colored kerchiefs, flickering each from the one preceding: swirling into harsh focus, fading into mushy senti-mentality, then intensifying once more. You pour another drink, grasp it tightly and ignore your wife's tentative bid for conversation.

Clutching Jo Anne Mills one hot summer night, juices boil-ing, strange odors entering and alerting you. Brushing her rose-bud breast, Jesus. Mouths open, tongues tasted of warm old pennies. Your body alive for the first time, tingling, swelling, needing something you're not even certain of. But her parents' car stalled on a railroad crossing with a diesel engine bearing down, and Jo Anne's door jammed; before she could escape, the train destroyed her while her mother watched, helpless. You didn't find out until you returned from a vacation trip with your folks—you'd dreamed of Jo Anne's taste and feel every clandes-tine moment—and you rushed to telephone her, only to hear her mother's sobbing collapse when you asked for Jo Anne.

And, throughout your reverie, imposing, demanding attention is Lea. You avoid her, sliding around or slinking away from her memory, concentrating on others, conjuring some you'd forgotten, some who slip back to life in you after too many years: Blue Boy Bennie who rubbed his heart medicine on the sprained ankle you faked to explain a defeat suffered in a school track meet. Bennie who could only watch and who would sacrifice the green medicine just to feel he was part of things; we used to joke about him. Oh Christ, you'd forgotten him. He died in the ninth grade and his parents were too poor to give him a decent funeral; they'd spent what little they had to keep him alive, buying the green medicine he rubbed on your ankle. Mike Gorden, hit by an automobile in the fourth grade; he was in Cub Scouts with you. Even the little pale girl in the second grade who cried a lot and didn't take recreation with the rest of the class: Patsy. She went to the hospital and a year or so later, after you'd really forgotten her, she died. Leukemia, you heard your mother whisper into the phone.

Lea rushes back, back into you, an accident in your life, she shouldn't have happened but did. Your buddy couldn't make a dance he'd asked her to attend with him, so he convinced you to do honors. And you did, for three years: a lifetime, an old lifetime of yours that ended too soon as surely as had Bennie's and Mike's and Patsy's.

You finished high school together and entered college together, you opened a joint savings account; you planned, you built your lives around one another, for one another. She'd put you through grad school after you'd both graduated, but you wouldn't have any children until you'd finished your doctorate. There'd be no hurry.

That first time, on a secluded hillside in the country park, she cried. I don't know what to do, she said. I love you so much and I want to show you, but I'm afraid. You knew, as you reassured her, that desire made a liar of you. Then, later, you did love her and it meant so much more to love and to share the secret experiences with only her.

That day you had quarreled, so you stayed on shore while she skied behind her father's boat on the crowded lake. They were behind the island, then they didn't buzz back around. You noticed all the boats seemed to have stopped behind the island; the lake quieted and you heard a siren. (Somehow, you knew.) You finally asked an ashen-faced fisherman what happened. A boat killed some guy over there, he answered, just chewed him all up. (Vaguely, you knew.) You walked slowly to the other side, hoping that they'd suddenly cruise to shore and tell you what horror they'd seen, Lea excited, her father blasé, but you saw instead an ambulance and a sheriff's car, and you saw Lea's father crumpled next to a blanket-covered body weeping, oblivious of the holiday crowd milling around him. And you knew. On the greasy water you could still see a fading red memory.

If only you hadn't quarreled. If only you'd have ridden along with them as spotter. If only you could have died with her. Your own breakdown, the years you drifted, the strange jobs and places and the army, somehow it's not enough, it's not important.

For the moment neither is the girl who helped you put your life together again, who actually did put you through graduate school and who bore your babies and your burdens. Maybe it's because she moaned her first terrified yes to someone else somewhere else. Maybe. Or maybe it's because she's real while Lea is only a maudlin memory anymore, a way of being nineteen or twenty for a bittersweet instant.

Still, you can't resist, you're not strong enough. You don't want to give in to her memory, but you love her and you can't help yourself; you have to whisper a terrified yes to the glimpse of guilty joy her presence brings. Something in you opens and fills, something intensely real, and for a moment you know her once more, but in that same moment you're no longer certain about yourself.

White Lightnin'

Warm Up

ONLY ABOUT 10 PERCENT OF THE KIDS at King High School are white, so I sure didn't expect to see a pale face when I heard that name, Aiida. At our school, white girls are named Morgan, or maybe Ashley, or Sara, or even Brandi, but not Aiida. I don't want to sound racist, but that seems like too...well...too creative a name for most white families to use. To me, white names tend to be bland as lettuce. Black names tend to be more like hot links—Marchetti McLemore, Larryjane Jones, Desheila Larrieu Gray, Hiawatha Marlette Washington, and my favorite, Pearl Vengeance Collins, all of them runners I've coached.

Anyway, there was that little white girl, Aiida Holmes, at the first team meeting. She was tiny, looking like maybe a seventh-grader. All the other kids gave her the eye, but she seemed to ignore them. They were trying to figure her out, I think. Her blondish hair was, well, if not kinky, then...ah... densely wavy. But her nose, her lips, her eyes, her complexion and, yeah, her dialect, were all white. She probably just had a perm.

At that initial gathering each of the potential runners filled out insurance forms, medical forms, and I have one that I've made up that I have them complete too. It asks about any past running experience. The little white girl wrote that she had run the 660 in junior high school and that her best time had been 1:59. Not bad. Not very good either, but at least she could run some—if she'd really broken two minutes. Maybe she could provide a training partner for LaWanda, our senior.

That year for a change I had five girls out, so we'd actually have a full cross-country team. And I also had seven boys. You have to understand that King is a meat-and-potatoes sports school: football, basketball, baseball, and track. Cross-country, my sport, doesn't attract much attention. I was so tickled when I saw the sign-up sheet and realized that I'd have two full teams for a change that I once again asked the school's activities director if she'd urge the cheerleaders to attend our home meets. She laughed.

Anyway, that first day, Garfield, the team clown, sat in the back of the room and made smart-aleck remarks about the new girl. Now, he can't run a lick, but he's got the fastest mouth in town, so I stopped the giggles when I said, "Garfield, you'll train with the girls today." If Aiida could really run 1:59, he'd be in for a dose of reality.

After a long silence—the other boys chuckling at him—the clown said, "Ahhh, coach"—he always said it with two syllables, "coa-itch"— "you jivin', right? You ain't gon' make me run with no chicks."

When we met for practice that afternoon I realized that while we might have a full squad, our girls didn't figure to be contenders. Arletha, Crystal, and Janice—she was white too— were all out for the team to lose weight. It would be a triumph to train them well enough so that they'd be able to even jog three miles nonstop by the season's end. LaWanda, my lone returnee, a strong 400-meter and 800-meter runner in track, was a mature, gifted young athlete but unenthused about cross-country, and she was more than a little haughty toward the younger girls. She'd sat with the varsity boys during the meeting.

The only mystery was that new girl, Aiida. When she at last emerged from the gym in running shorts, though, my heart sank. I'd hoped for too much. Her pale, skinny legs were knock-kneed and she was pigeon-toed. No way she could be much of a runner. Oh well, she'd probably just made a mistake when she'd filled out her form. I figured big-mouth Garfield was off the hook.

Once the actual running started, however, she proved me wrong. Aiida did everything I asked in practice, and with each successive interval finished farther and farther ahead of Garfield. Moreover, LaWanda couldn't get away from her—a new experience for that young woman.

It was no thrill for Garfield. "Coa-itch," he panted after the sixth of eight easy quarter-miles with two full minutes' rest, "that Aiida girl bad. She white lightnin'." Garfield can be funny, and that expression immediately became Aiida's nickname, although I saw her look at him strangely when he called her that.

Mile One

After practice later that week, I asked her why that nickname, "White Lightnin'," seemed to trouble her, and she said, "Last year in junior high up in San Francisco almost all the kids were white. Some of them said I was black. Now almost all the kids are black, and they say I'm white." She shrugged. She saw right through an American illusion.

Feeling guilty about my own earlier speculation, I said, "Well, some people, ignorant ones mostly, they want to classify other folks by comfortable categories—black/white, male/female, Christian/Muslim. They use those things to create illusions: you're black so you can't play quarterback; you're white so you can't play wide receiver—it's all nonsense. Look at me, black as midnight and I'm part Irish. I ran the 10,000 meters in college and our best sprinter then was white.

"Everybody in America's mixed some way, whether they know it or not. What matters is what you are as a person and what you can do," I told her. "Folks who judge you because of what racial category they assign you to, they're fools.

"And you, Miss Aiida Holmes, are just fine as far as I can tell, by the way," I added. It was a big speech for me, but my own earlier willingness to classify her...well, it didn't make any *difference* what I thought her racial blend was. Talking to her, I was telling myself off as much as anything.

"Anyway," I added, "you're *real* white compared to Garfield."

She smiled. "He's nice though…and funny too."

"And slow."

Aiida laughed.

A potentially greater problem arose during the first three weeks of practice when it became clear that Aiida was indeed, as Garfield put it, "bad." To my astonishment and pleasure, she was even faster than her 660 time the year before would have indicated, and I had to assume that, little as she was, she'd matured since then. The team lifted weights three times a week, and she was also much stronger than I'd anticipated. But mostly it was her determination on the track that impressed me. She was tough.

She impressed LaWanda too. That senior had been the queen of running around our high school for three years, so she was even more shocked than I was when that skinny little blonde kept up with her. Every time I saw those two tour the track in unison, I'd marvel that from the side Aiida's stride was beautiful. From the front, though, it appeared tortured, but you couldn't have told LaWanda that. By the end of each workout, she was clearly struggling to stay with the newcomer.

It was the first time in her King High School career that she found herself challenged. One afternoon I heard her gasp to Arletha, "I *hate* that nappy-head bitch! I'm gonna kick her ass!"

I immediately confronted her: "You kick it on the track, girl. You kick it by outrunning her if you can, but don't let me hear about you or anyone else hitting on her. This is a team. We'll win or lose as a team."

I figured she might quit after that warning, but I underestimated LaWanda. She sulked a bit, but to her credit she responded by training harder than ever as the season wore on. She didn't avoid White Lightnin' and she didn't make excuses when she finished behind her. In fact, she grew up in the best sense of the term. But she couldn't shake her tenacious little teammate.

Mile Two

By the time we raced the Riverside High Rams—our first
league meet—we had seven girls on the team. Two transfer
students had joined us. Both were from Southeast Asian
immigrant families, and both told me they were out for the
team so they'd have extracurricular activities on their records
when they later applied for admission to universities. The odd
thing is that Bao-Mei Tran and Thriphavanh Nhouyvanisvong
were both pretty good runners, although they were novices.
Thriphavanh—Garfield, who couldn't say that Laotian name,
had nicknamed her "Jawbreaker"—in particular was a gifted
athlete.

That afternoon against the Rams we ran the junior varsity
boys and the varsity girls together in a single race, but of course
scored them separately. As usual, Riverside had twenty or more
girls, plus a gaggle of younger JV boys, so the start was a mob
scene. Over the cheers that always accompany the starting gun,
I heard Garfield's voice: "Get 'em, Lightnin'!" I had to laugh. I
think he was a little sweet on her.

I couldn't tell exactly where our girls were positioned as
the crowd disappeared around the first corner and began to
climb the tough hills that make our course the least popular
in the league. I jumped on my mountain bike and pedaled the
shortcut to the top of the highest hill, a little past the halfway
mark on the route. I like to encourage the kids at that point,
and to check on how we're doing too. Well, I no sooner
arrived than two strong-looking boys from Riverside rounded
a bend and began the pull; this is one of those long hills that
grows steeper at the top just when runners are struggling.
Another boy from Riverside appeared, then…then Aiida, her
skinny little legs looking awkward, rounded the corner.

I don't think I'd ever seen one of our girls who didn't walk
at least a part of that stretch we called "cardiac hill," but
Lightnin' was right on that Ram's tail and ever so gradually,
her face etched with discomfort, she eased by him. When that
boy saw a girl passing him, he redoubled his efforts, but she
was stronger and soon she crested the hill and accelerated the
downhill, opening a huge gap.

When I looked back, LaWanda was struggling up that hill, ahead of all of Riverside's girls. I couldn't believe it. The Rams were a perennial power, and our girls were going one-two against them. Then Jawbreaker and the first Riverside girl rounded the corner running stride for stride. Wow!

Arletha, who'd already lost a lot of weight, was maybe the biggest surprise of all. She finished ahead of their sixth girl, and we won the team result by a single point. We'd never before beaten them in cross-country.

"Man," declared Garfield, his arms around LaWanda and Aiida, "you two somethin' else! Tore 'em up! Tore those Rams up! Now you wait till you see what I do to their boys!"

After all the races were over, Riverside's coach approached me and said, "I don't want my junior varsity boys running the same race with your girls anymore. It's too hard on them when the girls beat them. You should hear the excuses and fake injuries they've come up with to explain how those two aces of yours got away from them."

"Sure," I said. "No problem."

A week later, I had a problem when I urged that the cheer-leaders begin attending our home meets. I wanted them to bol-ster our runners as they bolstered our football players.

"No way! No way!" sang Carolina Baker, the head cheer-leader. When I asked why, she responded, "We're not cheering for any *nerds* and *girls*." There was more to the conversation, but it didn't change her response. I got a little strong in my response to her.

Mile Three

It took half the season before I figured out Aiida's racing strat-egy. She always went out fast and pushed until she was really hurting, then she picked up the pace. Finally I asked her about that. She sort of blushed—she wasn't real talkative—then replied, "Well, I just figure if I don't feel very good, the other runners don't either, so..." She shrugged and that shrug said it all. She dealt in pain, and no runners in our league—

male or female—handled it as well as she did. Aiida was the toughest athlete I'd ever coached.

I spoke with her mother one afternoon and she told me that her daughter had become a runner when she grew fed up with other kids making fun of her legs. "My little girl's surprisingly aggressive," Mrs. Holmes said. "I think she'd make a poor choice if you were looking for an enemy," the tall, fair woman smiled.

"You're telling me," I agreed, and we both laughed. "Where'd she get that great cardiovascular system? She has wonderful endurance to go with that grit."

"I was a competitive swimmer, and her father—we're divorced—was a good miler in college."

To Mrs. Holmes, though, I remarked only, "They always say if you want to be a champion, choose your parents carefully."

She laughed with me.

After our meet with St. Elizabeth High, I just happened to be standing near three of their JV boys, who had earlier been blitzed by Aiida. She and LaWanda strolled by and one of the boys said, "There goes the 'studette' of the league," and I had to laugh. Lightnin' didn't look much like a studette; she looked like she should be out selling Girl Scout cookies, not running junior varsity boys and varsity girls into the ground.

Both Aiida and the girls' team were unbeaten in dual competition that season, so I was really looking forward to the league meet. LaWanda, who made a crusade out of staying up with White Lightnin' in practice, was in the best shape of her life and was closing the gap between them; she'd be a strong contender for second place. Jawbreaker was still our number three runner, Bao-Mei was number four, and Arletha was number five. We were ready.

Although she was surely coachable, I did have trouble forcing little Aiida to ease her training for the big meet. She was a workaholic, even if she was tired or sore. I'd noticed that she'd begun icing both knees and one hip after every practice, and I said, "You better lighten up, child. I don't want you burning out."

Garfield, who as usual was hanging around Aiida, said, "She already light enough," then he giggled, and she did too.

They really laughed when LaWanda, who'd overheard his comment, said to the team clown, "Yeah, but you ain't, fool."

Then it happened: ten days before the championship, the girls were doing speed work—110-220-330-220-110 ladders with long jog rests—when Aiida slowed and began limping badly. LaWanda slowed too and put her arm around her. I jogged across the field to see what was wrong, and Lightnin' said only, "My hip," and began weeping like someone angry more than like someone hurting.

Finish

Mrs. Holmes and I sat in the office of Ron Dinucci, King High's team physician. He didn't keep us waiting long. While Aiida was dressing, he entered, smiled sadly, and plopped onto his swivel chair.

"Well," I asked immediately, "will she be able to run in the sectional meet?" I assumed Aiida'd miss the league championship, but knew that she'd be granted a hardship slot to the next higher level, the sectional championships. She was, after all, unbeaten.

Ron exchanged glances with Aiida's mother, then said, "She'll never race again. She probably won't ever jog again. She's ruptured her hip capsule. We'll need to repair it surgically. Aiida was born with shallow hip sockets and all that torque you saw when she ran was not only damaging her knees, it was destroying that hip. The other side's not much better.

"We'll get that bad one resected right away, but there'll definitely be no more hard running for her."

All of a sudden I felt awful, and not because our chances to win the league meet were crushed, but because I had pushed the little girl even though I could see her poor mechanics. In a sense, the injury was my fault. I said that to Mrs. Holmes.

She placed a hand on one of my forearms, and said, "No, coach, no one has to push Aiida. She's a self-starter. Whether you know it or not, you probably kept her from hurting herself sooner." Then she turned toward Dr. Dinucci and asked, "Will she be able to do other exercise, to swim for instance?"

"Sure. There's no reason she can't."

"Good. When can you schedule her surgery?"

We hosted the league meet that year, so I went on about my business, arranging for officials, marking the course, even again requesting that the cheerleaders show up—no luck. My whole team, boys as well as girls, seemed distracted by Aiida's injury. Our workouts were horrible.

Two days before the big meet, the little girl on crutches returned to school. We'd all been visiting her at the hospital, of course, but somehow seeing her hobbling around campus really broke my heart. It was so unfair for someone that young and that dedicated to be so afflicted.

On the day of the big meet we had a good crowd. Our dual meets were held on Wednesday afternoons, but this championship was on a Saturday, so parents and friends were in attendance, and the other schools brought plenty of boosters too. I was preoccupied, being meet director as well as coach, so I told LaWanda, as team captain, to make certain everyone was properly stretched and warmed up. I really didn't notice that Aiida wasn't among the spectators until after I got the junior varsity boys' race started.

The girls' race would be next, so I called my kids together.

"Listen, make sure you've warmed up. There're only six of us, so everyone counts." That's when it dawned on me that I hadn't seen Lightnin', and I wondered if she'd suffered a relapse. "We need each of you to run your best," I continued. "You're all in top shape, so just go out and *do it*. We *can* win this thing!" They were quiet, and I could feel their tension.

I glanced around once more and noticed Jawbreaker's mother, attired in a Laotian dress that made her look like a photo from *National Geographic,* but I couldn't spot Aiida anywhere. I felt a bubble of worry rise in me. That girl was a team player all the way; she wouldn't miss the chance to support her teammates at this meet, unless…unless she was hurt again. That was my fear.

Then I heard Garfield say, "Coa-itch. Look who's comin'."

Behind the crowd, slowly making their way from the parking lot, I saw Mrs. Holmes and Aiida. I had to smile, then grin, because that pistol of a girl, crutches and all, was dressed

in a homemade outfit that looked suspiciously like a cheer-
leader's uniform, and she carried two purple-and-gold pom-
poms.

When her teammates saw her, they whooped, sprinted to
the girl, and surrounded her, laughing and cheering. "Coa-itch,"
grinned Garfield, "the pep squad here!"

"Gimme five!" called LaWanda, and she slapped hands with
Aiida.

"Gimme *six!*" demanded Garfield. I swear that boy is from
a different planet, but I laughed.

Black hands and white hands and brown hands were slapping above their heads, and their laughter sounded the same
no matter what the kids' colors. Then Garfield howled, "We
number one!" and the others joined his chant.

All the other coaches and runners, and their equally tense
boosters, were watching my kids with something like awe.

Behind Aiida I saw Mrs. Holmes sort of dab at her eyes,
then smile. My eyes were moist too, but I knew King High
School's Harriers would do just fine.

The Affairs of Men

Now here's a truth: there is a tide in the affairs of men. And it will drag your ass right out to sea and dump you, if you aren't careful.

Leon Stokesbury

I HAD JUST COME IN THE DOOR that evening, returning from my evening walk with Pepper, when the telephone rang. I unhooked my old dog's collar, then picked up the receiver. "Hello. This is Dominguez," I said.

"Jess?" The voice was scratchy and weak. I couldn't identify it. "This is Jim. Listen, I…"

"Jim? I didn't recognize your voice, *esé*."

"Must be a bad connection."

"Right. What's up?"

"Listen, Jason and I are gonna be up your way. He's gonna go to a triathalon workshop. Can we bunk with you?"

He knew he didn't have to ask, or even call. "Hell no!" I snapped. "I don't want my livestock buggered again."

"I'll bring my own Crisco."

That got me and I laughed as I replied, "Well, that's thoughtful. When'll you arrive?"

"Tomorrow evening late. If you've got time, I'll take you and Carol to lunch while Jason's at his workshop. We'll have to get right home after he finishes."

"We'll make time. Besides," I added, "I'm not letting my wife loose around a horny bastard like you."

"But I'm bringing that Crisco…"

"I keep forgetting that."

"See you tomorrow, buddy."

We hung up and I walked to the family room and plopped into my favorite chair, my snow-snouted pooch, who had stood patiently at my side while I talked to Jim, following me and curling at my feet. "Jim's coming up," I announced. "He and Jason are going to spend tomorrow night with us."

My wife's face was immediately lit by a smile. "Is Sylvia coming too?"

"I don't think so. He didn't say anything, but she's probably busy with classes. I think he's just bringing Jason up."

"It'll be great to see him."

Jim Bennett had been my best man when Carol and I were married; I had been his when he married Sylvia. He had been my closest pal since high school and, although we lived nearly four hundred miles apart, our families got together at least twice each year, once in the summer, the other time at Christmas.

I waited impatiently that next evening and, as always seems to be the case when I'm anxious, our guests arrived later than we'd anticipated. Both looked tired. *Hola pinche vato,* Jim had growled when I opened the door, his patented fake Mexican accent.

Su madre, I smiled, then hugged first him, then Jason, who, like my own boys, always seemed delighted at the banter between his pop and me.

"Hi, Uncle Jess," he grinned, nearly as big as me now. Jim and Sylvia's kids all called Carol and me "Aunt" and "Uncle" although we were not blood relatives.

While Carol scrambled eggs with chorizo for them and Jason hustled upstairs with Miguel, our oldest boy, I popped a beer for Jim and—Pepper at my heels—joined him in the family room. He was looking around.

"Hey," he said as I handed him the brew, "you didn't have to take all your black velvet paintings off the wall just because a white guy was coming up."

"I figured since I was going to have to put up girlie calendars to make you feel at home anyway, why not? How's Sylvia?"

Still chuckling at my remark, he answered, "She's fine. Busy as hell as usual, but fine. She sends her love."

"And the kids?" I asked as Pepper hobbled in from the kitchen and plopped next to me, his large chin resting on one of my feet.

"You've still got that old dog," Jim smiled. "Hell of a guy, isn't he?"

"He's been a great pal."

"Anyway, all the kids are fine. Courtney's a senior this year, and you knew that Stephanie was in Spain on an exchange, didn't you? I sure hope she doesn't marry no damn *Mescin* while she's there." He couldn't help smiling as he said it.

"I don't think she will," I responded thoughtfully. "She'll probably just come home with a gingerbread baby in the oven for you to take care of." He laughed.

"How about this bunch of yours?" Jim asked. "Miguelito looks good—like his mother, thank God—and big."

"Yeah, he's starting at tackle this year, and Bobby's starting at noseguard on the freshman team. Linda's in seventh grade and Jimmy's in fourth. They're all pretty good students."

"That's great. You're still a good Catholic boy—all those kids."

"I'm still a Catholic boy. The 'good' part is debatable. How about you—all those kids? You didn't let anything go dry either." It was an old joke between us.

"My baptisms never took. They sprinkled me and dipped me—my folks joined a new church every time they moved: Church of Christ, Assembly of God, Church of the Nazarene—and none of 'em took."

"Well," I grew serious, "at least your marriage did. Be grateful for that. You know Manuel and Betty are splitting, don't you?"

For a moment his shoulders drooped and he looked at the floor. The news seemed to hit him even harder than it had me. "No shit?" he finally said.

"No shit. He called about a month ago—on a Saturday—and said she was filing for divorce the next Monday. And she did. He's been on the phone almost every day since."

"How's he taking it?"

"Not good. One minute he'll say, 'Hey, it'll be great. I'll meet new gals.' Then the truth'll come out almost like a scream and he'll say, 'What did I do to her? Why's she doing this?' It's pretty painful."

"And Betty?"

"She's not talking, not about the divorce anyway. And, of course, we haven't got a clue about what went on in their marriage, so what can we say?"

"That's rough," he grunted, and for a moment his eyes seemed to wander.

Jim drove Jason to San Rafael for his triathalon clinic that next morning, dropping him off. He planned to pick his son up at five that afternoon and to continue home, the long drive south. I drove with them down to Dominican College where the clinic was held.

On the way back up to Petaluma I said, "It's a little weird, isn't it, you driving halfway up the state to take your kid to a *triathalon* clinic. When we were his age there wasn't any such thing. Hell, that word, *triathalon*, didn't even exist. All we wanted was to sneak some beer and get laid."

"I expect he likes to sneak beer and tries to get laid," grinned Jason's dad.

"That's all we did too, *tried*. But I just mean that our kids live in a world so different from ours: Stephanie in Europe— hell, Carol and I've never been there…"

"Sylvia and me either."

"…and Miguelito planning to attend computer camp at UC this summer. In fact, they all go to some kind of camp: tennis, soccer, hell, *camp* camp it seems like. And they've all got braces on their teeth and the right labels on their clothes. I don't know…Hell, our folks took both of us out of school to pick cotton when we were sophomores, remember, and coach Denton nearly died? Half the damn team was gone."

"I remember and I know what you mean. I don't really get all the stuff that's happening—all these clinics and camps and *consciousness-raising* deals of Sylvia's and, hell, even computers. It all beats the hell outta me. I just try to hang onto what I *do* savvy, a little core of stuff so I can keep going." He lit a cigarette so I rolled down the window on my side. "That's something else," he added, "nobody smokes anymore. I don't get it."

"We quit, both of us, after Carol's dad died. Lung cancer."

"I'd rather not think about it."

"But, you know, I'm like you: I just try to hang on to something. That's why Manuel and Betty splitting really shook me up. My dad used to say—and I didn't understand then—that in this world you have to hold onto your ass with both hands: *Dos manos, esé, dos manos.* I understand now. Boy, without Carol I'd just fall apart. Our marriage is the one thing I hang on to."

"Yeah," he grunted.

I winked then, a little embarrassed at how emotional I'd become, and said, "But don't tell her."

Instead of breakfast we all merely had coffee and juice that morning. A couple of hours later we ate brunch at a waterfront café. We lingered there, gazing across the Petaluma River toward old buildings being restored downtown. "You guys really like it up here, don't you?" he asked.

"It's home," Carol replied. "One thing Jess and I wanted was a stable place for the kids to grow up and this has been it." Her parents had come to California from Oklahoma, and had drifted from crop to crop during her childhood. My own parents had done the same thing after migrating from Mexico to pick vegetables in the Salinas Valley before I was born. Both of us had seen enough wandering by the time we'd met at Arvin High School.

"How about you, Jimmy?" she'd asked. "Have you ever regretted staying in Arvin?"

"Naw." He paused to light a cigarette. "I've worked steady, commuting to those oil fields, and we've lived good—not rich, but real good. You know what gets me, though? Think about it, all our kids—yours and mine—will probably go to college. You guys both went to the junior college and now Sylvia. None of our folks even graduated from high school. I thought it was really great whenever I did that, but now..."

"And Sylvia is about to finish her degree at Cal State Bakersfield?" I asked.

"Yeah," he nodded, "next June."

"I really admire her," Carol said, "going to college after the kids grew up."

"They weren't exactly grown up," Jim disagreed mildly. "Stephanie was in the fourth grade, Courtney in second."

"But she's done it," Carol said.

"Yeah, she's done it," he agreed, then he inhaled deeply from his cigarette. "I'd always kinda hoped we could have one more, another boy, but..."

That afternoon, while Carol was at the grocery store, Jim and I watched a football game on television and sipped a couple beers while Pepper sprawled between us on the family room floor. Our conversation covered old high school games we had played, the fates of several classmates, the remarkable growth occurring in Kern County. Living near wine country, I'd recently become interested in California vintages and had taken a night school course on the subject. I told Jim about it and he marveled: "Remember when we worked for Giumarra's grape shed and you used to spit in the wine tanks?"

I had to grin. "Yeah, but that wine was strictly brown bag."

"I don't recollect you ever smelling the cap when we used to buy long dogs of white port in high school."

"Ugh!" I held up my hands like a man trying to avoid a beating. "My liver still screams when it hears those words: white port."

He laughed. "It oughta. How about Thunderbird?"

"What's the word? Thunderbird!" I chanted. "What's the price? Sixty twice!"

"Good times, man," he grinned. "Remember that time when Carol and Sylvia drove us home from that party and just left us out in front of your house?"

"What's the word?" I repeated.

"*Never again* is what I said," Jim replied. "I never had such a hangover. God!"

"Now they smoke dope," I grinned. My old dog climbed to his feet and hobbled into the kitchen.

"At least they smoke something. Nobody else seems to."

"We really don't have many friends who do anymore," I agreed, "but it really doesn't bother us. That's why we keep the ashtrays."

He put out his cigarette. "Have you guys tried marijuana?"

"Yeah, way back when I was in the army in Texas," I told him. "Nothing special as far as I was concerned."

"Me too. Sylvia has some women friends at the college, and they bring some over every once in a while. I like beer better."

"Amen."

The football game Jim and I had been watching had just ended when Carol returned from the supermarket where she'd done our weekly shopping. Jim looked at his watch, then stood and stretched. "Well," he sighed, "time to pick up Jason."

I stood too, saying, "Damn. I'm sorry you guys can't stay one more day. We could hit a few wineries tomorrow."

Just then Carol came to the kitchen door and called me, her voice anxious: "Jess, come here. It's Pepper."

I turned. "What's wrong?"

"Come see."

My old dog sprawled on the floor, legs extended stiffly, eyes open but stunned, tongue lolling. His breath was rapid and shallow. "My God," I murmured as I knelt. Pepper was unable to respond to my touch or voice, although I thought I glimpsed recognition in those eyes. "Call the vet, hon'," I said to Carol, and I hefted the awkward animal. "Tell him I'm on my way."

Miguel had been rummaging through grocery bags in search of treats and he stood tensely next to us. "*Mijo*, go start the car," I said to him.

"Jim," I puffed, toting my dog toward the front door, "I'm sorry, *ese*, but I've got to get Pepper to the vet. You have a good trip home and we'll see you at Christmas like always."

His eyes were troubled and his right hand suddenly extended and gripped my left where it supported Pepper's hip. "Jess," he said, "I've gotta tell you guys something before I go. I don't want you to hear it from anybody else. Sylvia has left me."

"God, Jim, I…"

"She says I haven't grown. She says I'm holding her back." A tear spilled from one of his eyes.

"God…"

"I don't understand," he said. "I don't know what's going on anymore. I just don't get it," and his free hand brushed his eyes, then reached like a blind man's, groping.

The Trial of God

THEY TRAMPED THE LAST SHOVELS full of earth over Marvella
Turner beneath a large willow on the banks of the Kern
River, and Holloway again complained, "We really shouldn't
oughta done it thisaway, Dale."

"Why not?" snapped the thin man who had dropped to his
knees next to the damp mound. Leaping to his feet, Dale
Turner challenged Holloway. "You want my wife buried off in
some potter's field? Is that what you want? No sir! Not my
Marvella. She come out here a free woman and she'll go to
her rest a free woman! Here at least her own folks buried her
and carved her a marker."

"Take 'er easy, Dale," urged Long Jim Jordan, who rested
on his shovel.

"That's our damn problem. We take ever'thang easy," Turner
asserted. "And what's it got us?"

"It's all right, Dale. It'll be all right," soothed Long Jim.

"No it's not. Nothin' is!"

Holloway had backed a few steps away. "Dale?" he asked
quietly. "Cain't we at least read over Marvella?"

"Hell no! There ain't no damn God that lets little kids die
and their momma too!" He burst toward Holloway and
grabbed the man's ragged shirt. "Or if there is He's nothin' but
a damn killer! A killer!"

Long Jim and Clinton Wells and B. J. Tedrow dropped their
shovels, rushed to Dale, then eased him away from Holloway.
"Come on, Dale. Holloway means good. Besides, we got a
long walk back to camp," Long Jim said. "Marvella woulda
liked this place. You done her proud."

155

"Yeah," snorted Turner, shaking himself free, "I done her *real* proud. We shoulda stayed in Arkansas."

But they hadn't stayed in Arkansas, or Oklahoma, Texas, or Missouri. Instead they strode across a California floodplain until, from the crest of a thick levee, they saw their bedraggled community of tents, of wood, and cardboard hovels, of immovable automobiles in which some families lived, the whole scene looking as though it had been dropped from a great height to splatter on the scrubby land.

Dale Turner kept moving with angry resolve, but the other men paused atop the levee. "Poor Dale," said Holloway.

"Yeah," answered Long Jim, "he's had the worst luck, but ain't none of us been spared."

Below, in the camp that they could barely see through rising ground fog, folks moved slowly about with a lethargy borne of hunger. Between the men and their ragged homes sliced a canal, their lone source of water, and beyond the camp, hidden by the thickening fog, spread the pastures of a dairy. It was the dairy farmer they blamed for the sheriff's raids they suffered. True, they stole an occasional bucket of milk from one of the heavily laden cows, but only because their children needed it. They could not sit with starving children on their laps while milk-laden cattle grazed a few yards away. There had even been talk of butchering a cow but that had quickly been quashed. They had trouble enough without giving the law such a provocation.

Dale Turner crossed the weir that served as their bridge over the canal, then sloshed into camp. He was cold to the bone, and not just with California weather but with the helplessness that consumed him. There was no work to be found around Bakersfield. Most of the people who had filled the camp during the picking season were long gone. The handful remaining owned no vehicles that operated or possessed no money to buy fuel for cars that did. Even their number had dwindled as the cold, foggy winter enveloped them and sickness killed the old, the young, and the weak so regularly there seemed to be a death every day.

Dale had just buried the girl he had loved since they were kids, and he'd buried two children earlier in the winter. He stood in front of his tent next to the carcass of the truck that had carried them—buoyed by hope—into this godforsaken valley less than a year before. His one remaining child, Jenelle, squatted on a board surrounded by mud. She wore only a flour sack tied at her waist with a length of rope, and her mother's old sweater. Shriveled by illness and malnutrition, she looked like an infant although she was nearly four years old. Dale scooped his daughter up and stood holding her, surveying the bleak landscape. Why in hell had they come to California?

Still, sensing the dairy pasture across the camp from his full of ripe cows, and hearing cars full of, he guessed, comfortable people buzzing by on Chester Avenue a little to the west, it was clear to him that God had not forsaken California, he had forsaken them.

Tule fog continued rising from the surrounding fields and marshes, thick and grainy like a wall of cold sand that chilled through all clothing. Unlike anything folks had seen before moving west. This fog seemed to them a particular torture, a diabolic miasma that separated them from the world, from hope. Long Jim, Tedrow, and Clinton had gathered wood on their trek from Marvella's grave, and they built a bonfire near the camp's center, but few folks ventured from their hovels to warm themselves.

To one side of the flames stood Dale Turner. His daughter had joined a small cluster of children near the fire, so her father, alone with ravaged eyes and sunken shoulders, looked like one of the drowned trees beyond the levee, gnarled and withered yet unwilling to fail, defying itself.

Long Jim, concerned over his friend's desolation, wandered to him and offered a chaw from a twist of now-precious tobacco, but Dale refused. Jim was about to suggest they walk to their weir and try to catch a mess of crawdads for supper when Dale spoke, his voice strangling: "Jim, what would we do with a guy that done what God's went and done to us?"

Backing away a step, Long Jim blinked at his friend.

"What would we do to a guy that went and killed our kids and our wives and our friends? What would we do to a guy that starved folks and made 'em live like this?"

Searching Dale's face, Jim shuddered. He sensed that his friend was on a brink, pushed to the very edge by Marvella's death, and he was not sure how to help him back, but he was determined to try. "I reckon, if we suspected a guy," he answered gently, "we'd arrest him and put him on trial so's we could be damn sure whose fault it was." He wasn't certain he'd said the right thing.

Dale's eyes glistened. His mouth was an anguished slash. "We'd give 'im a trial, maybe, if there was any doubt, but there ain't no doubt who done this. God done it."

"I doubt!" A resounding voice startled both men. It was deep and certain, seeming to emanate from somewhere behind the flames, or from the flames themselves. Jim and Dale fell back a step, glancing at one another before peering from the fire itself into the surrounding gloom.

"I doubt!" boomed the voice as a dark figure began to materialize beyond the flames, through heat shivers so that it wavered and curved like a specter. "Who're you to question God?" it demanded. "Who're you to accuse Him?"

Dale stood his ground, glaring at the still vague figure in the fog. "What do you know about it?"

"I know you accused God!" The figure was closer now, just on the other side of the bonfire, and the cluster of children withdrew, scurrying for the tents and shacks and stranded vehicles. Jenelle clung to her father's leg.

"I heard you accuse God!" challenged the stranger across the fire. His darkness planted a kernel of apprehension in the bellies of the men, even Holloway, who had wandered from the shack where he lived. Not merely the long coat and full trousers, but the stranger's entire mien, a cast that appeared shadowed even in the dense fog, troubled them. He held a worn Bible. "How *dare* a flyspeck like you question God?" roared the stranger.

Dale Turner's wiry body was coiling when Long Jim and Tedrow grabbed him. Clinton scooped up Jenelle and hurried her to his own tent.

"What's this?" asked Holloway.

"This guy's stuck his nose where it don't belong," growled Dale.

Holloway, his eyes darting from face to face, finally addressed the dark stranger. "Are you a preacher, mister?"

The stranger ignored Holloway, riveting his attention instead on Dale Turner. "All right, you've accused God. Now prove it!" he demanded. "Prove your accusation."

"That feller's a preacher," whispered Holloway to Tedrow.

"Damn rights I'll prove it!" Dale shouted. "I'll prove it and lick you too!" Long Jim and Tedrow again held him.

"You three men act as a jury," instructed the scowling stranger, nodding toward Jim and Tedrow and Holloway. "I'll speak for God, and he"—the word hung like spit from the lip of a cuspidor—"can accuse. Let's see what he can prove."

"Prove?" Dale's angry voice suddenly elevated into a wild giggle. "Prove? Hell, just look around. You got eyes don't ya?"

The stranger ignored him. "You three will act as a jury?" he asked. The three men glanced nervously at one another. Long Jim finally replied, "I don't see what good this'll do."

The stranger surveyed him for a moment, then responded. "It's the truth we're after here. Truth is worth the trouble."

"The preacher's right, Jim," urged Holloway, nodding.

"Let's do it," Tedrow agreed.

Jim looked toward his friend. "Dale?" he asked.

"Damn rights! Let's lay 'er out."

"All right, stranger, you can have your say," Long Jim relented. "We'll be your jury. But this'd better not be no game."

The dark figure ignored the implicit threat and addressed Dale Turner. "Now what, exactly, gives you cause to accuse God?"

"What gives me cause?" Dale mimicked the stranger. "What gives me cause?" he repeated facing his friends, the jury. Then, turning toward the stranger once more, Dale shook his head. "What the hell's wrong with you, hoss? Don't you see good? See them scarecrows yonder? Them're our kids. Look at them piles of junk; them're our houses. See these two bony bastards?"—he extended his thin, hard fists—"them're hands that work and work and for what? Cause my ass!"

The dark stranger appeared unmoved. "That's your case?" he asked. "That?"

"You want more? You want the whole story about how we come west to save our families and got this instead? Piddlin' little work and it for starvation wages, and folks treating us like trash and our kids and our wives and our friends dyin', is that what you want?"

"Did you ever thank God for the work you did get?"

The suggestion staggered Dale, who faltered back a step before catching himself. "Thank Him? Are you nuts? We never got a livin' wage ever! Should we thank God for lettin' us starve slow instead of fast? You're all words, mister. You got a answer for ever'thang. But we cain't eat no words, and words won't bring our dead back, so shut the hell up and get outta here!"

Long Jim was quick to place himself between Dale and the stranger; Tedrow quickly joined him, but Dale did not move. He stood as though rooted, glaring through the flames. "Why did them poor little kids that never hurt nobody have to die? Why did their momma have to die? Answer me that."

The stranger's voice softened. "To save them," he replied.

It was Long Jim's turn to sound confused. "Save 'em?"

"To save them from the pain of *your* deliverance."

"Like hell!" roared Dale Turner.

After a pause, the stranger remarked, "Like hell, yes, like hell indeed," then paused once more before continuing. "God knows the tortured path of your salvation. He knows where your free will'll lead you and He can save an innocent child the desperate suffering that awaits you."

Long Jim was suddenly alert, awakened by one of the preacher's phrases. "Free will, huh," he snorted. "One ol' preacher back home he usta all the time talk about free will too, even when all we could do was stay and starve or leave and hope, he talked about free will. See, he's half sore 'cause folks was havin' to take off and his flock—meanin' his salary—was shrinkin'. Finally, when enough of us pulled up stakes, the preacher he had to leave too. Was that free will? Naw. He was a-followin' God's Call. So us poor guys got free will, but you preachers, you got the Call."

For the first time, the dark stranger seemed nonplused. Finally he cleared his throat and proclaimed, "You're talking about one frail human being. I'm talking about God!"

"Me and Dale and the rest're talkin' about us, mister, and what we've went through. We ain't talkin' outta books."

"Let's run the bastard off," urged Dale Turner, and no one, not even Holloway, demurred. The fire was burning low, smoking heavily as it reached damp wood near the ground. Combined with the ever-thickening fog, it all but obscured the stranger. "What the hell's the good a all this talk?" Dale demanded. This time Long Jim and Tedrow nodded in agreement.

"If that's the best you can do, stranger," Long Jim warned, "you be on your way. We got better thangs to do than listen to you."

From the swirling fog and smoke the stranger seemed to resubstantiate, waving his Bible at them. "You fools! You think God's on trial here, but he's not! You are! And you're finding yourselves guilty!"

"Hell's bells!" Dale Turner shouted as he burst away from his friends and scrambled directly through the embers, then grappled briefly with the stranger—the latter dropping his Bible while they struggled—before clouting him solidly on one cheek, knocking him spinning back into the fog. There was a roar like a sudden tornado that caused the others to flinch and nearly buckle. An instant later smoke swirled from the remains of the bonfire and a dart of flame screamed from the embers and through the fog in the direction of the stranger. "What the hell?" gasped Tedrow.

As the noise finally faded the men stood upright and glanced at one another with blank eyes. "You shouldn't oughta sock no preacher, Dale," Holloway whined.

"What's that?" asked Tedrow, pointing at something near the remains of the bonfire. He strode over and picked up the stranger's Bible. "Would you looky here," he gasped as he fanned the book's pages. Each was blank save for what appeared to be the charred print of a cloven hoof.

Ishi's Dream

Morning, August 9, 1911

"WHAT THE...? BUSTER! Hey, Buster! Quick, bring that lamp, willya? And the shotgun!"

"Never mind, boys, you don't need no gun. I pushed him with a stick, just pushed him and he fell over. I propped him back up before I called you boys. He's weak as breeze, maybe sick, I dunno..."

"The gun! Get me that damn gun! And watch it, they're tricky."

"He don't look tricky. God, I never seen nothin' like him before."

"I tell you, he's used up, boys. You don't need that gun."

"He's a redskin, ain't he? Cover him! You boys keep him covered while I call the sheriff!"

"At least get him something to wear, willya? Buck naked, he's gotta be froze."

"Damn, what a piece a work *he* is. What a specimen."

"The poor guy...I wonder what the heck happened to him."

Excerpt, *Butte County Record,* August 14, 1911:

...a wild man, probably an Indian, was captured at a slaughterhouse near here on Thursday last. Sheriff J. B. Webber reports that the wild man is now securely locked in jail, but that not even other Indians have been able to speak to him. He also said that the wild man has not eaten or drunk and rarely slept. Nonetheless, he appears to be in capital condition, according to Sheriff Webber.

Dusk, July 17, 1911

On that day, after I crawled from the earth's bowels where I had been hiding, I squatted on a hillock gazing far below toward the flatland where a snake-demon puffed and grunted. That monster, at least, had not invaded the Canyons of the World. Then I heard the dogs...

How many shouts and crashing plunges later? My arms and legs tight and quivering with fatigue, I at last no longer heard them. My lungs burned and my eyes could not focus. I squatted amidst boulders in a dry creek bed and sucked air, resting my head against stone. Finally I curled there like lizard-brother, too empty to stand.

Among those rocks, with dogs and savages no longer pursuing me, with my mind rushing to understand the shouts and howls, the flashes of trees and stones, the shadows and lights through which I had fled—so fast and fierce that my mind could not grasp it—I had fled without thought. Now the thoughts that could create order evaded me because I could not relieve the chase by speaking of it. I could tell no one...not talk through the terror. No other human beings were left, only me.

Me, trapped in the Silence.

I knew the hair-faced savages had found my camp and what was left of my food. I knew I could not return for my bow or basket and dried fish. I knew I could tell no one these things.

Finally, in my exhaustion, the spirit creatures came to me. *This is no longer our land,* they said. *It has been contaminated by savages.*

"But it *is* our land. We were built here," I insisted.

It has been contaminated. You must fast. You must cleanse it by cleansing yourself.

I awoke alone.

When I stood, my legs still shook and my belly burned for water. I climbed slowly toward three-tree spring. There, I knelt and sipped and sipped, trying to draw the Earth's strength into myself.

Above me wind whispered old names, but I had no one to talk to: Old Elk had first brought me to this place when I was a boy. We had watched bear-sister with two cubs sip here, then slowly amble off while the little ones tumbled and played. And we had discussed what we had seen. He told me that bears and humans had been the same in the Land of the Beginning but bears had traded their language for strength and beauty. Humans had remained weak and ugly because we had chosen to keep our language. It had allowed us to become The People, to laugh and to love. In those distant days there had been no Silence.

Kneeling before the spring, still feeble, I acknowledged at last that speech was dead. The People were dead. I rested my forehead against the rough bark of a tree. Everyone but me had gone to the Land of the Dead to escape the savages. With no one to talk to, I was no longer a human being. I was a speechless spirit like the slugs and worms, lost in what had been our land, and hunted by pale savages.

The Spirit Creatures had been correct. I needed to fast. I needed to find my way to the Land of the Dead so I could again be one of The People, so I could at last hear real words and share dreams and become human once more. After searching every measure of the Canyons of the World, I had found no other human beings, no path to the Land of the Dead. Perhaps this truly was no longer our land. Without our voices it was empty, and that hollow cry of the distant snake-demon that sometimes invaded our wind made it even emptier.

Without seeking food I walked down the creek, over a high ridge, careful not to expose myself, and then down into another creek's deep crease and up yet another ridge.
I paused and gazed back at memories too painful to savor, touched my breast, then placed my hand over my mouth that no longer sent language. A person could not truly live without language because Earth Mother and Old Man of the

Ancients had built The People with it. Without it, voice was empty wind. Then I departed from the Canyons of the World for the first time in my life.

I wandered all that day and the next, hungry and weak, far away from our canyons, far from the sacred rocks where Old Man of the Ancients originally met Earth Mother, far from the peak where Turtle found the sacred mud when all the Earth was ocean, far from the sacred cave where Coyote was trapped when he tried to trick Earth Mother. Twice I saw distant snake-demons in the distance. I was skirting the domain of the hair-faced savages searching for the slice in sound where the Land of the Dead was tucked.

That night I slept under a great tree near a stream. Below me, where the land was flat, I watched a hair-faced savage walking behind a horse that pulled something and made clouds of dust. Blackbird bands followed him as they once followed Fox following Coyote following Bear on their dung-rounds. Even here, in the land of the savages, Spirit Creatures like Blackbird could be found. That comforted me.

Another long day, and another, and another—for many days—I wandered far from the Canyons of the World, remaining in the hills on the edge of the savages' flat territory, eating little, drinking little. My vision grew foggy, my mind wandered, and once…twice…I thought I heard the Spirit Creatures calling, but when I searched for them I found nothing.

I could not lie down that night. Instead, I leaned against a rock and began thinking about my Death Song. That, at least, would be real language, the time a lone voice could be heard.

As my mind swirled toward sleep, the Spirit Creatures called me: *The Land of the Dead lies south beyond where the savages dwell. The hole in sound is far over there where the clouds begin on the mountains Crow built. Have no fear. They will take you there in the belly of a Great Snake. Have no fear. It will be a strange and wondrous world. The People await you.* And I saw my mother. And my father. And Elk. And lame Hawk Wings, my friend. And The Woman who carried my child. I saw my Child. I saw all the Last People for whom my hair was cut and my body covered with ashes. Then I was again in the Great Silence and my heart lurched.

Dawn, August 9, 1911

There was no reason to wait. I could no longer bear the quiet of sleep. In cold darkness I arose and walked directly downhill into the domain of the savages, stumbling with fatigue but ready to face them and their horses and their dogs, ready to face anything that would end the Silence.

By the time I reached a large lodge of the savages, I could no longer walk. My legs and my heart were empty, so I crouched against a post and listened to the dog talk, louder and louder, and I began to breathe my Death Song: "Take me, O Winds and Trees! Take me, O Rocks and Streams! Take me Mother Earth and Ancient Father to the Land of the Dead, take me."

Soon the dogs were howling and snarling around me, and savages, slowly at first and making the empty sounds with their mouths, surrounded me. They pulled the dogs away, then one poked me, another kicked my back, but I said nothing to them, only quietly continued breathing my Death Song. I closed my eyes and did not move.

When I opened them, the savages' chief stood before me with hair on his face. He made the empty sounds, then another savage placed cold bracelets on my wrists. Then the chief took me to two horses with a platform behind them. He helped me onto the platform and it began to move—was this the journey to the Land of the Dead? No, only a Great Snake could do that.

Other savages rode their horses alongside as we moved across the flat land. Ahead I saw a village so large it had to be the Land of the Dead, larger than all the villages of the Canyons of the World combined.

And the lodge into which I was taken seemed larger than the rest of the world: how could so much emptiness be inside? Although I did not break my fast, savages took the bracelets from my wrists, then brought me food and gave me covers. They came, the savages, in many colors and shapes and sizes, and they made many different empty sounds, but none had Language. Some appeared almost to be human beings, but their sounds, too, were empty.

I was not certain whether I was awake. At times the Spirit Creatures spoke to me, at others I opened my eyes to things and places unreal. I closed my eyes to the familiar Silence. I opened my eyes and savages again approached me, or did I close them before they arrived? I could no longer tell.

Each day, the chief and other savages returned, many I had not seen before, and tried their empty sounds. The chief and two of his warriors began to smile at me and to touch my arm, lightly, like brothers. They brought more covers and more food and more water. They acted almost like human beings. Friendly savages? Surely this was a dream.

Telegram from Professor A. L. Kroeber to J. B. Webber, Sheriff of Butte County, August 31, 1911:

Newspapers report capture wild Indian speaking language other tribes totally unable to understand. Please confirm or deny by collect telegram and if story correct hold Indian until arrival Professor State University who will take charge and be responsible for him. Matter important account aboriginal history.

Noon, September 1, 1911

Several times I heard—much closer now—that snake-demon calling, and I crouched to hide. The demon did not find me.

Then a new savage visited. He sat beside me on the bedding place and held a skin before his face. He began to mouth sounds empty as wind, then glance at me, then mouth more sounds and glance at me again.

Suddenly, he spoke a real word: *Siwini,* touching the bedding-place frame.

For a moment I could not breathe: the Silence was broken. My eyes warmed and I, too, touched the frame of the bedding-place, for it was constructed of *siwini* and this savage knew it.

I wanted to roar! *"Siwini!"* I said, rubbing the frame. *"Siwini! Siwini! Siwini! Siwini!"*

He grinned and repeated, *"Siwini!"*

For a moment I had to put my hand over my mouth, then I said *"Siwini"* again and we laughed together. Perhaps his Silence had ended too.

He said another real word and I had to laugh; after all the Silence, this was almost too much. I grew giddy. He said another word and another and I kept laughing. This savage— or *was* he a savage?—knew at least some of the language of The People.

Finally, I had to ask, *"I ne ma Yahi?"*

He stared at me a moment with eyes blue as a creek, then smiled and said, *"Ne I ma Yahi."*

Ah, he *was* human, sent in the guise of savage, perhaps to take me to the Land of the Dead. He was a human and I could speak to him. I could not stop myself—words burst from me: I told him how my woman and child drowned, how the old woman died, where Elk was lost; I told him how I sang their Death Songs and sheared my hair and rubbed my body with ashes; I told him how sound had grown empty then and that deer were fewer and that the great bears were nearly gone; I told him mountains were weeping and springs were bitter and even earth was turning to powder since The People no longer walked the Canyons of the World. I spoke so rapidly and fiercely that I could scarcely understand myself because another human being was listening.

He appeared overwhelmed, blinking and looking down at markings on the skin he held, his eyes confused. Finally he looked up at me and raised his hand, so I quieted, grinning and panting in my excitement, and he said slowly, *"I ne ma ishi?"*

I had to laugh. I had been speaking much too fast for him. Perhaps he was just becoming human because he still looked like a pale savage. *"Aha,"* I replied, *"ne I ma ishi."* Yes, I am a man.

After that he called me "Ishi." I called him that too, but he said no, his name was "Waterman."

I repeated his name, and he smiled. We touched hands.

When he left I spoke with the Spirit Creatures, asking if at last I had found the Land of the Dead in this vast inside space with a savage who was becoming human. *Be patient,* they advised. *Await the Great Snake.*

Afternoon, September 3, 1911

Just after I heard that snake-demon calling once more and hid, Waterman returned, bringing an old man to me who looked like a human being except he had hair on his face like a savage. His name was "Batwi." Although he was from another clan, he could speak like a human being, though not always clearly and well. I could speak rapidly to him, and he could speak understandably to me. In fact, he could not resist bragging of the wonders the savages possessed as though they were his own. When I asked if this was the Land of the Dead, Batwi laughed at me.

No, this could not be the Land of the Dead, I realized. I had not found The People, but only this specimen; I had not entered the Great Snake. But this was not the pit of savages either. I was no longer certain these were savages at all...Perhaps they were demons? They looked just like the ones who had killed my family, but did not act like them. These fed me. These gave me covers to warm my body. These smiled at me. One had actually spoken with me in real language, freeing me from the Silence.

I began to wonder if they were merely *saltu,* non-humans, but not savages or demons. Anyone can become a savage or a demon, I knew—some in my own clan, I had heard from elders, had done such things. Perhaps the pale hair-faces who killed my family were *saltu* turned to demons, while the rest were *saltu.*

If that was true then "Waterman" could be a *saltu* trying to become a human being and "Batwi" could be a human being trying to become a *saltu.* This may not have been the Land of the Dead, but it was a strange one.

Dawn, September 4, 1911

Waterman brought me clothes like he wore—layers and layers, more covering than I'd ever imagined; the weather wasn't even cold. He handed me clothes for my feet too, but I could not put them on and lose touch with Earth. He tried to convince me to pull the footclothes on, smiling and gesturing, but I only told him no, and soon he understood. Then we climbed on the savage chief's platform behind his horses and moved through the village of savages...of *saltu*?...until we joined a great throng of them at a large, flat hut next to two stiff lines on the ground. The lines were straight as arrows and longer than breath.

But what gripped me was the number of savages...of *saltu*. They were everywhere. I had never seen so many creatures in one place before—not squirrels or minnows or even ants—more savages there than all the human beings who had ever lived since Old Man of the Ancients first blew life into our words. I could only cover my mouth in astonishment and say, *"Hansi saltu."*

Batwi, who pretended to know much, merely nodded and agreed, *"Aha."*

I asked him what we were doing there.

He gave me that knowing look again, then told me we were going to visit another village of the *saltu*.

There are *more*? I asked in astonishment.

Many more. We go to their greatest village.

Greater than this? It was beyond imagining.

Oh, *much* greater.

I covered my mouth again. Some things could not be understood.

From far, far way I heard a lone cry, high and hollow: the snake-demon. It was louder now, closer, but I noticed that none of the *saltu* seemed frightened. I turned toward Waterman and he seemed to understand my fear, so he smiled and placed a hand on one of my arms. My feet felt the earth shuddering, and I asked Waterman what it was. He smiled, patted my arm, and told me to wait, and not to be frightened. It would not hurt me.

I will not be afraid, asserted the older man. Nothing frightened brave Batwi, according to Batwi anyway. I had to chuckle at him, and so did Waterman.

I knelt and touched one of the hard lines on the ground; it was quivering like an angry man. From the distance I began to hear not only that high, hollow sound, but a deeper one, a panting, a grunting, a wheezing, perhaps a roaring, and, in spite of Waterman's warning, my breath grew quick.

Then far away on the plains I noticed something black moving toward us—a mere dot at first, but growing as it slid our way. The dot spewed smoke and I squinted to see it more clearly, and then it turned: it was the head of the snake-demon. My breath caught. Waterman again touched my arm and smiled.

Batwi the brave blinked and shuddered at the snake's loud approach, but my body was wood, and I was beginning to understand. This *was* a dream. Perhaps that high, hollow howl the snake-demon made *was* the hole in sound that led to the Land of the Dead. Perhaps this was not a demon but the Giant Snake promised by the Spirit Creatures.

Perhaps I could at last complete my journey to the Land of the Dead...

Postscript

Ishi, Batwi, and Waterman entered the train and were transported to San Francisco. They arrived on September 4, 1911. Ishi lived at the University of California's Anthropology Museum until his death at noon on March 25, 1916. When he died, saltu and savages mourned.

"He was the best friend I had in the world," said Waterman.

Two-Headed Man Hangs Self;
One Head Depressed

IT WAS IN ALL THE PAPERS and even on TV news. You must've read about it, a strange deal. Them grocery-store gossip sheets they had headlines on it too. But didn't none of them carry the true facts, because didn't none of them even *know* the true facts. Like I said, it was a real strange deal.

WASCO—Authorities in this Central California town report that the body of Roscoe Monroe Miller, 32, was found hanging in the garage of his home last week. Mr. Miller, who had two heads, left a note indicating that he was depressed over a recent jail stay.

A reliable source, however, indicated that a fierce struggle occurred between Mr. Miller's two heads, known locally as Roscoe (left) and Monroe (right). "They never got along too good," acknowledged the source...

Me, I'm the source, and I'll tell you one thing don't many people know: it wasn't no suicide at all. No sir. It was cold-blooded murder.

About gettin' along, they never. Monroe he was in the Rotary Club with me and he was a born-again Christian, but Roscoe didn't let himself get Saved. In fact, he'd sneak a drink in a minute if old Monroe dozed off. And womanize. Poor Monroe wanted to keep his purity, but Roscoe wouldn't have none of it. Now you're askin' yourself, what kind of woman would want to do *that* with a two-headed guy? Well, the answer is all kinds and lots of them. It must've been the novelty, or maybe just ol' Roscoe's golden tongue, or maybe the fact that both of them boys was good-lookin'.

Sundays was bad because in order to go to church in the mornin' Monroe had to agree to go honky-tonkin' in the afternoon. About a month ago, Monroe he'd had enough and he took to singin' hymns or prayin' out loud every time Roscoe would dance with one of them queens he loved. Well, they went out to the alley and had one hell of a fight, right hand punchin' the left head and vice versa. Not much footwork, you can imagine, but a lot of punishment.

They come home that night not speakin' to each other, slammin' doors, and without no lady (which it was a change). Roscoe he was real sore because he hated not to have some gal curled up in bed with him. He commenced drinkin' right there at home and wouldn't go to bed like Monroe wanted to, and another fight busted out between them before they finally turned in, too pooped and beat up to do anything else. Monroe had surely found a way to wreck Roscoe's sinful Sunday.

But the next week in the middle of prayer service at the Assembly of God, Roscoe he begun hollerin' cuss words: "Shit on you pious bastards! Dirty sons of bitches! Ass-kissin' scum suckers!" Poor Monroe tried to put a hand over Roscoe's mouth but got socked in the eye for his efforts and they took to fightin' again right there in the church. Same as usual, there wasn't much dancin' but one hell of a lot of punches, them heads noddin' a little to duck but that's all. It was hard to tell who scored the knockdown, but somebody did, and the elders finally pinned them—those heads tryin' to bite each other—and broke the deal up, then told Monroe that until he could control Roscoe it would be better for him to worship at home.

That night, Monroe didn't even wait until they'd went inside Roscoe's favorite honky-tonk: he commenced singin' hymns right out on the sidewalk. Roscoe told him to shut up, and Monroe he sang louder. It wasn't long before they was at it again, rollin' around in front of the bar with arms hookin' at one another until the bouncer he come out and grabbed them, shook them like they was a doll, then said to Roscoe, "I don't want you back here till you can control that hymn-singin' jerk."

They was both sore that night. For Roscoe to go two weeks without a woman was real tough. For Monroe to miss church at all was even worse. They slept with their faces turned away from each other I'll bet.

At work the next day Roscoe he commenced fartin' while Monroe was waitin' on customers, and that scattered them real good. Monroe tried to reason with him, sayin' it was *their* livelihood he was hurtin', but there wasn't no chance he'd listen, and poor Monroe was real sorry that he'd let his brother eat chili on Sunday.

Later, while Roscoe was tryin' to finish a brake job at the station, Monroe he kept droppin' tools. Roscoe'd pick them up and Monroe he'd drop them again. Wasn't neither boy accomplished much that day, not much good anyways.

Well, it went on thataway for a couple weeks, all the townfolks keeping their noses right in the big middle of it. Then that young schoolmarm got "abused" and we all forgot about the feud between them Miller boys and followed the investigation of the crime, the worst one ever here in Wasco. Cops was lookin' everywhere for clues, and even county sheriffs was sniffin' around. The poor gal was so shook up that she couldn't tell them much and, for a while at least, it looked like a dead end.

Then Monroe he confessed that Roscoe'd done it. "He just forced me to go with him and he overpowered that poor woman," he claimed. It was sensational. The whole town took to talkin' about it. I mean we all *knew* old Roscoe was the womanizer.

Roscoe he never took it laying down. He told the cops and anyone else who'd listen, "Bullshit! This pious little phony done it and dragged me along. He's always poundin' his pud in secret but this time he just decided to try a real woman! He let me get drunk so's I couldn't control myself, then took me with him. He just figured he could lay it on me. Besides, he pisses and moans about me drinkin', but he loves it just the way he loves the ladies. He does crazy things when we're drunk."

Well, there you have it. That teacher she begun to remember that a two-headed guy'd done her, but not whether one head was in charge, let alone *which* one. The cops they was stumped, and the town chose up sides. Me, I favored Monroe. He was strong in the church even if he was a little odd. Roscoe he was the ladies' man, and I think he just went after one lady too many. But some guys said that Monroe he was a pervert that prayed and strapped his blade at the same time. And clever, they said, clever enough to trick old Roscoe. Me, I don't know.

They was out on bail when Monroe got hung. But he figured that the worst deal a Christian could ever do was commit suicide—I know because I heard him say that lots of times—so I know he never done it himself.

The way I figure it, Roscoe he waited till poor Monroe was asleep and got up real careful like he did whenever he had to take a leak in the night, then crept to this chair under a beam in the garage. Somehow he rigged a rope there without wakin' Monroe, and he slipped the noose over the other head and jumped off the chair. That's how I figure it.

It don't sound fair? Well, if you're lookin' for fair go to the baseball park, bub, because there's nothin' fair about this life.

Anyways, don't pay any mind to the newspapers because it wasn't neither of them boys depressed; no, they was pissed. And there really wasn't no struggle, I just made that up to tell reporters. Whenever we found 'em dead, Monroe had this shocked look on his face but Roscoe he looked like he was grinnin' to me, even if Sheriff McCauley did say he might've been screamin'. And there was the smell of liquor about him. Besides that, the suicide note it was in Roscoe's handwritin'. I think.

Them are the true facts. Like I said, it was a real strange deal.

The Day I Punched Ernest Hemingway

OKAY, SO I READ *The Sun Also Rises* twice and took it seriously. I read Poppa's others too, but that was the book that actually convinced me to become a writer. I mean, if *he* could do it, so could I. I'd been barhopping ever since I turned twenty-one. I was a fisherman and a hunter. I was popular with ladies, and I was tough. It was just my bad luck that there hadn't been a war for me to fight in because I'd have been good at that too. I was a natural.

Well, I bought a tweed jacket and had leather patches sewn on its sleeves. I began wearing cords and smoking a pipe. I even bought a beret from this Basque guy I knew in East Bakersfield. At Amestoy's Bar, I started ordering Pernod. Fred, the bartender, asked me what was wrong with beer the first time, and I explained that I was now a writer. "Oh," he said.

Just to play it safe, I subscribed to the *New York Times Book Review*—I don't see how anybody *reads* that thing—and *Reader's Digest*. I also bought a dictionary so I could look up words I didn't know because I wanted to laden (a new one I learned) my conversations with literary language and the names of good books.

Before long it became common knowledge that I was a writer. I'd just repair (another new word) to Amestoy's on Saturday afternoons and sit at one of the round tables in my tweed jacket, leather-protected elbows on the wood, with Pernod, an open steno pad, and a pencil in front of me—I knew real authors didn't use pens—and sensitively survey my surroundings. When guys like Bucky or Spud or Manuel drifted to my table, I'd say "fine" a lot: "Yes, it was a fine place. He was a fine chap."

I talked about running the bulls in Pamplona, and one of the Ansolobehere cousins, Juan, who had actually lived in Spain, would join me and we'd swap tales. We agreed that grace was the key to performing well in the *corrida* and that no contemporary *toreros* possessed it. "They all imitate El Gallo," I argued. "Dancers, not real men."

Of course, we didn't have many bullfights in Bakersfield and the closest I'd ever come to one was the time Dominguez's cow had stomped me back in high school. She didn't have much grace and neither did Dominguez: he'd laughed his head off.

After a while, though, people who didn't understand that I was *incubating* my novels started asking to see what I'd written. The truth is that I was ready to produce something, a story about this white hunter from Africa who goes to Spain to run the bulls, gets caught in the Civil War, is hurt, meets a beautiful nurse, takes her on a cruise where they catch a giant fish, then they part sadly at the end because she's married and has this sense of honor. It would be dynamite. I could just see them standing in the rain in Paris waving goodbye.

I intended to begin work on it soon, but I couldn't find time since I was by then attending local literary parties regularly and entertaining followers at my table in Amestoy's almost every night. Fred even introduced me to some new customers as a famous writer and they listened quietly while I explained how to stalk a cape buffalo. I bought a second pipe and occasionally drank red wine—"grappa." Besides, my lack of publication didn't seem to be a big problem; I figured I could hire this English teacher I knew to actually write it after I provided the ideas—he had the time—and I was sure *Reader's Digest* would publish it. Except he wouldn't go for it; he was not a fine fellow.

After a while, though, most of my crowd just began to drift away. There were a few who didn't, of course, but my table became less and less crowded. A couple of stock car drivers started hanging out in Amestoy's and everyone wanted to drink with them. Moreover, I read an article in *Reader's Digest* that said smoking a pipe gave you tongue cancer, and I lost my beret. The luck it was bad.

Then it happened. Late one Saturday afternoon, the bar's door burst open and three men swaggered in. One was tall and dark, another was short and dark, and the third, the third was this husky, white-haired, white-bearded man. They were speaking Spanish.

I was sitting alone sipping grappa, my steno pad open. On it I had written "chicken—vegs—napkins—grappa—lettuce—Cheerios." I dropped my pencil immediately and stared at the white-haired fellow. He looked fine. I knew who he couldn't be, but he looked so much like this photo of Hemingway I had at home that I couldn't take my eyes off him. Finally, I stood and, carrying my grappa, I approached the three.

As I slipped next to them, I heard the shortest man call the oldest one "Poppa."

Well, there it was. On a Saturday afternoon in 1959 in Bakersfield, California, Ernest Hemingway had entered Amestoy's Bar and I was there to greet him. It was fate and it was fine.

"Poppa," I said as soon as there was a lull in their conversation, "I'm a writer myself." I extended my right hand.

The old man swung his heavy head toward me and fixed me with two red eyes. *"Qué?"* he said.

"The weather, it is fine," I said.

"Fock you," he mumbled.

My right hand hung there in front of me, and he turned his back. The tallest of the three said something about me in Spanish.

I tapped Poppa's shoulder. "Listen," I said, "I'm trying to be friendly." The hint of impatience entered my voice. Nobody treated me that way in Amestoy's.

The big head turned and again grumbled, "Fock you."

"Listen, Poppa," I said, working to control myself.

"Who you callin' Poppa," demanded the shortest man.

"Mind your own business," I ordered.

"Take off, asshole," the tall one hissed.

"Oh, you want part of this too?" I growled, my fists balling.

"Quién es esta puto, hijo?" Poppa asked the short man.

"No sé, Poppa. Algún loco."

"*Loco* your ass, shithead," I shouted and swung, missing the short guy but thudding Poppa's shoulder.

"*Pendejo!*" he shouted, then seven hundred pounds of badger landed on me, punched my mouth, stomped my butt, danced on my chest. When Fred finally broke it up and hurried them away, I sat on the floor for a long time, the other customers lurching around me. "What the hell happened?" the bartender demanded.

"You know who that was?" I said through a puffed lip.

"I don't care as long as they don't come back."

"That was Ernest Hemingway."

"Who?"

"Ernest Hemingway, the writer."

"That old Mexican? Oh. Well *you* better stick with writin' and leave the fightin' to him."

"He needed those other guys to help him."

"They pulled him off."

I stood up and wiped my face with a bar towel, then dusted off my tweed jacket and cord pants; I'd spilled grappa on them. I returned to my table and Fred brought me another grappa. I waved it away: "Bring me a draft," I said. For a moment, I stared at my grocery list, then I picked up my pencil and, my breath still quick from the fight, I boldly crossed off "grappa" and wrote "beer" above it. To hell with Spain and Hemingway if he was a chickenshit dirty fighter who needed other guys to help him. That was all phony stuff anyway and he was the biggest phony of all.

I was sitting there the way you do when you've had your ass kicked in a bar, gazing into my glass of beer and sucking on my swollen lip, when I was swept by this great idea for a novel. I wouldn't write about Pamplona or Africa or Paris, I'd write about Bakersfield. It would be about this family that comes from Oklahoma or someplace to California during the Depression in this old truck—an old lady, a son, a daughter, maybe some little kids and a preacher—and they just have bad luck, can't find good jobs working in the fields. Pretty soon the son gets in trouble, maybe the preacher gets killed, then they're all caught in one of those big floods like we used to have. It would be dynamite.

That Last Antelope

*From the moving car, I'm not certain what I see twinkling there,
through heat waves in the distance; I lift the binoculars and ask my
bud Tom, the driver, to slow on this nearly deserted road. He does,
and after a few moments scanning the burnished scenery I make out
the rump patches and the tawny bodies of several pronghorns, seeming
to prance on the distant edge of perception.*

*This is 1998, but I am gazing into the past because free-roaming
antelope haven't been seen in this central California country since
early in the century...*

TONY RODE THE LITTLE PINTO down the old stage road into the
long, rocky draw, lurching past wild grapes and cactus paddles.
About halfway down, he stopped at a green spot on the shelf
where a spring puddled. While the pinto drank, Tony's breath
burst white in the cool morning, and far ahead on the road
he could see one of those newfangled automobiles moving his
way. Well, he'd be well out of the hills before that contraption
reached him. No need to hurry.

Below him the land opened into that great valley, as far as
he could see: barren plains to his left, then the gleaming slash
of Kern Lake, then distant Buena Vista Lake surrounded and
connected by a thick green band of tules. Beyond that
loomed low hills so barren that horny toads carried umbrellas.
Straight ahead to the north, dotted by a few farms—but more
all the time poaching on open range—and ranch houses, there
was prairie and more prairie except—far, far to the north—a
few dark trees where the sloughs of Kern River curled

through Bakersfield. On the east were the Tehachapis and the Sierra, big, muscular mountains.

If he looked closely, squinted, he could see specks on the nearby prairie, range cattle, and he knew that vast herds of sheep were grazing the foothills all around him. It wasn't empty, this valley, and a man could hire on with a ranch and breathe here. Tony had wintered near the mission in San Gabriel, working in a tack store, but the stench of autos and the clatter of people had nearly driven him crazy. This time he would hire on year-round with an outfit and stay. He nudged the pinto and they lurched on down the rocky draw until the sloping land at last seemed nearly level. They veered west then, away from the stage route along the foothills toward San Emidio ranch, where he knew they'd be hiring vaqueros.

Almost immediately he passed a clutch of wild-looking cattle, four slick-eared calves and five cows. They wouldn't be slick-eared for long, those calves. He and the rest of the boys'd have them notched and cut and branded before summer. A few hundred yards farther—he'd jumped several large jackass rabbits in that distance—and he surprised another bunch of cows in a thicket of low trees. A good year for calves and rabbits too, he noted, and that meant a good year for cowboys, lots of work.

The sun had worked its way over the mountains behind him and he could see a heavy haze rising from the marshes near that distant lake. Just ahead, Big Arroyo opened and there was a stand of willows at its mouth where he had often rested in shade during scorching summer days. He could see a thin finger of smoke and figures there and assumed it was some of the boys from the ranch, so he turned the pinto south. As he closed on the trees, however, he saw no horses. Closer still and he knew it was a bunch of Indians—two kids scrambling away and a woman squatting there next to the small fire. Well, they had no business here on ranch property.

As he neared the small encampment, two rough-looking men who had been posed near the trees stepped forward and waited for him. Three other women, one carrying a baby, and two more children scurried behind the trees. Those two bucks stood below him, their hair long and tangled, their eyes smoldering like a treed cougar's. The men's lean, dusty bodies were covered by only rabbit-skin shirts and frayed, store-bought britches. Behind them near the willows was a small shelter of branches and their meager belongings—a few baskets, some leather bags, not much. And there were two under-fed mules tethered there too.

"What're you people doin' here on ranch property?" Tony demanded.

The younger buck glanced at the older, then said, "Catch rabbit."

"And catch calf or two, I'll bet. You better get your butts off this property or me and the boys'll have to run you off."

"Catch rabbit," the younger buck insisted, and he pointed behind the tree where several skins and strips of meat were drying. The older man glared at Tony with undisguised disdain, like a damned animal.

"I wouldn't be here tomorrow if I was you," Tony warned, then he swung his horse around and moved west once more toward the ranch. He wanted to be there in time for a little coffee.

That next morning he was riding with Manuel and Shade, moving toward the foothills far west of the ranch house where the pipe draining a lone spring—the cattle's only water thereabouts—needed clearing. They would be plumbers, maybe well-diggers, that morning, typical cowboy work, and maybe carpenters tomorrow, since a windmill was down over toward Wheeler Ridge and it had to be rebuilt.

Below them as they traveled was that wide band of tules—rushes and reeds maybe fifteen feet high—that spread from the lake to a small flat with a few cottonwoods and willows. "That there's where the Indi'ns used to keep a camp in the old days," explained Shade. "Hell of a bunch of 'em—damn near a town. That was, oh, '71 or '72 when I first come out here. I don't know where they all went."

"I know where some of 'em went," Tony said. "Over to Big Arroyo. There's a gang over there on ranch property. Say they're takin' rabbits. I figure we might can run 'em off after work today."

"Why for?" asked Shade, who was the oldest rider on the spread. "That might be the last bunch still on their own. The rest of 'em, they're all on that big reservation now."

"Cause they're *there,* Indians, right on the property."

"Hell, they won't hurt nothin'. Maybe they'll thin out them damn rabbits some. Besides, you cain't blame for wantin' to stay free."

"Maybe *you* can't. They don't belong here."

Shade grinned. "Hell, *we* prob'ly don't. They was here before we was even born and they never hurt nothin'. Just leave 'em be. Right, Manuel?"

Manuel grunted, "To me it don' mean nahthing."

There was no talking to old Shade. He was half loco and he had an answer for everything. No point pursuing it. Tony would talk to a few of the younger boys when they got in that evening. They'd see the fun in running those damn Indians off. He changed the subject: "A nice elk steak'd sure taste good tonight. How's the herd this year?" Tony patted the carbine in its scabbard hanging from his saddle.

"Too many folks like them steaks," Shade replied. "There's still some elks out in them tules, but not many. Things ain't what they used to be. Back when I first come here, we killed almost eight hundred in one week, sent the meat to the city. But there was too many meat hunters. Now them elks're about gone."

That old man could complain more than any two guys Tony knew. No point in talking to him. "Hey Manuel," he finally called, "how 'bout a little elk steak?"

"To me it don' mean nahthing."

What a couple of pistols Tony'd got stuck with on his first day. He determined to ride silently to the spring.

A quarter-mile later, Shade said, "Maybe you could shoot one a them white deers down there."

Tony glanced and saw, beyond a distant road where one of those damned automobiles slowly moved, a vast flock of sheep that seemed to extend as far as he could see into the distance toward Bakersfield. "Jesus," he whistled, "where'd all of 'em come from?"

"More ever' year," Shade said, "ruinin' the public range. Usta be they'd stay up in them hills or over toward the far mountains, but they're down here now, all over."

"What's the old man say about it?" Tony asked.

"How don't like it none, I'll tell you that much."

"I'll bet."

An hour later, the three vaqueros finally crested the final barren rise toward the Carrizo Plain and saw the green patch that marked the westside spring. Tony counted maybe a dozen cows and calves lying in around it, then he saw a white flash, a tan form far too large to be a rabbit, that was streaking away. "What the...?"

Shade squinted, then said, "I'll be go to hell! It's a damn pronghorn antelope. I ain't seen one on this range for years."

"De veras?" Manuel grunted.

"No shit," Shade assured him as the fleeing animal disappeared into a fold in the rolling country.

"Ain't that somethin', Manuel," the old rider observed. "Why hell, they got thinned out here about as fast as grizzlies did back in the old days. Where the hell'd that little guy come from?"

They had stopped their horses on the rise, and Manuel pushed his sombrero back and crossed one leg over his saddle horn and commenced rolling a cigarette. Finally he replied, "Out on the Carrizo maybe. Juan he seen some there last year an' he tol' me some hunters they still go there."

The Carrizo was an enclosed valley just over the desert hills to the west and it had been spared the pressure that had ruined hunting here in the huge Tulare Valley. Tony hadn't ever seen an antelope hereabouts, although way up north of the Buttonwillow spread maybe eight, nine years before, he'd jumped a little band of them and killed three before they'd managed to run out of range. It seemed like a long time ago.

That lone pronghorn had long since disappeared, and Tony patted the scabbard alongside his saddle and said, "Well, a little antelope stew might taste good if that guy was to show up again."

"That there's the last one, Tony," pointed out Shade. "Let's just see he drinks without no one shootin' at him, all right?"

It was not a request, Tony knew, and he resented anyone telling him what to do. Hell, it was just like living in a damn city.

Manuel, the dark vaquero, nodded then said, "*Sí*. Don' do heem nahthing. He ees the last one."

Shade swung off his big bay and said, "Let's go to work, you two."

That evening, too tired to feel like riding to Big Arroyo, Tony nonetheless told a couple of the younger boys about the Indians he'd jumped the day before. They seemed interested in the possibility of a little sport but knew they'd have to defer it until a job took them near Big Arroyo. The old man had plenty for them to do right now.

A week later—Big Arroyo still not visited—work led him back to the westside spring, where he'd seen that lone antelope. He was sent out to make sure those damned shepherds weren't trailing their flocks up there to drink. That was one thing the old man wouldn't stand. Riding alone this time, Tony had tarried to plug several jackass rabbits with his carbine, although he did not bother to collect them since they were mere Indian food. He had squeezed off a shot at but missed a great condor soaring far overhead. Despite Shade's claims to the contrary, he was certain those ugly birds snatched calves.

When he finally crested that desert rise, he halted his pinto. There, sipping at the tank, was that antelope, or at least *an* antelope, and it did not seem to sense his presence. It would be a longshot, but he silently slipped the carbine from its scabbard and leveled it at the animal's tan shoulder. Just then, the pronghorn looked up, exposing a white patch on its chest, and Tony moved his sights there but did not pull the trigger for, squinting, he saw its small spiked horns, its large dark eyes, its delicate muzzle. "The last one," Shade had said. So what?

Tony squeezed the trigger and the rifle cracked. A plume of dust exploded behind the startled animal, which jumped, then streaked with jerky, surging speed that immediately took it out of range. Frustrated, Tony fired once more but wasn't even close. Those damn things're sure fast.

Work didn't bring him back to the westside for another couple of weeks. By then many of the boys had seen that pronghorn and all of them had talked about it. They seemed a little awestruck at its existence because it had been years since any had been observed on this range, and it wasn't natural to see just one because they lived in groups. This was surely a survivor from the last of the great herds Shade and the other old-timers remembered, maybe the last one. Men who Tony knew would shoot lizards for the fun of it spoke almost reverently of this animal. No one discussed hunting it, so he kept his counsel. If it was the last one, he'd be the guy to get it, by God.

Anticipating an encounter with the antelope that day, he had borrowed a spyglass from Antonio Salazar, and he held it at the ready when his pinto climbed that final rise before the westside spring. To his disappointment, he noted only a half-dozen cattle milling around the tank, so he urged the pinto forward. He checked the pipe and cleared some trappings from the tank. That finished, he listed in the notebook he carried the number of calves he had seen, then once more pulled that spyglass from his saddlebag and, closing one eye, he scanned the vast, beige panorama, not really expecting to see that antelope, but what the hell.

He sighted nothing to the west, to the south, to the north. When he scanned the east, however, looking for elk as much as anything, he saw something else: farms were marching toward the lake from Bakersfield, covering open range that the old man's stock had grazed just a year or two before. Hell, if that kept up, there wouldn't *be* no place left in the valley for cattle. He was half tempted to organize the boys to go raid those damn dirt spreads.

Just as he dropped the spyglass, his eye caught something else. He sighted again, closely this time, and, sure enough, one of those dirty Indians was on that flat near the tules where Shade said there'd once been a village—on ranch property, by God. Well, Shade wasn't here to talk his nonsense, so Tony determined to take care of them himself. Urging the pinto down the slope toward Buena Vista Lake, he covered the ground to where those devils were camped.

"You boys can't seem to stay off'n this ranch, can you?" he demanded.

That same surly young buck gazed up at him without fear and did not respond. He looked the same except that, for some reason, his hair had been shorn and his skin looked like he'd rubbed ashes on it. Tony could see no evidence of the others and for a moment he wondered if he hadn't walked into a trap. "Where's the rest a your bunch?" he demanded.

That buck didn't blink. "Gone dead," he said.

"Gone dead?"

"Big sick gone dead."

Then Tony noticed a bloody hide hanging from a tree snag not far away in the tules. "Uh-huh, and you boys been big sick gone dead a few calves, haven't you?"

The buck did not reply and his eyes did not leave the mounted man's.

Looking away from that thin Indian, Tony studied the hide. For a moment it didn't register, then his throat suddenly swelled and he roared, "Son of a bitch, you killed it! You dirty digger! You killed it!" He struggled to pull his rifle from its scabbard, and the buck immediately darted into the tules and disappeared, leaving only that fresh hide hanging on the snag.

"You savages!" Tony howled. "You damn savages!" And he fired into the dense, green rushes, shooting again and again until the rifle's hammer at last clicked against a hot, empty chamber. They aren't even human, he thought. They aren't even *nothin'*. They killed the last damned antelope. His breath puffing, he reloaded. He knew that he'd never find the redskins in that vast wilderness of tules, so he glanced one last time at that fresh tan-and-white hide, then turned the pinto. He'd come back with some of the boys to root out that damn digger and settle with him once and for all.

The Cottonwood Tree

MY FATHER'S FACE LOOKED LIKE a pale yellow raisin. Only three months had passed since I'd left Dad with Uncle Martin. Although he was eighty-two years old, and suffering from a half-dozen ailments, he had retained the lean, vigorous appearance he'd had when I'd delivered him to his younger brother's house in San Francisco back in June.

I stuttered like a damn kid when I greeted my father. "How...how are you, Dad?"

"Can't complain. Good of you to come, Cecil," he said as we shook hands, that feathery tenor of his no different from my first memories of it some sixty years before. I'd always been amazed that a man of my father's size, a man who had ramrodded cowboys and vaqueros all his life, had been saddled with a voice like a castrato.

"It's that time," I said. "You all packed?"

"You bet. Martin gave me a hand."

My uncle stood at my elbow. He was ten years younger than Dad—"the baby of the family"—and still practicing law. A third brother, Miles, who was eighty-seven, had retired from the university in Berkeley way back when. He'd been a distinguished professor of mammalogy and he still lectured occasionally as an emeritus prof. All three were widowers.

"Well," my father urged as with some effort he rose to his feet and placed his thoroughly broken-in Stetson on his head, "we'd better get on the road if we want to make the ranch before dark."

"Right," I agreed and reached out to give him a hand, but he shrugged off my offer. Uncle Martin winked at me.

The three of us walked to my car parked on the steeply sloping street, me eyeing my fragile father who seemed on the verge of stumbling all the while. I loaded his luggage into the truck, shook hands with Uncle Martin, then climbed behind the wheel.

Dad eased himself into the passenger's side and his brother snapped the door closed. Through the open window the two old men shook hands. "Thanks again for everything, Martin," Dad said.

"Always a pleasure to have you here, Milton," smiled my uncle. "I'll try to visit the ranch before it turns too cold and we can visit that Indian site you found."

"You bet. We'd better get along, Cecil."

"So long," waved Uncle Martin. I noticed as we pulled down the street that Dad's brother stood on the sidewalk in front of his house and watched us, something he'd never done before.

"Let's head straight home today, Cecil."

"Sure," I replied, staring at him briefly.

Little talk passed between us as I motored out of the Bay Area megalopolis. We crossed low hills into the Central Valley, then across that flat agricultural landscape into the Sierra foothills. Finally, we lurched into the high country, the big double-cab pickup easily accelerating even on the steepest grades. I began to wonder if Dad was fading, but when we reached the turnoff at Donner Summit, that squeaky voice requested, "Pull over here, will you, son?"

Son? When had he last called me that? At sixty-one myself, I rarely think of myself as anything but grandpa, so that word startled me.

I eased the truck into the view area next to the road. I was preoccupied as I had been throughout the trip with returning him to the ranch and calling our family doctor; that notion had been swirling in my mind like a rattlesnake in a gunny-sack while we drove across much of California's girth. We sat in the cab, seeing Donner Lake and the scattered houses and the railroad plat of Truckee below us, the vast panorama of granite and trees and water. Not far over the high mountains just east of us was the high desert of the eastern Sierra and our family ranch, the one founded by my great-grandfather and great-grandmother a century before. "Hell of a view," I said.

Without turning toward me Dad replied, "You bet. Years ago, the three of us boys, plus Momma and Poppa, all rode up this on horseback with mules carrying our supplies. We were just kids the first time, and we rode all the way from the ranch to Sacramento, then we took a paddle-wheel steamer down the river to San Francisco. Years ago..." His voice faded, then he added, "Except for the highway, the place hasn't changed at all. Wonderful country."

"Remember the first time you brought Bird and me up here? That was on horseback too." Bird's my younger sister, Brigitte.

He grinned. "You bet. Your mother wanted me to take the old flivver, but I said no, I wanted you kids to experience this land the way I had, and she gave in. She was always a good sport," he grinned. He seemed incapable of mentioning my mother without smiling, a fact that always left me feeling good.

"She was," I agreed.

"You know, Cecil, I saw the docs at the university medical center in San Francisco while I was visiting Milton and they told me I'm gonna cash 'em in before long."

I jolted not because an eighty-two-year-old man would soon die, but because my dad would. He had always kept his private life private. "Why do you say that?"

"Well, I've been feeling punk for a while," he said. Then he grinned. "You know, I've been old so long that I just kind of thought I'd keep on being old. But I'll be in good company dead, damned good company. It'll be good to lie down with Katie again, and with little Matthew."

Katie was my mother. Matthew was an older brother who'd died in infancy. They were buried side by side under a cotton-wood tree at the ranch. Dad had years before outlined his own grave's site on the other side of Matthew so the baby could sleep between his parents. "That little cuss used to pee on my back when he'd bunk with us," Dad had once explained. Their first baby had been sickly, and my folks had told me they'd cuddled him nearly every night.

I, too, felt somewhat relieved by the prospect of my father and mother and brother being once more united, but the unvarnished fact of his death hung there. I could not think of life without him.

"Well, let's get back on the road," my father finally broke the silence. "I could use a cup of Bird's coffee."

Our ranch extended from just across the Nevada line toward the high desert between Reno and Carson City. It was the largest and oldest continuously operated spread in the region. The main house sat almost on the state line on a bench above a river canyon.

My sister and her husband, Les, assorted of their brood, plus all the hands and their families lived there. Bird and Les actually ran the ranching operation and related dealings. They had long since moved into sheep and were developing beefalo. Our family had financed the region's first successful vineyard too, and we grew both potatoes and sugar beets, plus enough hay to sell in California. Recently a couple of my nephews had, in partnership with a Japanese corporation, opened a vacation development in the mountains north of the ranch, and one of my nieces, a mining engineer, had reestablished some old claims to our collective profit. Dad paid most attention to the beef, and we were one of the few big cattle outfits that steadily turned a profit.

I lived in North Lake Tahoe and kept a town house in Carson City, the state capital. My father had been a senator there throughout much of his adult life, retiring for good when he was seventy-eight, never having lost an election. My younger daughter, an attorney, plans to run for the same seat next year. My son, like me, is also an attorney, and I run the corporate offices there in Carson in our complex of buildings just east of the capitol building. One unkind editor has suggested several times in print that our place was the real center of power in the capital.

My son seems both to believe and enjoy that possibility. He's a good kid, a good businessman, but not much of a rancher; he favors Italian loafers with no socks, not cowboy boots, while I still scuff around in Justins, an enduring joke between us: "Are you *sure* you're my kid?"

"I don't know. Ask Mom."

Since retiring from state government, my dad had made it a practice to regularly visit the bar in the Capital Hotel and hold court there, where his presence always guaranteed a full house. This trip, though, he only wanted to return to the ranch.

Bird had coffee on when we got in. She kissed Dad, then walked arm in arm with him into the kitchen, where we all plopped at the rough wooden table that had been our family's gathering place for as long as I can remember—since long before I was born, surely. To me, that plank table symbolized our lives: sturdy, unpretentious, enduring. When we were kids our parents had kept Bird and me busy shoveling out corrals, mending fences, bucking hay. It had come as a great surprise when, at about the time we were carted off to college in Reno, we learned that we were the products of a rich, influential family. We'd never had domestic help, and even when my father was at the height of his political powers, he had worked shoulder to shoulder with fieldhands when he was home. He believed that manual labor was sacred. Anyway, it was a lesson my sister and I had learned well. Blue jeans and cowboy boots were still our costume, pickup trucks our vehicles.

We all drank hot coffee laced with brandy that afternoon while various kids and grandkids trooped over and around us, kissing Dad and me, taking no obvious notice of his deterioration. The old man slumped in his chair, his Stetson hanging from a corner of it. He said little.

When Les came in from mending fences, he talked briefly with Dad, telling him they'd cleared that spring that had stopped flowing and asking him what they ought to do about this or how to deal with that—cowboy talk. It was all business as usual except that the shriveled old man was obviously very sick. Only a few minutes after Les arrived, Dad said he was tired and shuffled to his room.

"He looks awful, Cec'," my sister said as soon as our father departed.

Her husband agreed. "He sure as hell does."

"Listen, Bird," I urged, "call Doc Johnson out, will you? Invite Oleta and him to dinner so it doesn't look so ominous to Dad, but let's find out what's going on."

Bird glanced around like she was about to reveal a deep secret, then said, "We already know, Cec'. Doc told Les and me that Poppa's got metastatic prostate cancer and that it's just a matter of time."

For a moment I could say nothing. Finally, I managed only, "So that's it. We can get him down to one of the big cancer centers…"

"Doc says it's irreversible and that aggressive therapy would kill an eighty-two-year-old man faster than the malignancy would. Poppa's known about the disease for a long time."

"That doesn't surprise me." I puffed for a minute, sad and angry, then said, "And I know he's eighty-two and that he's had good life, but he's our father, Bird."

"Yes, Cec', he is…" and she reached across the table and took both my hands in hers. "Yes he is."

The first two or three days after he returned home, Dad perked up. He'd arise early, Bird told me, just as he always had, drink his coffee, then ride his old gray out to the cotton-wood tree to Momma and Matthew's graves. Later he'd survey those beefalo calves, maybe gab with the hands. At noon he'd drink a little soup—he didn't seem to have any appetite for solid foods, my sister reported. "He just plays with his food at dinner, Cec', maybe downs a few bites."

I had to get back to the business, and when I returned the next week, he wasn't eating much at all, just drinking his morning coffee—laced with brandy and honey by Bird—and sipping a little soup. It was pretty discouraging. I brought out a case of his favorite ale and, while he was grateful, he didn't show much interest in it. He looked like a sick, sick old man.

The next day Uncle Miles arrived, having driven his large Lincoln over from Moraga. "There's one damn highway cop who'd give his eyeteeth to catch me behind the wheel," chuckled the eighty-seven-year-old driver, "but he'll have to add about 40 IQ points to manage it." My father stood to greet him and I saw shock in my uncle's eyes, but the old professor's voice didn't betray a thing. "It's about time you got back here, Milton, and earned your keep. No wonder my stock in the company hasn't been producing what it should...these knothead kids of yours." He grinned at Bird and me.

"You better talk to Cecil, there. He's the boss now," Dad grinned.

"Ahhh, that boy never had sense enough to pour piss out of a boot," replied my uncle. "If I could find a lawyer in this state who wasn't a relative of yours, I'd sue the hell out of you for malfeasance."

Dad was grinning: "You can't even spell 'malfeasance,'" he snapped.

"Well," chuckled Uncle Miles, "I think it starts with an M..."

It was their typical exchange, always teasing, always sparring, and I was grateful to Uncle Miles for holding up his end of it. Later, the two of them rode out to the cottonwood tree together.

Two days later, walking Miles to his car, I thanked him for visiting.

"No need, Cec'. No need. I've been the man's brother for eighty-two years, plus the months Momma carried him, and I've loved him in my way nearly all that time—except for a couple of scraps between us. We need to be together in this."

He hooked one of my arms with one of his. "You're still young by our family's standards and I know this'll sound funny to you, but your dad'll be the first of us boys to die since Matthew nearly ninety years ago. And don't worry—he knows and he's not afraid, not Milton. To me, though, it seems like he's being plucked away just when he's starting to figure out what it's all about. Your spirit doesn't age, but your body breaks down. Isn't that a hell of a note?

"But maybe if a man knows too much it's time for him to die. He was always much the smartest of us, and became the wisest. Staying with the ranch did that, I think, kept him focused and kept him in touch with the earth in spite of his political career. He stayed closer to life and death than Martin and I did."

He glanced at me then and I noticed that his faded blue eyes glistened. "I'll miss him, Cecil," he said.

"So will I, Uncle Miles."

"I know, boy," he said and he patted my back. As old as I was, it felt both good and right, him doing that. "I'll be back whenever you need me."

He wheeled his large silver Lincoln down the ranch road, dust billowing like exhaust behind it. I'd seen that same dust rising from horses, from wagons, from Model As and Model Ts, from bicycles ridden by kids, even from an elephant way back when one of Dad's friends who owned a traveling circus brought one out and gave Bird and me a ride. Just at the point where the lane turned toward the county road stood the cottonwood tree, gaunt as my father.

Three nights later, Dad slipped dramatically. He suddenly needed large, then larger, doses of pain medicine, and twice Doc Johnson drove out. "There's nothing we can do but keep him comfortable," he told me. "If this gets to be too much, we can move him into the hospital," he added.

"No!" Bird and I snapped simultaneously.

Doc raised both hands as though in supplication: "Just a suggestion."

Soon Dad slipped into a coma. Bird and I initiated a death-watch, taking turns—four hours on, four hours off, and refusing the offers of others to spell us. We injected him with painkillers as we'd been instructed, and just tried to be there. On the next night, his eyes opened and he said, "Katie? Where's Katie?"

"I'm here, Dad," I said, stroking his forehead.

"Where's your Momma? I want her to come to bed with me."

At well over sixty years old, I blushed. That was my mother he was talking about, and I understood exactly his intent. Those were the last words he ever spoke.

Only three, three and a half hours later, just as Bird and I were changing shifts, we noticed that his breathing was becoming ragged. He began gasping. I jumped to my feet, not certain what to do, and my sister exchanged a wordless glance with me. Dad's breathing shallowed, shallowed until it became just a whisper. I placed both my hands over his on his chest, and Bird caressed his forehead. A respirator could keep him breathing, we both knew, but that wasn't an acceptable option, not for this man.

When he stopped breathing, we each gave him a final kiss, a squeeze, then hugged one another long and hard. I closed Dad's half-open eyes, then covered his face with that blanket just as Les entered the room and asked, "Is it over?"

"Yes," I replied as he embraced his wife.

"Should we call someone?" Les asked.

"No need, hon'," my sister replied. "Poppa's resting easy. We all need to sleep. We'll call Doc in the morning."

"Right," I agreed.

Bird and I talked afterward and we were both convinced that our father was aware of our presence during those final moments of his life. He lay on the same bed in which our mother and brother had died, under the same wool Navajo blanket that had likely covered them. Both Bird and I had been born in that bed. So had my father.

Our call the next morning was not unexpected and Doc, also the county coroner, arrived shortly after breakfast, examined Dad's body, then returned to the kitchen and signed the death certificate. "No autopsy needed," he said. "Milton died of natural causes. May I have a little more of that coffee, Bird?"

"Sure," replied my sister and she poured him another cupful.

Then he added, "Do you want me to take Milton in to Hal Everett's?"

Hal Everett was the local undertaker, a relative newcomer who'd taken over after Manuel Ansolobehere died.

"You and Les give me a hand with the bag and gurney, then you folks can drive in and talk to Hal when it's convenient."

"You bet," I said, and for an instant I thought I heard my father's voice.

Bird and I telephoned everyone we could think of and mid-afternoon drove to the little crossroads town fourteen miles from the ranch. On all four roads stood large billboards with airbrushed likenesses of the local undertaker on them: "Harold W. Everett, Funeral Director" was printed in bold letters. "Everett Mortuary. Chapel of the Sage. The High Desert's most thoughtful service. Credit available. Pre-need plans." You might have trouble reading the small print, but you couldn't miss that man's puss grinning at you, and somehow it galled me.

I'd met Everett at Rotary a time or two and hadn't liked him. Bird had suggested at the time that I just didn't cotton to little men on the make—men like our own grandfather had been—and that criticism stung me because it was at least half true. If there was one thing Dad had done when we were kids it was to remind us that hard work and blind luck, in about equal portions, had made us rich, not any great superiority or virtue on our part. Still, running the business in Carson City, it was difficult not to be turned off by folks frantically scrambling up the ladder we'd already climbed. And Manuel Ansolobehere never found it necessary to spread his face all over billboards.

The undertaker looked much like his large portraits, except that he was a small man. His clothing was impeccable and stylish—much like my son's, actually. His pink face and hands had the too-clean look of a hair dresser's, and his own coiffure was a swirled bluish-white that had been sprayed stiff as glass. His pale blue tie over a pale blue shirt and the shiny metal dingle-dangles on his shoes offended me, but I guess I was in an offended mood, on the cusp of anger from the time I shook his practiced hand.

We sat in his small office on fancy plastic chairs while he gently probed our private lives. We told him almost nothing. Dad's name and age and place of birth; our addresses and the names of other survivors. When he asked if "the Senator," as he called my father, was to be interred in Reno or Carson City, I said no, and he seemed disappointed. Finally, he asked if we'd like to view caskets. We agreed and he led us into a deeply carpeted room with muted music and light to match, directing us toward a massive copper coffin that looked like a sports car. "This," he explained, "is the top of the line, a casket befitting a man of the Senator's station. You'll notice the real silk lining, the inner-spring construction, the absolute hermetic seals that, in conjunction with the proper crypt, will preserve your loved one for a thousand years."

"For what?" I asked.

"I beg your pardon?"

"For what? What's the point of preserving a dead body for a thousand years? It sounds ghoulish to me."

He cleared his throat and I saw a smile crease Bird's face. "Well, that's really just a figure of speech. What I mean is that this will show the world your respect for the Senator."

"And how much does this little beauty cost?" My tone was not kind.

"Well, we prefer not to discuss cost during your hour of grief…"

"Well, to receive a large bill after it's too late to change my mind would *greatly* intensify my grief. My mother and brother were buried in simple wooden coffins, and that's what we want for my father. No inner springs, no hermetic seals, no crypt. We'll take care of the burial out at our ranch."

"Do you have a permit?" It slipped out, I think, because he immediately covered his mouth with one hand.

I rocked back on the heels of my boots and I heard my sister exhale. Before I could speak, she did: "Mr. Everett, my brother is an attorney. He's aware of what is and is not legally required in this state."

The undertaker's ears and nose reddened and a short silence ensued. I finally broke it: "You embalm Dad today. We'll prop him up in my pickup's cab and drive him back to the ranch— he'd like that. We've a man there who can build a coffin."

Bird gave me a familiar look that said I had, perhaps, gone too far, but Hal Everett—after another moment of silence— slumped. "I'll take care of it," he said.

Dad's body was delivered to the ranch in a simple wooden coffin that afternoon. Les, two of his boys, and I carried it to the table in the dining room, and Bird draped it with a Najavo rug our parents had bought as newlyweds.

That next afternoon, with the clan gathered, ranch hands from all our holdings, friends, and associates filling our house and yard, we hitched our old wagon to two large mules and carried my father to the cottonwood tree where my mother and brother waited. My nephews had opened a grave there on the other side of Matthew, and we lowered the coffin into it with two ropes. There was little weeping: Dad's life had been long and rewarding.

We aren't churchgoing people, never have been, but Alvaro Etchevarry, the local Catholic priest, was an old poker partner of Dad's and, as prearranged, he delivered a eulogy. "God, please accept this good man into your kingdom. He was our friend, our father, our brother, and we'll miss him. Don't let his rough exterior or that squeaky voice fool you, and if you need a fourth for poker, call him."

"But watch him closely.

"So long, old friend. We'll miss you but we'll see you soon. In the name of the Father, the Son, and the Holy Spirit, amen."

Every person attending—and there were plenty, I can assure you—walked to the mound of fresh earth, grabbed a handful or sliced a shovelful, and dropped it into the grave, and then Bird and I and our two uncles shoveled the remainder until the grave was completely closed. Everyone waited. Finally, we all returned to the house to eat and talk.

Those two mules followed us, pulling that empty wagon back to the barn. Behind them, silhouetted against the tangerine slash of a sun that would soon set, that gaunt cottonwood stood sentry over my parents and brother.

In the parlor, I grabbed a can of beer, avoided any long conversations, then escaped onto the porch and peered once more at the progressing sunset and that sentinel tree. Every spring, we'd wonder if it was finally dead, and each spring a few small brown buds would swell and burst. As I gazed at the tree I could just make out the shape of a few clusters on its limbs and even see a few birds settling on it for their night's roost.

A large Mercedes I recognized as my son's, who'd earlier told me he had a business dinner scheduled that night in Sacramento, wended its way out of the confusion of cars in the yard, then sped up the lane, dust billowing as he picked up speed and passed the cottonwood tree, causing the birds to rise briefly. Then they returned to their perches.

ESSAYS

The Cusp of the Future

I question if the next generation here will care for Shakespeare, or any other author, growing up in ignorance, far from school, church, or other institution of civilization.

William H. Brewer, May 5, 1863

As IT TURNED OUT, the barriers to civilization Brewer perceived proved ephemeral. Four disparate regions constitute California's Great Central Valley; in the over five hundred miles from Grapevine Grade to Mount Shasta can be found one of the most agriculturally varied, most technologically altered, most abundantly productive landscapes in the world. Its nearly fifteen million acres constitute two-thirds of all tillable land in the state, producing that amazing 25 percent of all table food consumed nationally. In it may also be found farmers and entrepreneurs as innovative as can be discovered anywhere and a society that has allowed countless migrants to achieve some version of the California dream.

But in this region, the dream itself is undergoing testing and change. Philosopher Stan Dundon summed up the findings of the 1986 California Academy of Sciences' symposium *Heartland in Transition* this way: "Awareness of new, environmentally sensitive agricultural technologies and an explicit concern for equity in the interest of Valley residents" may allow guidance of future agricultural impact "to provide both an environmentally and humanely better outcome." However, "short-range economic market forces will remain the dominant determinant in the future of the Valley," thus remaining

the major constraint *against* sustainable agriculture and, potentially, against an improved social and economic environment for
residents. Given adequate political will and openness to
change, however, many of the short-term demands may be
met and a lower-impact, sustainable kind of farming introduced.

Perhaps it is time to grow more farms and somewhat less
short-term produce. Certainly it is time to shed the nine-
teenth-century delusion that more—more acres of land, more
acre-feet of water, more lugs of rubber tomatoes—is inevitably
better. Big agribusiness in this region has the resources, both
financial and intellectual, to move toward less damaging, more
enduring methods of farming—but businesspeople must
believe, for instance, that it is not absolutely necessary to spread
thirty tons of pesticide on these fields each year. Old ways of
thinking do die hard, and no corporation makes expansive and
expensive changes casually.

Nonetheless, if the quality of life that has made the Valley a
fine place to live and raise one's family is not to be lost, then
local people must look at the larger picture. Do they *really*
want to dwell in suburbs indistinguishable from those in the
Santa Clara Valley or the San Fernando Valley? Do they *really*
want family farming entirely replaced by corporate agriculture? Do they *really* believe that immediate profits compensate
for cancer clusters and poisoned wells? Dundon suggests that
participation in planning and research by farmers who are
committed to this place "may be the most important factor in
reconciling the various factors affecting the future of the
Valley." In fact, all local residents should participate for,
although corporate boards elsewhere may control the deeds to
much land here, they do not know the call of a dove or the
chill of river water slicing from the Sierra Nevada or the
dawn smell of a freshly mown alfalfa field.

This final point is vital: deliberations concerning the Valley's
future should be made by all those whose lives will be most
directly affected—the shoemaker in Chico and the field foreman in Edison—not only the lobbyist in Sacramento. Effective
change cannot be exclusively the domain of theorists, of

technocrats, of corporate executives or their "house" politicians, but must include representative elements of entire communities. However, the expansion of possible alternatives for the future is, as Dundon points out, "a principal responsibility of research institutions."

The Valley now boasts eight colleges and universities, and they, along with other, less proximate institutions, have been producing native-born scholars deeply concerned with the future of this area; the generations for whom Brewer feared, they have increasingly contributed to a body of knowledge that may allow the heartland to continue as an economic and social force. Local folk, farmers and others, have the toughness, the inventiveness, the spirit to deal with their problems, but first they must face them squarely, casting aside old, obscuring illusions and prejudices. "We're so parochial. We want to live in our own little world," admits Aldo Sansoni. "Everybody else is wrong. No one else's problem is our problem....We on the farms and those folks in the cities need each other. We've got to stop viewing each other as enemies." And, of course, most Valley folk dwell in urban settings.

But it is not enough merely to think in terms of a rapprochement between growers and their urban markets. Agriculture is an international business, and Valley farmers produce quantities of food and fiber that exceed the demands of domestic markets. "Consequently," points out J. B. Kendrick, Jr., longtime chief of Agriculture and Natural Resources at the University of California, "for economic survival, it is imperative that our major crops and many of our specialty commodities find receptive and rewarding foreign markets." Productivity—and thus competition—is rising worldwide, but so is population, so is hunger. Kendrick goes on to caution that, in order for US agriculture to remain competitive in the international trade environment, "it must continually improve its productivity and its efficiency."

The catch-22 is that "efficiency" has traditionally been interpreted in the Valley to mean bigger, more concentrated holdings and fewer family farms, along with more and more technology. "The trend toward larger-scale farming is often

justified on the grounds that it is more efficient," Richard
Smoley agrees. "Small is not always inefficient," Chuck Geisler
of Cornell University argues. "Many inefficiencies in the large
end of the production scale don't get reported....They may
be energy inefficiencies, labor inefficiencies, environmental
trade-offs."

Finally, Dundon's suggestion that Valley dwellers themselves
must decide what they want. Do they prefer family farms
with somewhat reduced production but longer productive
lives, for example, or greater concentrations of land and power
in the hands of a few, with greater short-term production?
Local folk must determine which and live with the society
that results.

Residents complain that outsiders too often focus on negative aspects of Valley life in general, and agriculture in particular, while those who study the region complain that locals
prefer to wear blinders. Thus, for example, two recent books
by outsiders have railed against the physical and political
dangers of irrigation in the area without acknowledging the
positive aspects of life here; thus, too, many locals railed
against "outside agitators" and "communists" when farm labor
was being organized here, ignoring the patterns of agricultural
peonage that actually predicated the disruption.

Today, the issues cannot be avoided. If they are, Valley residents will by default end up with what outsiders—politicians
from elsewhere or corporate executives—prefer. The blinders
must be removed, justifiable criticism must be considered, and
important decisions must be made. Solutions for a great many
contemporary problems of both farm and town lie in progres-
sive, creative modes of thought here, not in the insistent hope
that technologists will save the day.

Francis DuBois is chairman of an eight-family cooperative
that cultivates six thousand acres in the Sacramento Valley.
His credo defies stereotypes of Valley growers and illustrates
the quality of mind that is now necessary and, happily, available. "Though we farmers, or our banks, own the farmland," he points out, "we are in truth only custodians of it.
We hold it in trust for future generations and we must not
exploit it, erode it, poison it, bury it, nor may we violate the

rights, dignity, welfare, and friendship of those who together with us farm this most productive of all the valleys in the world."

It is also important to recognize that no other region of our state—perhaps of our nation—better illustrates the cherished and enduring illusion that ours is a land of yeoman farmers, cultivators of the soil who draw strength from the earth itself. Here we have created what Henry Nash Smith identified in *Virgin Land* as "the Garden of the World": "The master symbol of the garden embraced by a cluster of metaphors expressing fecundity, growth, increase, and blissful labor in the earth, all centering about the heroic figure of the idealized frontier farmer armed with that supreme agrarian weapon, the sacred plow." In the Great Central Valley today, many farmers face the frontier of the boardroom and drive the sacred Cadillac, while campesinos do the plowing. Others, meanwhile, struggle to retain family farms, exhausting their bodies for the mystical intimacy with the soil that personal farming retains, and they do so despite conditions little more promising than those faced by Ishi. "In 1982, 4 percent of the farms that harvested crops—those of one thousand acres or more—brought in 56 percent of the harvest," Katharine Ulrich points out. That leaves a slim gleaning for the other 96 percent who farm in the Valley.

This is a land of paradox, full of friendly people whose sudden xenophobia can shock. Its open spaces lull those who do not realize that those straight irrigation rows and neat white houses starkly demonstrate the impulse to harness nature. Moreover, to the classic tension between the natural and the artificial, a third element is added here: the introduced. Despite increased urbanization, most of the Valley is covered not by plastic or concrete but by vegetation imported from elsewhere. Native grasslands are gone from this great, enclosed prairie, and so are most of the riverine forests and the wetlands, as well as many of the animals that lived in those habitats. Gone too are most of the Yokuts, the Miwok, the Wintun, and the Maidu. But the soil remains—the soil, the water, the sunlight, those and the people who still migrate here searching for the cusp of the future.

That future may be urban now that the Valley is the fastest growing section of the state. Sacramento, Stockton, Redding, Modesto, Fresno, Chico, and Bakersfield, once considered sleepy Valley towns, are cities surrounded by suburbs that are in turn swallowing farmland. "William Saroyan's quiet hometown will exceed the size of San Francisco by the century's end," Frank Viviano points out. To accomplish such dynamic and rapid growth, rich agricultural acreage is being covered with stucco houses and shopping malls, which in turn leads to marginal land being irrigated and plied with chemicals. But the amount of even marginal land available is finite, and K. Patrick Conner is correct when he writes:

Urbanization—or, more properly, suburbanization—now constitutes the single greatest threat to the Central Valley. For example, between 1976 and 1981, more than fifty thousand acres of prime agricultural land was lost forever to urban development. Each day, new fields are being paved over.

Increasing urbanization is not necessarily the principal force for change in the Valley, let alone the region's major dilemma—not with salinization, toxicity, soil erosion, land subsidence, racism, economic inequity, farm foreclosures, these and a host of other issues also pressing—but it is visible and undeniable and in many places illustrates the lack of substantive, long-range planning that has caused most of this vulnerable region's other problems. For instance, still another difficulty is looming because there will be fewer agricultural jobs for future migrants if the development of more and more automated technology in farming continues.

Nonetheless, migrants continue to stream in, and onetime migrant, the poet Wilma Elizabeth McDaniel, reflects that social reality in "Old Neighbor Reports on a Trip to Merced":

Everything has changed
he lamented
nothing like the old Merced

drive out any direction
all the new houses
big air base at Winton
strange faces

Oh, now and then you will see
an old Portugee ranch
with a tankhouse
and pomegranate bushes
in the yard
but don't expect it to be the
same
and all them little kids playin'
in the dust
ain't Okies now
they call 'em boat people

Forty years ago, Floyd Renfrow was an Okie child playing in the dust, and he understands well what it means to have remained in the Valley and made both a living and a way of life in that dust. "You know," he says in the parking lot of one of the grocery stores he now owns in Bakersfield, "my folks didn't have much whenever they came out here, but they worked real hard and saw us kids through school. It's been a real good place to live and raise my own family, a real neighborly place. I like this old Valley."

For well over a century, this old Valley has been plowed and irrigated and chemically infused to produce crop yields unimagined by the most optimistic of the region's early settlers. It has developed communities with opportunities and problems beyond the ken of the most prescient of its original boosters. Fields that once grew native bunchgrass now sprout mylar ribbons waving from short wooden stakes, those and the remains of trees strewn over what was once an orchard like bodies across a cratered battlefield—casualties in the intensifying combat between a growing population and a finite expanse of land.

This is not a static place. As new folks move in and as old folks recognize new realities, there is growth in awareness and in action. The recognition that flood irrigation may no longer be best, that chemical farming may do more harm than good, that other forms of agriculture may in fact offer viable alternatives to industrial farming, all these illustrate hopeful developments, as does activism of all sorts; not long ago, for instance, local growers sent twenty-five hundred fruit trees to farmers in drought-ravaged Ethiopia. The development of coalitions such as the Central Valley Safe Environment Network is especially hopeful, for it reveals an expanded awareness of regional issues. As John Latta, a Merced County rancher, suggests, "I think all farmers have to be environmentalists if they're going to survive on the land. You have to know what makes it viable. When the wildlife goes away, you're going to be gone pretty soon too." According to recent estimates, only 4 percent of the Valley's original wildlife habitat remains, and groups like the Nature Conservancy, Ducks Unlimited, California Trout, and the Sierra Club are trying to save it.

Based on his observations in the 1860s, William Henry Brewer was dubious about the Valley's cultural future, but it has—in spite of the continued enormous economic gap between haves and have-nots—allowed generations of poor migrants to achieve economic stability and to open up a world of wider horizons for their children. Kids of various colors wander barefooted over this rich soil and these paved streets, frequently together, with an easy multiethnicity uncomfortable to their elders; they still wing clods at one another, still gaze silently at dust devils dancing across the horizon, still plunge naked into irrigation ditches.

Many will indeed pursue possibilities unimagined by their parents—many will dream new dreams. And those dreams, with their power to expand not only the region's but the world's artistic or scientific or moral boundaries, those dreams, not three hundred varieties of produce or ubiquitous shopping malls, are the Great Central Valley's most vital crop.

Is California Part of the West?

with Janice Haslam

IS CALIFORNIA REALLY PART OF THE WEST? This is an academic version of "Who's on first?" Definitions of what's West—and, indeed, of what's California—are endlessly flexible, thus largely self-serving. Many folks are afraid of the Golden State's image, but most—Californians included—simply don't know enough about the state to answer the question one way or another.

At a meeting of the California Studies Association in Sacramento a few years ago, one scholar from Los Angeles complained, "I don't see why this meeting has to be held clear up here in northern California every year. It's a real hardship."

From the back of the room a voice responded, "This ain't northern California, it's central California. Try Yreka." He was right. That exchange among supposed experts illustrates what has become increasingly clear: our supposedly best-known and certainly most-publicized state is really not well understood.

California is the third-largest, most geographically varied, and most heterogeneously populated state, so large and so complicated that no one can understand all of it without considerable study. If someone says, "I've lived in California all my life, so I can tell you about it," keep your malarkey-meter running. In fact, growing up in one section of the state offers virtually no clue about another: Dunsmuir in the great northern forest is so distinct from Mexicali in the Colorado Desert as to suggest different continents. Bishop on the edge of the

Great Basin shares little weather or scenery or attitude with
Carmel on the cusp of the Pacific. The vast cattle ranches of
Modoc Plateau of the northeast are little connected to swishy
coffee bars of Walnut Creek in mid-state. In the nineteenth
century, Eureka and its damp environs were part of the north-
west, while San Bernardino's parched environs were part of
the southwest…and on and on.

Then there's the rebuttal: California? Hey, it's a matter of
attitude; Californians are laid-back, sybaritic, soft…except that
California requires enormous numbers of manual laborers…
all softies, maybe; it also produces far more college and professional athletes than any state, and far more Olympic athletes…softies too, perhaps. As Lee "Brownie" Brown, a
migrant from Texas, once said, "Yeah, it's an easy deal out
here, 'specially pickin' that cotton in 120 degrees or buckin'
that pig iron at 10 degrees. We sure got it made." There are
vast stretches of this state where life is hard indeed, just ask
John Steinbeck's Joads…and not only in the hinterland; try
Watts or West Fresno.

Theodore Roosevelt's hoary aphorism, "When I am in
California, I am not in the West, I am west of the West,"
proved that like many politicians he didn't know what he was
talking about, but he said it well. The terms of his confusion
remain rooted in an inability to recognize that there were—
and are—many Californias. At the very time he spoke, vaqueros and cowboys herded cattle over much of the state's open
territory; America's last "wild Indian," Ishi, struggled to survive in foothills east of the Sacramento Valley, which itself
burgeoned with yeomen farmers; miners still haunted this
state's deserts and foothills; and loggers were stripping the vast
forest of the north. Those sections were the West, period—as
the writing of Jack London, Arnold R. Rojas, Sally Carrighar,
Frank Norris, Theodora Kroeber, Frederick Faust, and many
others illustrates.

Then there are those who claim that California is "West
Coast, not West"; they are responding to illusion, not reality.
California is the western edge of the West, coastal only on its
far side. Geographically and culturally, the coast extends no

deeper inland than the edge of the Coast Range—still largely unsettled and dotted with range cattle. North of LA isn't northern California, and south of San Francisco isn't southern California; there is a (large) center, there are (large) sides, a (large) top and a (large) bottom. There is a real and varied California where real and varied people live without much fanfare.

As for that varied terrain, if folks don't think the northern forest, the Great Basin, the Mojave Desert, the Sierra Nevada, the Colorado Desert, the Central Valley, the Coast Range, the Great Basin, and much of the rest of the many components of the state are Western, then they'll have to come up with an odd definition of West. If Jedediah Smith or Francisco Garcés or Ina Coolbrith, Snowshoe Thompson or Grizzly Adams or Tamsen Donner, Joaquin Murieta or Ishi or the Dalton Gang—among many thousands of others—aren't Western, then who is?

One problem in understanding California is that, despite being only small parts of the actual province, Los Angeles/Hollywood and San Francisco/Berkeley dominate the state's image. Once perhaps the apotheotic southwestern city, desert Los Angeles now hosts more Hispanics than Costa Rica or Puerto Rico or Nicaragua, more Mexicans than any municipality other than Mexico City. San Francisco, meanwhile, seems daily to become more a Pacific Rim metropolis, with its distinctly Asian flavor. If we accept cities at all, no slam dunk given the Western bent toward rural romanticism, then those two are the West intensified, the West expanded, but
perhaps the West ruined as well.

Maybe it's the kind of literature produced in California that makes it appear non-Western. The final four books examined in Lawrence Clark Powell's *California Classics* may symbolize what other Westerners—and many rural Californians—fear or dislike about southern California: *Merton of the Movies* by Harry Leon Wilson, *The Day of the Locust* by Nathanael West, *After Many a Summer Dies the Swan* by Aldous Huxley, and *Farewell, My Lovely* by Raymond Chandler. LA? Faugh! Movies? Faugh! Detectives? Faugh! Where are the noble pioneers? As a matter of fact, they're here too, in books like William Manly's *Death Valley in '49* or William Heath Davis's *Sixty Years in California.*

In fact, before kicking southern California out of the West, remember it also gave western letters the first great surge of desert writing with books by John C. Van Dyke, George Wharton James, J. Smeaton Chase, A. J. Burdick, and the wonderful Mary Hunter Austin. And it was the source of much of the finest work on the Hispanic past, everything from Horace Bell's *Reminiscences of a Ranger* to Helen Hunt Jackson's *Ramona* to Gertrude Atherton's *The Splendid Idle Forties.* Nothing's quite as simple as it seems...or as we'd like.

Urbanization, not diverse population, seems to pose the greatest threat to older definitions of the West, but California's multiethnicity has long baffled whites harboring middle-American prejudices. Martha Jackson, who migrated to the Golden State in 1937, recalled:

> We thought we were just 100 percent American. I had never heard of an Armenian, I had never met an Italian, and I had never seen Chinese or Japanese or Mexican people.... We thought their grandparents didn't fight in the Civil War or Revolution.

She didn't understand that in California nonwhites—which in the 1930s often included Armenians and Italians—have been substantial and enduring pioneers, building much of this state. In coastal California, it has long been clear that the United States is a world country, not merely an extension of Europe. That may seem non-Western to someone from the homogeneous interior, but it is the logical result of a continental nation, of the West's western edge bordering an ocean.

Still, those of us from rural and small-town California understand why folks might have a negative image of the dominant LA–SF version of the state, since those two cities seem to be the most provincial sections hereabouts, concerned about little except themselves. In the late 1960s at an academic meeting in the Bay Area, the spheres of newspapers became a serious issue. One man asserted that since the *San Francisco Chronicle* was read more than the *Los Angeles Times* in Fresno, that town was clearly in the Bay Area's sphere of influence, but, he said, in Bakersfield the *Times* was more popular, so it was part of LA. The group hailed that insight.

The Central Valley's reality and importance were to them dependent upon its relationship to the two coastal metropolises, even though fewer than one subscriber in five hundred there read those out-of-the-area newspapers. Could it be that folks in the Central Valley were more interested in their own regions than they were in San Francisco or Los Angeles? A revolutionary notion!

Henry Nash Smith long ago pointed out "the covert distrust of the city and of everything connected with industry that is implicit in the myth of the garden," and of course images of California have epitomized that myth. As a result, a formula has arisen: California = phony urban; phony urban = non-Western. Even if that was true today, though, we'd have to acknowledge that places change. A pal said to me last summer, "Phoenix isn't even Arizona anymore, it's California"; heartfelt but dumb, since Arizona and everywhere else is what it is; it won't go back. I've also heard that the Sierra Nevada, the Great Basin, all the deserts of the state's southeast, the northern woodland, and so on, aren't really California, either—which means that some people aren't dealing with the real state but with a contrived version of it.

This state's fastest growing population is found in the long-ignored Great Central Valley—fifteen million acres, about the size of England—the world's leader in agriculture, a traditional hotbed of country music, and much closer to San Antonio than to San Francisco in the eyes of many locals, most of whom seem to prefer San Antonio anyway. Despite that population growth, valley farmers have added three hundred thousand acres to cultivation in the past decade. The region has transformed from the historic American Serengeti, roamed by vast herds of elk and pronghorns, penetrated by annual salmon runs, and scoured by grizzly bears, to the factories in the fields that Carey McWilliams exposed, roamed largely by nonwhite fieldworkers. It has epitomized Frederick Jackson Turner's conflict between the high social values of the primitive society of frontier farming and the importance of social stages as exemplified in urban industrial society. As Henry Nash Smith summarizes, "The capital difficulty of the American agrarian tradition is that it accepted the paired but contradictory ideas of nature and civilization as a general principle of historical and social interpretation." In the Great Valley that paradox seems to have been resolved, but not necessarily in a positive way, since social and economic conflict is endemic there.

Perhaps as a result of that churning, the Great Valley has been the source of the state's finest crew of native-born writers in this generation: Joan Didion, Victor Martinez, Maxine Hong Kingston, Luis Valdez, Gary Soto, Sherley Anne Williams, Frank Bidart, Joyce Carol Thomas, Richard Rodriguez, David Mas Masumoto, Leonard Gardner, among many others. Notice how many are women, are nonwhite, are from working-class families. That's evidence of the extraordinary enrichment of this state's letters since World War II.

The list of writers also demonstrates that not just regions are varied here. Westminster's Little Saigon and Latino towns such as Huron could also be across the world from one another; at any one time there are enclaves of this group or that all over this state—which is still America's favorite destination. Fortunately, second- and third-generations tend to move into the general populace, as the highest rate of ethnic and racial intermarriage proves. They move into the general literature too, as the list above well illustrates. In fact, the state's abundant literature—more publishing writers reside in California than in any other states—also reveals that maturing in one ethnic community offers few insights to maturing in another, just as coming of age in one social class exposes little about doing the same thing in another, and class is likely even more important than ethnicity in a state where the gap between haves and have-nots continues widening.

Our definitions of the West are as important as our understanding of California in deciding if this state is Western. If we root our definitions in the past, or in regional longing, how are we different from "code" Westerns, those stereotypical tales about cowboy life on the wild frontier? Los Angeles 1855 was certainly not Los Angeles 1999, and the same could be said of Fort Worth or Denver or Las Vegas or Santa Fe, and so on. Like it or not, those poor drunks cadging money on Gallup's streets are as Western as Buffalo Bill ever was, but not as mythic. Many of us don't like what Western cities have become, but we can't pretend that only mesas and saguaro count—an inherently romantic and dishonest vision—and still have any claim to the dynamic and viable region we call the West.

Texas and California in particular have been much shaded by stereotype and often by self-serving illusions too. Images of early California lean on romanticized versions of the mission past, or perhaps on the gold rush. The latter, in particular, contributed to the sense of California as a black hole where friends, relatives, and, most of all, values can be lost because so much is possible, even reinventing oneself. Leonard Slye comes west from Ohio and becomes Dick Weston, who becomes Roy Rogers, who becomes King of the Cowboys. In *Heretic's Heart,* Margo Adler writes about driving to the university at Berkeley, "saying various syllables over and over, like 'Oregon' and 'all.' I am trying to lose my New York accent; like so many migrants, I am trying to remake myself." Her parents weren't enchanted.

Because of the enormous power of twentieth-century, LA/Hollywood–San Francisco/Berkeley images, much of this state's actual history has been forgotten. Yet Lawrence Clark Powell says of LA in the 1850s, "It was the toughest town in the West, a cesspool of frontier scum." And the state's vast but often ignored interior, where virtually no Western movies have been set, featured covered wagons, outlaws, cattle drives, cowboys and Indians...the whole stereotyped Wild West scene, plus fewer stereotypical figures that are considered Western when they occur elsewhere: fur trappers, Spanish explorers, Basque shepherds, etc.

In the early 1850s, for instance, the famed bandit Joaquin Murieta rode into Stockton from the San Joaquin Plain and spied a poster offering a $5,000 reward for his capture, dead or alive. In full view of the populace, he crossed that figure off and wrote below it, "I will give you $10,000—Joaquin."

To the south, the Valley's only substantial community, Visalia, was an early cowtown. It was a rough-tough arena where notorious outlaws such as Chris Evans and John Sontag, as well as Bob, Grat, and Emmett Dalton, plied their trade. Then Eugene Kay took office as Tulare County's sheriff in 1890 and they met their match. Kay went after Sontag and Evans first, but before he could act, the notorious Daltons robbed a train nearby. The sheriff was up to the challenge, and although gunfights killed one of his deputies and wounded several others, he sent Daltons scurrying all the way back to the Indian territory, deposited Evans in Folsom Prison, and planted Sontag in a local cemetery.

Traditionally range-cattle territory, nearby Bakersfield by the turn of the century became the feeder-cattle capitol of the West. It teemed with vaqueros and cowboys from all over, as well as banditos such as the legendary Tiburcio Vasquez. It was also the scene of the final infamous Wild West shootout in the state. In 1903 at a Chinese temple— how Californian!—a fugitive highwayman named Jim McKinney got the jump on City Marshall Jeff Packard and his deputy, Will Tibbett, and gunned them down. McKinney himself was then leveled by a shotgun blast fired by Bert Tibbett, Will's brother and also a deputy.

What happened to the cattle industry in California? According to the Department of Agriculture, "non-Western" California produces more cattle and calves than all but four states—Texas, Nebraska, Kansas, Colorado—but cattle and calves rank only fourth among California's own agricultural products. In fact, the state retains more open territory than any other state besides Alaska and Texas, and more designated wilderness than any but Alaska.

Back in Bakersfield after the big shootout, the streets remained dusty and cattle the major industry, yet that bloody event served as a symbolic veering from frontier anarchy. The brave deputy, Will Tibbett, lay in his grave in Union Cemetery, but his son, Lawrence, matured in a rapidly changing state, became an urban man, and launched a career that would make him the principal baritone of New York's Metropolitan Opera Company.

There are books and books and books full of that stuff by everyone from historians such as Richard Dillon and Frank F. Latta to fictionalists like Larry Jay Martin and Robert Easton or poets like George Keithley and Edwin Markham.

But finally, this question isn't about facts, it's about illusion and perhaps fear. Those who don't know the state's vast stretches of open land, its abundance of rural towns, or its actual history seem to sense LA creeping toward them like the slimy critter in a Hollywood horror flick—which is exactly what folks in most of rural California also fear. As Pasadena's Richard Armour so well summarized,

So leap with joy, be blithe and gay,
Or weep my friends with sorrow.
What California is today,
The rest will be tomorrow.

Is California really part of the West? Is John Muir? Is Robinson Jeffers? Is John Steinbeck? And, yes, is Wallace Stegner, who lived in the Golden State for over fifty years and produced what most consider to be his finest novel, *Angle of Repose*, with California settings? Come on...

The dominance of urban, coastal California's image creates the illusion that the state is somehow not Western in a cultural sense. But among those who see past that deception, a more interesting question arises: What does this western edge of the West—with its churning combination of the staunchly traditional (a plethora of rodeos) and the decidedly nontradi-tional (great links to Asia) and everything in between—tell us about our dynamic, threatened region as we enter the third millennium?

Southwest:
Toward a Realistic Definition

TRADITIONALLY, THE AMERICAN SOUTHWEST extended from West Texas, where my father was born, through New Mexico and Arizona, and well into central California, where my mother was born: El Paso to Paso Robles. It also included southern Nevada, southern Utah, and southern Colorado: the entire diverse territory penetrated by Spain. The idea of the Southwest is most marked by arid geography, by significant and enduring Indian civilizations, and by mingled Hispanic and Anglo histories. In terms of geomorphology, settlement, even weather, it is of a piece.

There are subregional currents, of course—the importance in Texas of blacks in the cattle kingdom following the Civil War, for instance, or the centrality of Chinese to the development of rural California—and it can be argued that the region's most important determinant during the American period has not been landscape or weather but the discord caused when Anglos confront African, Asian, Hispanic, and Indian cultures.

For thousands of years before the first Europeans set foot here, Native Americans produced oral literatures and histories that were set in this place. The first significant European narrative set here was *La Relación* by Alvar Nuñez Cabeza de Vaca, which was published in Spain in 1542. In recounting his eight years of wandering lost through the wilderness and among the tribes of the region, this remarkable narrative sets a pattern for many books that would follow: year by year, Cabeza de Vaca came to understand, to respect, the native cultures he encountered. Lucy Hazard once suggested that American writers had to deal with three frontiers: land, industrialization, and the spiritual realm. The first and the last have dominated Southwestern books and, as would be true of so many writers of the Southwest who followed, Cabeza de Vaca traversed a wilderness of the spirit and grew as a result.

Even *La Relación* makes it clear that the Southwest should not be thought of as a single place but as a series of related places—Taos and Flagstaff, Moab and Mojave, Fort Worth and Sonoma. Some have suggested that it is where the mesquite or cactus grows, others have said it extends as far north as did Spanish or Mexican land grants. Some early purists restricted it to the range of adobe construction: California, Arizona, and New Mexico. One of New Mexico's most astute writers, Erna Fergusson, excluded California altogether, demanding, "Who would recognize its gargantuan congeries of Iowa villages as Southwest?"

What Fergusson actually did in her fine book *Our Southwest* (1940) was to confirm a new element—if a place didn't remain unspoiled, it was no longer Southwestern. In other words, she participated in a distancing from reality that has become increasingly a part of the accepted image of this region. If California in 1940 was no longer acceptable, the same place a century earlier was inarguably a Southwestern hub—a desert community founded by Hispanics. Of late, Texas has also been excluded from regional definitions: as water is imported and cities grow, as populations diversify and industry burgeons, we must pretend that San Bernardino and San Antonio have somehow moved to the Midwest or the East. That sort of thinking will soon relocate Albuquerque, Phoenix, and El Paso—all of them consigned to purgatory because they have the audacity to acknowledge and deal with contemporary urban problems. The physical setting of the Southwest is so overwhelming and its romanticized history so compelling that it constantly lures observers into soft-focused visions of itself: those enchanting mesas, those labyrinthian canyons.

Lawrence Clark Powell explains the accepted vision of this region when he writes in *Southwest Classics,* "Its heartland is Arizona and New Mexico, an area distinguished by a tri-cultural fusion of Indian, Hispano, Anglo, and by an unmistakable landscape, from dark-robed northern mountains and incarnadined mesas to the dove-colored desert which merges with Mexico."

"Merges" is a key word, for here the border is not a barrier but an intermingling, and the two nations have by no means settled the business of 1848. That Hispanic link, along with Catholic-Protestant tension, with undeniable if varied racism and class tensions, with thoughtless destruction and determined defenses of the environment, and with unresolved issues of conquest and pride, must be embraced by any significant regional definition. It is not merely a matter of geography. History cannot be ignored.

My mother's family came north from Mexico in the 1850s and we remain Southwesterners—*bilingue, mixto, y católica.* One paradox of this section is that Mexicans are central to its oldest—both Indian and Spanish—and its most recent history, since some families can trace their Southwestern roots back four hundred years while others arrived this morning—a constantly renewed first generation. There are so many different kinds of Hispanics in this region, and some of Mexico's problems and prejudices are being played out here, such as the confusion of race and social class. For example, the young workers who cross the border now are from Mexico's least advantaged classes—they are Indians and Mestizos. With them come conflicts of allegiance and demands on other Hispanics—difficult political and emotional issues.

It is curious that the Southwest's heartland—New Mexico and Arizona—is an area in which much of the Latin population is conveniently not identified with Mexico at all—we call them "Spanish" or "Hispanic"—or with problems of the never-ending migration, and that, I believe, is one part of the comfortable regional myth. Let California and Texas struggle with the merged economies of the two nations and with the growing illusion that there was at some ideal time a barrier that precluded illegal immigration.

Prejudice against Latinos is not new here. Three years ago I interviewed a ninety-one-year-old vaquero named Arnold

Rojas and he had this to say: "When the Americans came, the people who owned land became 'old Spanish families,' while those who had none—even if they were cousins—became Mexicans, doomed to suffer discrimination."

It is clear that intercourse between Mexico and the United States continues unabated. In 1987, Richard Rodriguez offered a striking analysis:

I think that history will replay itself here. I think that something large is happening, as large as the Mexican-American War. Josiah Royce said that the great failure of 1848 was Europe's, the inability of the Protestant north to wed itself with the Catholic south, to the Mediterranean culture that created New Spain and the mestizo.

I think Mexico will determine the region. That's what it will become, a mestizo culture.... We don't celebrate the mixed marriage in America, that is Mexico's creation. Say what you will about the cruelty of Catholic conquest, nonetheless in the south the two continents were wedded and it became impossible to tell where the Spanish ritual left off and the Aztec ceremony began. There was nothing like that in North America; the Protestant dream never reconciled the Indian to the white settler.

Now we are in some sense once more faced with that same predicament. My own instinct is that we will not fail again...

"Mexico will determine," Rodriguez asserts. That reminds me of Ross Calvin's 1934 book, *Sky Determines*, which in turn reminds me of something I witnessed a while back. Two years ago, under a stunning sunset in El Paso, I saw a gang of Latin youths—their heads swathed in bandannas—suddenly attack a group of men huddled with bedrolls outside a rescue mission near the Amtrak depot. The assault was fast and brutal and apparently unprovoked. It ended suddenly, just before two police cruisers arrived, and the sky remained clear and beautiful behind the scene. Sky determines, but so do poverty and hopelessness and the mingled currents of two countries that frequently function as one.

If the sky over Phoenix and Albuquerque and Los Angeles is at times now like halitosis, that is reality too. Calvin, like other astute regional writers—Fergusson and her brother Harvey, J. Frank Dobie, Mary Austin, Paul Horgan, Joseph Wood Krutch, Powell—was not naïve about social issues, but he seemed to believe either that the grandeur of New Mexico could transcend contemporary issues or that it could somehow avoid them and remain a haven. During the Great Depression, he wrote: "In the world of roots and clouds and wings and leaves there exists no Depression." On one level this is escapism; on another it is an acknowledgment of humankind's insignificance, something that this area's scenery encourages.

The American Southwest until the recent past has suffered from too many fans who rhapsodized over its landscape and ignored the kinds of issues Rodriguez confronts, its human and historic dilemmas. Indians in this area have been among the poorest and least advantaged people in the United States: the unemployment rate among heads of households in the Navajo Nation is 58 percent. Facts like that don't fit the soft-focused vision of the area, but they are real.

Texas and California, not without scenic wonders, have actually produced wider-ranging literature than has the region Powell calls the heartland, possibly because human dramas are more visible in those two populous states with their freeways and smog and rising crime rates.

Speaking of the artistic challenge of such thinking, Wallace Stegner observed a generation ago: "In the old days in blizzardy weather, we used to tie a string of lariats from house to barn so as to make it from shelter to responsibility and back again. With personal, family, and cultural chores to do, I think we had better rig up such a line between past and present."

A kind of siege mentality is implicit in the desire to dump Texas and California—if a place reflects the twenty-first rather than the nineteenth century then it can no longer be the real Southwest, no matter where it's located or what its history. Homogeneity too—only deserts and mesas—is part of the myth.

But this is actually a diverse region. A 1983 conference at the University of Texas in Austin dealt with that state's literature. Three distinct sections of the state were acknowledged: East Texas, which is southern (from Dallas east—including the work of Katherine Anne Porter, William Owens, and William Humphrey), West Texas, which is southwestern (Fort Worth west—Elmer Kelton, Loula Grace Erdman, and Larry McMurtry), and Tex-Mex (principally the Rio Grande Valley—Rolando Hinojosa-Smith, Carmen Tafoya, and Tomás Rivera are among its best-known writers).

We must remember that *Southwestern*—despite its component words—is not customarily a combination of southern and western cultures but is a unique realm, so that the subregional division of Texas letters also suggested chronological realities: the southern tradition in Texas is the oldest but is not southwestern at all; the western, which features the cattle kingdom, is the most pervasive and enduring; and Texas-Mexican in English and Spanish is the most recent and most intriguing. The conference concluded by recognizing the power of another force, a fourth literary tradition, as it were: the state's Mystique—Texas as symbol and myth. The latter was perhaps epitomized in a cable sent by an editor in England to Alastair Cooke in 1968: WOULD APPRECIATE ARTICLE ON TEXAS AS BACKGROUNDER JOHNSON STOP COWBOYS COMMA OIL COMMA MILLIONAIRES COMMA HUGE RANCHES COMMA GENERAL CRASSNESS BAD MANNERS ETC.

The assumptions about Texas revealed in that telegram might come from a famous novel, *Giant* by Edna Ferber, and that fact suggests an important question: What is the relationship of history to novel, of nonfiction to fiction? At their best, both are about truth. History employs facts to understand what really happened while fiction does not allow facts to stand in the way of truth. All historical writing is, after all, interpretive—that's why we study historiography. It's not a matter of history being documentary and true while fiction is made up and false. In fact, great fiction explores deep chambers of reality that often cannot be discursively described.

In a sense, Southwestern writers have a unique challenge and opportunity, playing against expectation and stereotypes, and at least some Texans have availed themselves of it. Discussing our nation's letters, Stegner has asked, "Why, when so much of our literature (for example, Hemingway) strikes us as dealing with a present which has no past, should Western books so often strike us as dealing with a past which has no present?" If pressed to select a single Southwestern book that counters such assumptions, *Goodbye to a River* by John Graves would be my choice. Graves explains his book this way:

> Though this is not a book of fiction, it has some fiction-alizing in it. Its facts are factual and the things it says happened did happen. But I have not scrupled to dramatize historical matter and thereby to shape its emphases as I see them, or occasionally to change living names and transpose existing places and garble contemporary incidents.

The book is travel narrative, history, poetry, folklore, autobiography, eulogy, and fiction—unique and unusually effective. For example, near Turkey Creek the author encountered traces of some famous Texans:

> Not far above the bridge a dude ranch stood, tile-roofed and Spanish-stuccoed with dark oak trim, near where the Newberrys and some others fought half-white Quanah Parker's raiders, a long running horseback fight. The Comanches got Elbert Doss, characterized…as a "promising young man"…
>
> Among the pursuers was a type usually described as "Bose Ikard (colored)."…In Weatherford Cemetery, Bose's stone says:
>
> "Served with me four years on Goodnight-Loving Trail, never shirked a duty or disobeyed an order, rode with me in many stampedes, participated in three engagements with Comanches. Splendid behavior."
> —C. Goodnight
>
> It was an Old Testamental God for whose perusal that commendation was issued, the stern Monarch in whose campaigns the stern generals like Mr. Charlie galloped. It seems clear, too, that Mr. Charlie considered that his

opinion of Bose Ikard (colored) would carry weight with that Monarch.

Graves is by no means the only important writer Texas produced. In fact, Texas seems to be one of the nation's most exciting literary realms right now. Larry McMurtry thrust Southwestern writing into the present in 1961 with *Horseman Pass By,* forever breaking the stranglehold of the past. At his best, McMurtry is the writer who has demonstrated the deepest knowledge of Texas and the Southwest's central social trauma (and drama)—the imperfect transition from rural to urban society. Ironically, when *A Literary History of the American West* was planned a few years ago, some older scholars insisted that McMurtry not be included because of his subject matter and language. He represented changes that they did not favor—a new, less-romantic Southwest.

Arizona and New Mexico have, of course, also given us some high-quality literature of late. The work of John Nichols, N. Scott Momaday, Mario Mendez, Leslie Silko, Rudolfo Anaya, Ana Castillo, William Eastlake, Esther Portillo, Tony Hillerman, Edward Abbey and Simon Ortiz, among others, is unique and powerful. Nonetheless, it is ironic that only that other Southwestern outcast, California—actually southern California for, like Texas, the so-called Golden State consists of several distinct regions—bests the Lone Star State for symbolic power, for general misunderstanding, and for numbers of productive writers. There exists in the minds of outsiders a stereotype of California that might include tanned blonds roller-skating from their marijuana patches to their hot tubs, but not desperate people chopping cotton in order to survive or Mexican vaqueros pulling cattle from Kern River's sucking sands. For every coke-sniffer in Beverly Hills there are hundreds (perhaps thousands) of migrant farm laborers desperately seeking to escape the cycle of poverty. Reality can be startling in the nation's leading agricultural and most ethnically diverse mainland state.

Southern California is a desert-turned-city as a result of water piped from elsewhere. It was called the "the cow counties," an adobe pueblo patrolled by vaqueros, and it remained Spanish-speaking until the 1860s when it harbored a strong movement to split the state in order to avoid dominance by English-speaking San Francisco. Today, after considerable historical twists and turns, only Mexico City boasts more Mexicans than does LA. In any case, during the mid- to late nineteenth century when it was still a distinctly Southwestern locale, "Los Angeles was," according to Powell, "the toughest town in the West, a cesspool of frontier scum."

How does a region lose its Southwestern designation? The pivotal work in southern California's literary history is Helen Hunt Jackson's *Ramona* (1884). Intended to expose the desperate plight of Mission Indians, the novel ironically became the major factor in the creation of a romanticized mission past, which promoters and developers exploited. This remains, in another pattern common to this region, a place where a romantic frontier past was invented post hoc and is now exploited.

Ramona led to promotion of a fake, soft-focused version of the Spanish period by promoters and was followed by a rate war between the Santa Fe and Southern Pacific railroads, a war that culminated in fares from the Missouri Valley dropping, dropping, dropping until on March 6, 1887, they reached a low point, one dollar to cross the vast wasteland that had not long before cost so many migrants their lives. As a result, SP in 1887 transported 120,000 newcomers to the Los Angeles Basin, and Santa Fe moved slightly fewer; over 200,000 residents were added in one year. As John Gregory Dunne observes, "If New York was the melting pot of Europe, Los Angeles was the melting pot of America."

Erna Fergusson might summarize matters this way: Hello Midwest. Goodbye Southwest.

But southern California didn't immediately become what it is now, and it was the scene of one of the Southwest's most important artistic developments: the literary reclamation of the desert. Those barren lands had once been crossed by pioneers too intent on survival to notice the unique beauty surrounding them. By the turn of the century, however, the arid lands could be studied and sometimes romanticized. It

was one of those interesting cases where changing circum-
stances allowed people to rethink, *re-vision* an area.

John C. Van Dyke's *The Desert* (1901) was the first in a
series of books that changed the way those ostensible waste-
lands were viewed. An art professor, he saw the arid land as a
painter might: "Pure sunlight requires for existence pure air,
and the Old World has little of it left. The chief glory of the
desert is its broad blaze of omnipresent light." Other important works in the literary reclamation of the arid regions were
A. J. Burdick's *The Mystic Mid-Region* (1904), George Wharton
James's *The Wonders of the Colorado Desert* (1906), and J.
Smeaton Chase's *California Desert Trails* (1919). The finest of all
desert books, however, the most mystical and eloquent, is
Mary Hunter Austin's *The Land of Little Rain* (1903). Only
later would Arizona and New Mexico's deserts also be noted,
and Austin was a significant figure in that emergence too.

The Southwest's most unique response to urbanization was
the detective novel. James M. Cain (*Mildred Pierce, The Postman
Always Rings Twice,* etc.), Raymond Chandler (*The Lady in the
Lake; Farewell, My Lovely;* etc.), and Ross Macdonald (*The
Drowning Pool, Underground Man,* etc.) produced fiction significant enough to force serious critical attention as well as a
new sense of the price exacted by obdurate urban reality.
Today Albuquerque's Hillerman is among the finest detective
novelists, and he blends the wonderful setting and the desperate social realities of the Navajo nation as a major component
of his stories. There, too, a world seems to be going mad.

Like it or not, cities and their effects have become major
thematic elements in writing by Southwesterners. And they
had better have. If we don't recognize that Los Angeles has
been a prototype for Albuquerque, for Phoenix, for Fort
Worth and Las Vegas, then we've all been kidding ourselves.
Since there is no reversing that process, then we'd better
understand it in order to avoid its most heinous excesses.
What is special, of course, is that outside most of those
cities—Paso Robles as well as El Paso—exists the wondrous
nature that brought so many of us here in the first place. Part
of what makes many Southwestern writers unique is that

we continue to approach nature with a sacred attitude—the same one held by native peoples. Eastlake opens his novel *Go in Beauty* this way:

> Once upon a time there was time. The land here in the southwest had evolved slowly and there was time and there were great spaces. Now a man on horseback from atop a bold mesa looked out over the violent spectrum of the Indian Country—into gaudy infinity where all the colors of the world exploded, soundlessly.
> "There's not much time," he said.

In *The Names* N. Scott Momaday writes:

> Monument Valley red to blue; great violet shadows, planes and prism of light. Once, from a window in the wall of a canyon, I saw men on horseback far below, two of them, moving slowly into gloaming, and they were singing. They were so far away that I could only barely see them, and their small clear voices lay very lightly and for a long time on the distance between us.

These are examples of classic Southwestern writing: rhapsodic and true. In each, we humans are on the landscape but are dwarfed by it, our perspectives are seen as less than cosmic.

Unfortunately, it is true that while we never want to lose the magical relationship with nature that this region promotes, it would be naïve not to acknowledge that urban kids—and more than a few rural ones—in the Southwest might be more familiar with crack cocaine and AIDS and gang violence—harsh urban realities. Therein lies the paradox: while promoters and even some artists persist in behaving as though the Southwest is unchanged—as, God knows, many of us wish it were—we must prepare youngsters to enter a world full of genuine peril and promise, much of which simply cannot be avoided by the expedient of climbing onto a horse or into a four-wheel-drive vehicle. Pollution, greenhouse effects, misappropriated water, and grinding poverty will not veer away from this region no matter its beauty. And, indeed, this enchanting landscape itself is under constant siege by commercial interests. It may, as Edward Abbey and Eastlake have urged in novels, be necessary to mount a counteroffensive so that the environment itself can be saved.

Ross Calvin closed *Sky Determines* this way:

And when the last Americano in the fullness of time follows the last Spaniard and the last red man into the shadows, this will still be the same poignantly unforgettable land of beauty, its arid mesas, canyons, and deserts lying perpetually beneath an ocean of pure light, and its Sky Gods still pouring frugally from their *ollas*, the violet-soft rain.

One can only hope that Calvin is correct, that the land can endure strip-mined coal on the Navajo Nation, dammed and flooded canyons in Arizona, mountains of garbage filling arroyos around Albuquerque, the sprawl of people and houses that pollutes the Los Angeles Basin. To this reader, however, Calvin is far too sanguine, much too passive. Southwesterners, especially Southwestern writers, had best involve themselves in political and social and environmental issues. To wait for the Sky Gods to act is to fall for a reductive fallacy that will soon exclude more than El Paso and Paso Robles from definitions of the area, that will eventually shrink and shrink the honored region until only Taos or Acoma remain, lone points in an anachronistic definition clung to desperately by romantics.

What Horton Hatched

MY EARLIEST MEMORY is of sitting on my mother's lap listening to *Horton Hatches the Egg*:

> I meant what I said
> and I said what I meant,
> an elephant's faithful
> one hundred percent...

As the only child of a working-class family during the Great Depression, I was read to constantly, and sung to constantly, and talked to constantly. Language and imagination were my companions.

Books in particular came to be magical instruments to me. My folks didn't own many, but my mother visited the Oildale branch of the Kern County Library weekly, frequently taking me with her. There I gazed at illustrated editions while she made her choices—both children's and adults' books each visit. As nearly as I can recall, she always allowed me one choice of my own.

Those books were revered in our house, often read aloud, frequently discussed by the adults, and I was taught to read before beginning classes at Standard School. As soon as I acquired my own library card—a rite of passage in my family rivaled only when I received my driver's license ten years later—I became a regular at our neighborhood library.

There I, like my pals, was encouraged and directed by generous ladies who seemed to believe that all we barefooted, we burnished, we generally disheveled kids were worthy of hope. What we couldn't recognize (but those librarians certainly did), as we dug through dinosaur books and pirate yarns, was that we had begun the process of sharing the accumulated wisdom of our culture...indeed, of our species. That idea was far too remote and elevated to have crossed our minds at the time.

But that is exactly what we Okies, we Bloods, we Chokers—whatever we were called then—were doing: building the foundation that has allowed us to participate in our shared culture. And in doing so, we have changed and shaped it. In our cultural hearts, we are all part African, all part Asian, all part European, all part of everything that filled those books that stirred our minds.

For me it started with a faithful elephant sitting on a lazy bird's egg, and with my mother's voice. Sadly, Mom is no longer with us, but that egg continues hatching, a library's enduring legacy: mother to son, son to granddaughter, granddaughter to...the world, *faithful, one hundred percent.*

Horton hatched my life.

Growing Up at Babe's

OUR LAST MEETING seems, in retrospect, fated. I had not been home for a long while and had not visited the gym for a couple of years, yet that day I drove to Bakersfield determined to catch a workout and banter with one of my few real friends, Babe Cantieny. I had just completed my first year of college teaching and was writing my first book, so I was full of my career; ties to my hometown had not lately loomed large on my mind, but I was determined to correct that.

When I didn't find Babe in the gym, I wandered downtown window-shopping until, unexpectedly, I spied him near the California Theater, or him in miniature, for he had shrunken. He was still the well-proportioned, muscular man I had known, but he looked more like a finely conditioned lightweight boxer than a bodybuilder. When I commented on his altered physiognomy, he gave me a crooked smile and said he was dropping a little weight for definition, then we moved to other topics.

We spent most of that afternoon talking, and he uncharacteristically brought up a couple of old misunderstandings, a couple of rough edges in our relationship. Babe wanted, it was clear, to make certain that we had everything in order, but it didn't dawn on me that he might also be saying goodbye. Our conversation, while deep at times, was not morose; we found a good deal to laugh about: the time a greenhorn challenged Charlie Bear Ahrens to a strength contest; the shenanigans we'd observed in the decrepit hotel across the street; the traffic cop who'd finally figured out that I was recycling an old parking ticket on my windshield for nearly a month while I worked out upstairs unconcerned about feeding a meter. It was a good day, one of the best.

A few months later, my mother sent me the clipping from the *Bakersfield Californian* that told me Marion "Babe" Cantieny, local businessman, was dead at forty-one. Then I understood what had occurred on our last afternoon together. Then, too, I finally admitted how important that short, quiet man had been in my life. I sat for a long time alone on my sunporch, too old to weep, reading and rereading the clipping: remembering, remembering...

I had begun lifting weights at Babe's Gym in June of 1954, seven years after Cantieny had opened it near the corner of 20th and Eye Streets. I was a 140-pound weakling who had not made the football team at Garces High School the previous season. A chum named Charles Tripp convinced me to train there, even though in those days weightlifting was considered hazardous; there were ominous rumors that a few workouts might leave you "muscle-bound," unable to tie your own shoes. Still, a friend at Garces, John Renfree, had used weights to go from a pudgy sub to an all-league tackle, and he seemed to tie his shoes with ease.

This was the dawn of the weight-training revolution that has so altered competitive sports. In fact, every athlete I knew in Bakersfield who lifted weights during that period did so at Babe's; he was without question a pioneer in introducing the technique to the area's athletes, especially football players.

Babe, himself, seemed quietly intimidating that first day when Tripp introduced us. All I could see were his bulging biceps as he sat behind his small desk in the cubbyhole he then employed as an office. He was all business as he made out a routine for me and walked me through it. Over that summer he twice altered my schedule of exercises to ensure full range of motion and development. I noticed that he was always watching to make certain that all of us did our exercises properly and that no one hurt himself. He was quick to correct flawed techniques, demonstrating them until you grasped the proper method.

Babe had a few close friends among his clientele, chums with whom I'd hear him open up, laugh, and romp a bit, but

basically he was private without being cold. I realized then
that he was far different, far deeper than the brooding adoles-
cents with whom inexperience had at first led me to identify
him. His silence was not a threat because he did not need to
threaten.

There were rules of conduct at Babe's Gym and they were
not breached, not twice anyway. Even in those days when
young bucks all thought they had to be fighters, I never saw
an argument get out of hand among the youthful studs
pumping themselves up. It was clear that nonsense wouldn't
be tolerated. Once—this would be in 1957—two large
Bakersfield College football players began wrestling among
the weights. Babe said only, "Hey!" and they froze. Later, I
walked into the dressing room while the two, each appearing
twice Babe's size, were gazing at the floor and the proprietor
was softly saying something like, "If you can't respect other
people's rights, don't come back." They came back but never
disrupted workouts again.

The atmosphere at the gym was convivial; as Mike Janzen
recently observed, it was like one big family. Babe's Gym
remains for me, over thirty years after I first entered it and
nearly twenty-five since I've been an active member, my club,
the only one I ever belonged to in my hometown, the only
one I ever needed. It featured a rugged but not raw male
camaraderie, with joshing and kidding the principal forms of
communication. Taking yourself too seriously was not tolerated,
although genuine problems were dealt with compassionately.

I especially recall how the older guys shaped up the
younger. Once, in my loudmouth youth, I referred to a
middle-aged musician's spouse as his "old lady," a cute term
that wowed my pals. He turned to me and asked, "Do you
mean my wife?" I was thirty years younger and twenty
pounds heavier than him, but I got the message. "Yes sir," I
replied; "Sorry." Doing the correct thing, I learned, was not
the same as backing down, and I don't think I've called any
woman that again. Mutual respect required, most of all, that it
be mutual. From such lessons is maturity built. They were
taught that way because mutual respect and acceptance were
the rule, not the exception—you had to *prove* yourself a jerk

in order to be rejected, possibly ejected—which was a reflection of Babe's own personality. If a guy couldn't be comfortable at the gym, he probably couldn't be comfortable.

About 1958, Babe fell on hard times. Big chains of workout salons (we called them "saloons") were opening in town, with high-pressure salesmen pushing "life memberships," which promised profit for the gyms in the guise of bargains for prospective members. The salons featured steam baths and plush carpets and newfangled exercise machines. Babe's customers were dazzled by the dramatically lower rates such joints advertised, and some began drifting away. Moreover, new customers became as rare as saints. Not knowing what else to do, Babe opened a second gym on Baker Street and tried to compete with the chains, even selling life memberships, something that would haunt him for the remainder of his days.

I was inducted into the army that year. When I returned home on leave, Babe had lost his gyms and, to a degree, his self-respect. It was a painful time because his family life had fallen apart too. But he didn't leave town or hide; he was in fact fighting back, determined to reopen the gym and to try to make good on the memberships that had been forfeited when his business had gone belly-up. "Your reputation is really all you've got," he told me, "and when something like this happens, it seems like everything turns bad, but you can't give up, you've got to work your way back." He did.

I had listened then as later because, without being heavy-handed, Babe had become an advisor to me, and his willingness to acknowledge his own frailties and problems made his counsel all the more valuable. He was the first adult who had ever really confided in me. When I was considering marrying a girl my friends advised against—"It'll never last..."—I talked to Babe, who also knew her. He told me about his own failed marriage and suggested that many of the conventional, romanticized generalizations about marriage were bunk. "Marry someone you can get along with, that's what's most important. You can have the hots for anyone, but be sure you get along. Then put away the past—everyone's got one—and start from scratch. You two will be okay. I think it will work."

I married her and, nearly twenty-five years later, remain grateful that I did.

In one limited area, the student became teacher. Babe, like most white men of his generation, harbored misgivings about nonwhites. This is not to say that he was a racist—he certainly was not—but he had little experience with nonwhites and, like many in those unenlightened times, accepted certain stereotypes. In any case, I was, as he once called me, "the resident liberal." We talked often and not very expertly, I'm afraid, about race and ethnicity. Some others in the gym hinted that they'd resent having to work out with nonwhites. When push came to shove and a black East High football player climbed the twenty-eight steps to the gym, Babe signed him up, gave him his routine and, without saying a word, let it be known that he would, like the rest of us, be given the benefit of the doubt.

That occurred, of course, well before the civil rights movement grasped the nation and rattled Kern County, so Babe's act, however insignificant it may seem today, was a long way from business-as-usual then. We talked about that, Babe and I, during our final afternoon together and, while he had by no means joined the NAACP, he acknowledged that I had been correct when I'd urged him to judge each nonwhite as he would each white, individually. I'm glad that I was able to return some small slip of wisdom.

During my initial summer of training at Babe's Gym, once I had realized that Babe was friendly in his quiet way, I'd begun working out during off-hours when there were few others present, and that had led to conversations with him, perfunctory and superficial at first, then deeper and more candid. Eventually I admitted feeling that I had let my father down by not sticking with football the previous year, and he sensed correctly that my too-frequent bravado hid an aching insecurity. He advised me gently and earnestly, then one day asked if I wanted to play baseball. With special friends, when the gym was otherwise empty, he'd pitch a cork—the missile spinning in odd and unpredictable directions—while a batter flailed futilely with a narrow stick. It was a laughing time but, more than that, it was a symbol of acceptance. And if Babe could accept me, I could accept myself.

I played football for Garces the following season, even made a contribution; I went on to play a bit in college and in the service, my lean frame bulked up to a massive 165 pounds. I continued lifting at Babe's—except for those years away in the army—until I departed for good in 1961. I still lift three days a week using the routines Babe taught me, at home now with my own kids, none of whom, alas, ever was lucky enough to know Babe. And I still weigh 165; while I'm wearing my hair thinner and my wrinkles deeper, I continue to wear the same size clothing. Best of all, I can still tie my shoes. The habit of fitness came early, and it came from Babe's Gym.

I write this remembrance on Babe's old wall desk, the very one at which he noted in his precise hand my routine that summer afternoon in 1954. He gave me the desk when I went away to college and it has seen me through three degrees. Moreover, all of my books, all of my stories, all of my articles—my entire career, really—have been written on it. Like my past and my town and my friends, with all their imperfections, it will do. I don't expect ever to replace it.

Reflections from an Irrigation Ditch

THAT DAY THE WATER RAN crystalline between the rows of potatoes. My bare feet were sunken in one channel's soft bottom between furrows while that cool, clear current pulled brown smoke from them, flowing parallel to other ministreams toward a far, perpendicular ditch that would catch the runoff we called "tailwater" and channel it along the country road toward a reservoir at the property's corner. I was eight years old then, and I pretended those artificial currents were racing, choosing a favorite—the one already ahead—and urging it toward distant victory, then exulting.

My Uncle Pete straddled a row next to me, a shovel leaning against one shoulder, his feet planted in two streams. He reached down and pulled a young potato from the earth, washed it in the clear flow, then opened his pocketknife and sliced me a sample. "Try it, Gerry," he urged. "It's sweet as all get-out."

We were standing only a short mile from where the foothills of the Tehachapi Mountains began sealing the southern end of California's Great Central Valley, near the point where desiccated Caliente Creek slipped from the high country to curl around those same foothills and to fade almost unnoticed onto cultivated land, and where it still occasionally and unpredictably reminded farmers of its existence with a stunning winter flood. West of us, the apparently flat terrain gradually, ever so gradually, sloped—agricultural patch after agricultural patch—until it was lost in shimmering heat waves that hid distant Bakersfield.

I accepted the proffered piece a little reluctantly—it might be a trick, since my uncle had already begun initiating me into the rough world of masculine joshing. Finally, I bit into it and immediately made a face. To my palate, spoiled by Saturday matinee candy, the potato sliver tasted starchy and bland.

"What's wrong?" he asked.

"It tastes crappy." Toleration of such mild profanity was another aspect of our growing male camaraderie.

My uncle's lined, leathery face smiled then, and he popped a thick slice into his own mouth and crunched it. "You'll learn," he said. "There's nothing better than something fresh out of the ground. Nothing better." He was not an especially articulate man, but on this subject his words were unambiguous and as clear as the water in which we stood.

He knew the soil, Uncle Pete did, its tastes and its smells, for he had been raised on a farm near Shafter and had earned his living as a field foreman for various spreads in Kern County. The land here was too expensive to ever allow him to acquire a place of his own, a frustration that led him to try other work but to always return to farming, to always remain close to the earth even if it belonged to someone else.

When, many years later, a severe stroke felled him and my uncle was consigned to a chair in a room in a house in a city, yearning, ever yearning, for the open country and open life he so loved, I came to understand how sweet that potato had tasted. The final time I saw him, after another devastating stroke left him connected to tubes and machines in the intensive-care unit at Memorial Hospital in Bakersfield, his consciousness supposedly blasted, his eyes nonetheless followed me with torturous certainty—my uncle was in there, lurking. By then I had grown, and that long-ago slice, that crystal water, and that rugged and imperfect man had become as precious as breath itself. Too late. Too late.

A couple of years after sampling potato from my uncle's knife blade, I wore something irreplaceable into an irrigation ditch just across that same field. My mother treasured her high school class ring more than I could imagine. Many years later in a repeated, sadly revealing series of episodes, she would tell each of my children to enjoy high school because those would be the best years of their lives.

But I knew nothing of that when I begged, cajoled, whined, pleaded—used every persuasive trick in my only-child's repertoire—until she reluctantly agreed to allow me to don her ring, a twist of tape at the back of my finger to secure it, an admonition twisted into the back of my mind, *"Don't you lose it!"*

For a while—a day or two, maybe a week—I treated that ring, that finger, that hand, like the Gifts of the Magi, protecting them in a pocket when I walked, removing them only to thrust into the faces of startled acquaintances—"It's *real* gold!"

That following weekend, however, back out at the ranch, I was romping with my cousin in an irrigation ditch, pretending we were professional wrestlers—a new fascination—bouncing, battering, splashing, and wallowing, a good old-fashioned romp. Eventually, we were called in for lunch, so after hosing mud from ourselves we walked to the yard where sandwiches and lemonade awaited us in comforting shade.

I had just seated myself at the picnic table when I heard those words: "I hope you didn't lose my ring with all that roughhousing." In a moment that remains slow-motion and precise now, over forty years later, I glanced down at my bare finger, then came as close to swooning as I ever would.

I don't recall exactly what happened to the sandwich or the lemonade, but we—my mother, my cousin, my aunt, and me—spent most of the afternoon in that well-churned ditch. Later my uncle and a couple of the fieldworkers joined us, but we found nothing. The ring was gone.

I was not punished, not physically anyway. My mother was too devastated to do more than gaze at me and moan, "I *begged* you not to wear my ring." She remained strong enough to physically restrain my father, but considerable time was to pass before I felt the shadow of that lost keepsake fade from our immediate relationship. On a deeper level, it never has, for at certain sad times even today she reminds me of it.

But I managed to put things into perspective when I was seventeen because of two events. The first was an occurrence worthy of *Ripley's Believe It or Not:* I came in from a day of maneuvering a tractor over a distant field and found Aunt Marje and Uncle Pete examining something at the kitchen table. My uncle had been plowing the field just behind the barn and had hit an old irrigation casing. When he'd climbed from his big yellow Caterpillar to pull cement shards from the earth, he had noticed a small, black lump: Mom's ring. Unfortunately, even after being cleaned up, it bore only faint resemblance to her golden memory, but at least it had reappeared—the consequence of hundreds of candles lit for St. Anthony, Mom later claimed.

That same summer, a girlfriend lost my high school class ring while waterskiing. She climbed into the boat after a spill, realized it was gone, then began weeping softly. I was afraid she had been hurt and was relieved to learn she was okay; the ring's loss troubled me but not deeply. I certainly didn't want it lost, but there was nothing I could do about that. I did, however, worry about telling my mother. Eventually I was deprived of that girlfriend too, by the way—a far more painful and consequential experience.

Mom was predictably upset about the loss of my ring and she built pagodas of melted wax, but this time St. Anthony was otherwise occupied. For myself, I had already determined that high school was no more than an early station on a much deeper journey. Mom, who had matured during the Great Depression, had enjoyed few of the abundant opportunities my generation took for granted, so when I'd lost her ring in that ditch, I'd also displaced her dreams and a small token of her worth. My own ring was no such talisman for me.

There was a time, however, when I certainly could have used a charm. At twenty-one, I was floundering, having lost the aforementioned girlfriend and having flunked out of college, both by dint of profound immaturity. There had been other girls then, too many of them really, and I had met but did not then date the one who would eventually be my wife. Just as well that she and I didn't grow close during that pained period, for my life was swerving without focus. Childish illusions that had previously sustained me had blown away like Valley fog, and I found myself back at an irrigation ditch with Uncle Pete.

He employed me to dip, slice, and plant seed potatoes. I also watered twenty-five acres of sugar beets and eighty more of barley, did some discing, some plowing. I planted many personal seeds too. One shirtless afternoon, for instance, straddling a vat of corrosive sublimate solution while pulling sacks of soaking seed potatoes from it, I slipped and was immersed. Fifteen years later, a surgeon would carve a black lesion from my chest, identify it as cancer, and tell me that I was lucky indeed that it had been removed so early. We talked about what might have caused it, and I remembered that sun, that vat, that youthful invincibility—all unarguably gone.

My habit of working shirtless indirectly led to an episode that Uncle Pete never forgot. We often rattled our pickup after work to a beer bar called the Buckhorn. One early summer evening, we were guzzling brew with other farmers when a woman who looked like she had gone two falls with the Masked Marvel slid into the group, slapping backs and laughing in a voice that could remove warts.

Uncle Pete was a good-looking man, and the formidable lady paid him increasingly serious attention. He did not act especially interested, but did seem to enjoy kidding her. Finally, she said that she'd like to take a ride with him to see the farm where he worked—this long after dark. He winked at me, then said, "If you do, you'll have to dress the way Gerry does—no shoes, no socks, and bare to the waist."

For a minute she posed expressionless, then smiled. "Well, I just *might*," she said, and she reached down and removed one large shoe.

"Time for us to hit the road," my uncle said, the hint of an edge in his voice.

I was halfway through a draft beer and feeling no pain, so I hesitated, but he wasn't kidding. I hurried after him, that woman's excoriating laughter in the background. Once in the truck, I asked why we'd left so suddenly.

He grinned. "Two more minutes and that honky-tonk heifer woulda been buck naked. No thanks." Time passed and the woman grew larger and homelier, her clothing scantier, and her ambitions ever more prurient as the anecdote was told and retold. At the time, it had seemed an event of small moment, but twenty years later it had been legendary.

In truth, there were few laughs during that stay on the farm, but those long days in the fields, those hours directing water, shoring up ditches, and those nights of exhausted, easy sleep were what I needed. Eventually, I decided to volunteer for the army, an experience that would abolish the final vestiges of my childish delusions and help me gain perspective. After a couple of years I returned home, discharge papers in my pocket, determined to complete college and to write.

Many years later, marriage and career in full flower, I drove my family by the ranch where my aunt and uncle had lived and worked in the open country near Arvin. It was a hot, late summer day with a mirage floating ahead on the blacktop, and I stopped our car on the county road marking the western boundary of the field where I had once yearned to be someone else somewhere else. Across the dusty green of unripe cotton, I saw the old house shimmering, the barns, the water tank, plus a scattering of dark trees and, well behind them, dehydrated hills where we had hunted. There was a man shimmering in heat waves far off across the tract, wraithlike. He was irrigating, most likely. He did not look familiar but his job did.

At twelve I had chopped cotton in this very field, my first grown-up job, and I wanted to tell my kids about it, to give them a potato slice, but this fevered view was all there was. I remained uncharacteristically mute.

"Let's go, Daddy," urged Alexandra. "It's hot."

"That's where I worked when I was little."

"It's hot, Dad," Fred said.

"Yeah," I agreed, "it is." They had never chopped cotton and never would if I could help it. But I had. I started the car and, after one more longing look, drove away.

Homage to Uncle Willie

Bend, Oregon, 1987

I HELPED MY UNCLE from bed into his wheelchair, then through the narrow bathroom door and onto the commode, leaving him there and wandering toward the kitchen for coffee while he did his business. I filled my coffee cup and walked into the dinette, where Jan smiled sadly up at me from the table. "How's Bill this morning?" she asked.

"The same." We touched hands, kissed, then I rubbed her back for a moment. He was my blood kin not hers, but there was a deeper link between them; they had over the past twenty-six years built a great and singular intimacy, he the father figure she had craved, she the daughter he needed. They were kindred souls. Now his life was drifting, drifting away...he knew it, we knew it...and there was nothing any of us could do except make the best of things there on the lip of the abyss.

"I'll go check Willie," I said—he had always been Willie to his brother and sisters and to me, Bill to everyone else. Although not only Jan but his dedicated step-granddaughter Debbie and a registered nurse named Karen were available, when I was present it became my role to attend to Uncle Willie's bathroom needs. This was unspoken, blood's responsibility to blood: if life itself could not be defended, at least dignity could.

In the bathroom, my uncle had managed to lift his butt slightly and was trying without success to wipe it. He looked up—his head appearing shrunken on the large rack of his shoulders—then reluctantly handed me the tissue. I completed the job, flushed the toilet, and muscled him back into his wheelchair.

He plopped there and puffed, half of his face blank and drooping like molten flesh, the other bright and angry enough to melt itself, and said with abject frankness, "I never thought I'd need someone to wipe my ass."

That afternoon, Jan and I bundled him up and the three of us repaired to a locally famous eatery for lunch: blackened catfish, red snapper Vera Cruz, sautéed prawns washed down with a good Sonoma chardonnay. My uncle was a gourmand who years before had taught us, two small-town kids, to love fine food and wine, so that meal was important, a ritual validating our enduring relationship.

With the grace that characterized him, Willie managed repartee with the waitress and something resembling his traditional conversational style: "Glorious salad, isn't it? Utterly glorious."

The following day, we bade him goodbye and returned to California. There were a couple of uncomfortable telephone conversations in the days that followed; then, about a month later, Debbie called and told us Willie had slipped into a coma. While Jan and I were packing to travel north, she called again.

My uncle was dead.

Oildale, California, 1941

I remember Pearl Harbor and Willie. He and his brother, my dad, were playing badminton that Sunday morning and I, four years old, was watching. When my mother called them, her voice was strange and she took the time to hurry out to the yard, scoop me up, and carry me into the small house on Arvin Street they then rented. Inside, we all sat around the radio.

I have no recollection of what was said that morning, although I do have a clear memory of tense, hushed tones that frightened me. Everyone in the room had wondered what would happen next: Would the Japanese invade California? Could America rebuild her navy? Would Willie and Pop survive the inevitable war?

As it turned out, my father was deferred—his job in the oil fields was considered vital. His younger brother was not so fortunate. A draftee the previous year, Willie had been out of the army for only six days on that December 7th and would be back in by the end of that month. "It was a short leave," he would say with a wink much later, "but a glorious one." The next four and a half years would take him to the Aleutians, Italy, France, and Germany. He would be wounded twice.

Oildale, California, 1945

In the midst of the welcome home celebration, Uncle Willie handed me three souvenirs: a Sauer 9mm pistol (sans firing pin), a German gas mask in its cylindrical metal container, and a German combat helmet; I have them today. He gave me no war stories, however, and never did in the forty-two years that followed.

If asked he would talk about his service, though not at length, and his tone was usually bemused when he did. The Aleutian service seemed most memorable to him—"Utterly horrible: wind blowing all the time and not a tree in sight"—although what was left of postwar Europe's cultural centers intrigued him too. Not surprising really, since in the manner of people who came to maturity during the Great Depression, Willie was inconsistently educated. He had finished high school and taken a few college courses while working, but had never embarked on a degree program.

He was, nonetheless, a serious reader, aware of and intrigued by Western civilization as well as current events and, even before entering the army, he had become an inveterate opera fan—a condition tolerated within our family as an eccentricity on the order of foot fetishism, embarrassing but not evil. It was also good for a few laughs since my uncle was tone-deaf. "He can't carry a tune in a bucket," observed my father, no Caruso himself, and it was true; Willie couldn't even hum along to recorded music. Nevertheless, he transferred his love of fine music to Jan and me, but that would happen many years later.

Santa Maria, California, 1951

At my maternal grandparents' house in my folks' hometown, Uncle Willie talked about his high school athletic career. "We both went out for track, Speck and me," he revealed, "and we both ran the quarter mile. We'd always sandwich the field: Speck first, me last."

Everyone laughed, then Mom explained, "Your father always looked like he was ready to kill someone when he ran. Bill used to kind of lope in last with a big grin on his face."

Willie nodded, then added, "Of course, Speck was one of the fastest there was in through there." He sounded genuinely proud of his older brother. "An utterly glorious runner. He made it to the state meet when he was only a freshman." I was considerably impressed.

Overshadowed and ignored in the conversation, however, was the fact that Speck's little brother, easygoing Willie, had himself become one of the nation's top swimmers during the early thirties, when he won the Far Western 100-meter breast stroke. My uncle's framed photo was for years the centerpiece in the local swim club's trophy case, but you'd never have learned that from him.

Earlier that very day he had been swimming with a humorous, rawboned woman named Ruby. She was one of a parade of girlfriends he had escorted since returning home from the army. His love life was the subject of seemingly endless family speculation; more than once I heard my mother and aunts discussing it in excited tones. "How was she dressed? No? *Really?* It's certainly time for Bill to settle down."

During that period I was urged to refer to any of Willie's girlfriends as "aunt." It was an ongoing joke that he treated with great good humor. I seldom saw him upset about anything, and me saying "Aunt Ruby" or "Aunt Geri" certainly didn't bother him, nor did my mother's persistent, "When are you going to set the date, Bill?" He'd just smile.

Sunburned and a little tipsy from the beer they'd consumed, Uncle Willie and Aunt Ruby were discussing their adventures at Buena Vista Lake, while my mother and Aunt Marje continued to make none-too-subtle references to matrimony: "Swimming together? That's pretty intimate stuff, Bill. Set the date yet?"

Just then Aunt Ruby, emboldened by the suds she had sipped, said, "Well, Bill rowed us way out to the middle of that darned lake. We were drinking beer and I had to go"—my mother's face suddenly tightened and she moved as if to cover my ears, but I grinned—"so I said, 'Bill, you've gotta get me back to shore right away.' That *character,* he just kept rowing and laughing, so I showed him."

"You go in the other room," my mother ordered, her voice unambiguous, so I reluctantly slunk toward the kitchen, calling over my shoulder, "What'd you do, Aunt Ruby?"

"I peed in the bailing bucket."

"That really *showed* him," laughed my dad.

"Oh, I didn't *show* him anything. I made him turn his back," grinned Aunt Ruby.

I was by then being thrust into the kitchen by my quivering mother, who hissed, "Don't call that woman 'aunt' anymore!"

Oildale, California, 1956

Christmas Eve and the Tom and Jerries were flowing. My father was always a menace when drinking and that night, true to form, he launched another diatribe against his stepmother and those he believed tolerated her. "I've got too damned much pride to kowtow to that bitch," he snarled, hinting that his good-natured brother had done just that. Pop never understood why Willie didn't seethe as he did.

"I've got better things to do than to think about her," my uncle explained. "That's all ancient history."

My father would have none of it. "Goddamnit, that woman *abused* us."

"Thirty years ago, my boy," Willie pointed out. "It's all over now."

"The hell it is."

"Well, Speck," commented Aunt Marje, my mother's sister and not one to back down, "no one ever gave your stepmother more trouble than Bill."

"Whadya mean?" Pop snorted.

"I mean the Waldorf!"

Everyone in the room burst into laughter and even my father, after a hesitation, had to smile. "Yeah, maybe," he admitted.

"What's that?" I asked.

"You tell him, Bill," urged Marje.

He grinned. "Well, along about the time dear Momma"—Uncle Willie often used the word "dear" with satirically devastating effect—"was pushing Pop around pretty good—when was it Speck, 1925, '26?—she decided that she'd just trump the Santa Maria Inn for some imagined slight and put up a fancy hotel of her own, run 'em out of business, so she had a big sign that said 'Future Home of the Santa Maria Waldorf—*Leone Haslam,* Proprietor' put up on one of the lots she owned. Well, a few days later was Halloween, so a couple of pals and I went out to old Dad Hailey's place and borrowed a broken-down outhouse he had in through there.

"We loaded it up on the wagon I used to make deliveries from the store and hauled it to dear Momma's lot, then took down her sign and put up a great big one of our own: 'Santa Maria Waldorf. *Leone Haslam,* Prop. No reservations needed. Quality corn cobs provided.'"

My mom's mother interrupted him, laughing so hard at the memory that tears were streaming from her eyes. "The one thing that woman couldn't stand was not being taken seriously. I'll tell you, she laid low for a while after that."

"Then what happened?" I asked my uncle.

"Oh, dear Momma figured out who had to have done it, so she gave Pop hell and he said I had to haul that privy away right now, so my pals and I loaded it up, that big crowd there to cheer for us, and we paraded through every street in town on our way back to Dad Hailey's. By the time we finished, we'd poked an utterly glorious hole in her balloon."

"You should've seen Bill," added my mother, "sitting there on that wagon with the old outhouse and the sign, grinning and waving to everyone." Her laughter was rich and deep.

"Yes, my boy," smiled Willie, "it was quite a parade."

South San Francisco, California, 1961

Newly married, Jan and I visited the Bay Area where I had to straighten out a problem with the admissions office at San Francisco State. We were staying with my uncle, by then a widower living alone in a comfortable two-bedroom home. Although I was in my mid-twenties, an army veteran embarking with my wife on a course of studies that would one day lead both of us to degrees, my parents insisted on looking askance at my marriage and on speaking of me as though I was still a foolish youngster: "He'll be sorry."

My uncle took us for lunch at Sabella's on the wharf and we delighted in pirate's salads—heaps of crab, of shrimp, of scallops on beds of fresh greens; neither of us had ever seen, let alone eaten, anything like them. He walked us through tourist attractions—Chinatown, the Academy of Sciences, Fisherman's Wharf, the DeYoung Museum, the Japanese Tea Garden—and seemed gratified doing so. As Jan would later observe, "Bill's greatest pleasure came from sharing his pleasures." We would continue the jaunts together until Willie moved to Oregon twenty-six years later. Today neither Jan nor I can visit those places without fondly remembering my uncle.

In 1961, however, we were less certain of ourselves, young adults who had chosen to forgo steady employment in the oil fields, the house and car that were sure to follow, and to gamble on the somewhat belated pursuit of education in a large, alien city. Uncle Willie provided our halfway house.

There was no condescension, there were no reservations in his acceptance of us. He allowed us to use his residence as a home base, to live with him until we found a place to rent, and he acted as our advisor when we sought advice; he was our friend, our mentor, our haven. It was clear that he trusted us and had confidence in our abilities to succeed. Although he surely noted unrealistic expectations and foolish performances, he did not admonish. He actually acted upon a belief that we were smart enough to learn from our errors.

Moreover, Willie immediately and without hesitation integrated us into his own jovial and profoundly multiethnic circle of friends, which included mixed couples, something we rarely if ever saw in our hometown. My uncle seemed color-blind to a degree unheard of in Oildale, although he and his friends were in the habit of identifying—often inaccurately—everyone ethnically: "When I was in the veterans' *house*pital"—a pronunciation unique to Willie—"there was an Italian boy on one side of me in the ward and a Greek boy on the other. Well, those two got to arguing over this beautiful little Spanish nurse we had in through there..." and so the stories went.

In any case, my uncle's gang congregated at his house most Sundays for lavish spreads of food and drink and conversation. Best of all during those years, he always insisted that Jan and I take all leftovers home, so despite our meager income, we ate well indeed. His friends, especially Ethel and Tom Martinez, also adopted us, giving us everything from slabs of meat to jugs of wine. Never had it been so comfortable to be young and poor and in love.

South San Francisco, California, 1963

We became parents sooner than we'd planned. As a result, I had to leave school, all but one night course anyway, and work full time while Jan cared for Frederick. There were rumblings in the family that it was time for Gerry to grow up and accept responsibility, time for him to come home, go to work in the oil fields and support his family properly instead of living hand-to-mouth in San Francisco. But my uncle did not agree: "Well, my boy, you two seem set on getting that educa-tion, so stay with it. We'll always be able to work something out if you go broke. I have a feeling you two will be good for it." As it turned out we did indeed go broke, he did indeed help us, and we were indeed good for it, all unbeknownst to the rest of the family. With Uncle Willie, our privacy remained private.

Many years later, PhD well in hand, I slipped and revealed to my father that Jan and I had once in an emergency borrowed money from his brother. Pop seemed both hurt and angry: "Why the hell didn't you ask me instead of Willie?" he demanded.

I mealymouthed an answer, not admitting that his money dangled strings thicker than octopus tentacles. Willie never imposed provisos.

Every Friday night during the period when I had returned to school to complete my BA, Uncle Willie had us over for dinner. Those evenings he occupied himself grilling steaks or chops, pouring wine and commiserating at length with my wife about what our golden egg had lately accomplished, about her work—she was then putting me through school—or with favorite topics such as gardening, cooking, and travel. He seemed to have driven every back road in California and to take special delight in discovering out-of-the-way places. Willie also refused to limit his interests to traditional masculine topics: while he was an inveterate sports fan, for instance, he dearly loved flowers and cooking and was gifted with both. I was less flexible, so while he and Jan talked, I'd usually raid his liquor locker, then plop with a beer in the living room to watch television—we had no set of our own, so it was a treat.

One Friday, brew in hand, I sat in front of the TV with Frederick playing in a cardboard box at my feet. He was a happy baby who rarely cried, and I glanced at him with a young father's continuing pride, then at the screen, then back at him. With an uncertain thrust our son suddenly stood in the box, holding onto its sides while his chubby, bowed legs wobbled. "Jan! Willie!" I called. "Come look at this."

Just as his mother and uncle emerged from the kitchen, Frederick let go and stood for the first time with perfect pink hands free at his sides, grinning.

A moment later, he plopped onto his bottom and Jan scooped him up and planted a wet kiss on his cheek, so I did the same to her and, for an instant, I felt my uncle watching us. Although he had two stepdaughters, he'd had no children of his own and his marriage had been sadly short; Eleanor, his wife, died only a couple of years after they were wed. There was gravity in his gaze, perhaps wonder, but he too was smiling. That look taught me a volume about what it meant to be family.

Petaluma, California, 1976

After attending a country parade in nearby Penngrove, we celebrated the bicentennial in Petaluma, the small town where Jan, our five kids, and I then lived—a traditional barbecue-watermelon-fireworks day. That bicentennial my wife and I had reason to celebrate the American Dream for we had lived a version of it. We were by then a long way from Kern County's oil fields and packing sheds; my career had blossomed and I was a professor of English at Sonoma State University as well as the author of a couple of successful books. My uncle took great pride in introducing me as "Professor Haslam," and I took even more pride in his obvious satisfaction.

He seemed to be almost the only member of his generation in the family not overly impressed and, consequently, overly resentful about my good fortune. From him I never heard that litany of frustration, "School doesn't teach you *everything*." In fact, our relationship had changed very little. I deferred to him in the many areas of his expertise and he did the same for me. In other realms, most notably politics, we agreed to disagree—Jan and I liberal, Willie conservative—although we often debated our disputed positions without rancor, an unheard of feat in our family. I referred to one of his favorites as Richard "Millstone" Nixon; he called one of mine "President Peanut."

Jan and I shared a passionate commitment to the civil rights movement and disillusionment with America's erstwhile war in Vietnam. We were members of the NAACP and, while Willie was particularly sympathetic with the demands of nonwhites, the specter of lawless demonstrations deeply disturbed him. It seemed to him, and to many good people of his generation, I suspect, that the national fabric was being rent. In his view, demonstrations invalidated even just movements. My wife and I disagreed, feeling that the national fabric was at last becoming a quilt of varied colors and that demonstrations were the only way the disenfranchised could penetrate the nation's consciousness.

Moreover, Jan and I were also Sierra Club members, dedicated, perhaps overly idealistic environmentalists. I was especially proud that Ansel Adams had personally sponsored our membership. We went 'round and 'round with Uncle Willie about various matters: "Those loggers have to work. You people've got no right to deny them a living," he'd say.

"They've got no right to destroy unrenewable resources like first-growth forests when there's technology available to harvest other trees."

"Those working people can't put that in their pots."

"But their bosses can. Those're the villains in this thing and they use the loggers as a screen so we can't see the corporate boardrooms and the fat profits."

"Gerald"—I knew matters were deepening when he called me that—"there are hundreds and hundreds of miles of utterly glorious forests in through there. No one wants to harvest all of them, but we can't suddenly change history and economics because your generation living in cities and going to colleges has decided trees shouldn't be logged. The whole economy up north is based on logging and those people have a right to a living. They're more important than trees."

"First-growth redwoods don't have to be logged anymore. There are second-growth forests and tree farms everywhere..." We never agreed on that issue, but when stakes with mylar strips appeared on Mount San Bruno just north of his house, Willie was outraged and we were in total accord.

"Goddamnit, they want to develop every square inch of land in through there. They don't give a damn about the quality of life. Those developers'll say anything to rationalize making more money, their only real goal." He supported the petition that placed development on the ballot, campaigned for the measure, and was delighted when it passed and development was halted.

South San Francisco, California, 1980

After dinner, the three of us sat around the table sipping the dregs of wine. I winked at Jan as I began to tell a joke. My goal was to prompt my uncle to reciprocate, because he always told dialect stories and all his dialects sounded the same—Other Lingo, I called it.

After I finished my yarn, he launched one: "There was a Jewish boy, a colored boy, and a Portugee boy who got killed and they all arrived at the pearly gates at the same time. St. Peter looked at his book and he said, 'I don't know about you boys. I'm going to have to think about whether you get in or not.'

"Well, that Jewish boy said, 'Leestena, eefa you leda me een, I geeva you a meelliona bucksa.'

"St. Peter said, 'Well, thata sounda hokay to me.'"

That triggered laughter, since even St. Pete was now speaking Other Lingo.

"That colored boy got in on the action too: 'I geeva you two meelliona eefa you leda me eena.'

"'Hokay, you geda eena,' St. Peter says. Then he thinks, 'Wella, I might asa wella leda thata Portugee boya eena too.'"

Now St. Peter was even *thinking* in Other Lingo and we were rocking with laughter.

"So Peter asks that colored boy, 'Where'sa thata othera boya?' The colored boy looks around and says, 'I theenka he looka for a co-signera.'"

By then all three of us were roaring. He could sure tell a joke.

Victoria, British Columbia, 1986

After another delightful day, I rued my complaint prior to this trip: "We won't have any vacation of our own," I had whined, genuinely aggrieved because our precious and scant private time seemed to be slipping away.

Homage to Uncle Willie

Jan had been adamant. "I told Bill after his stroke that we'd take him to Canada. He wants to go back to Vancouver Island and after all he's done for us, we're taking him." My wife was generally a pliant person, willing to compromise, but for Uncle Willie she was absolutely committed and inflexible.

Just as I was planning a subtle counterattack of spousal sulking, she employed her major weapon: "Remember our last trip to Canada?"

I remembered. In 1965 Jan and I were attending Washington State University and the four of us—two children by then—although much closer to the fulfillment of our dreams, were even more impoverished than before, surviving during the summer on county commodities and what I could earn doing library research for professors. Uncle Willie had driven north with a great CARE package of food, then taken us for a ten-day tour of western Canada at his expense.

My wife didn't tell me how self-indulgent my attitude toward the Canadian trip was; she didn't have to. I, of course, came to my senses. Not only had Jan been correct to make me aware of my selfishness, but she was also correct in her assumption that the journey with Willie itself would be pleasant. It was. He remained an excellent companion and guide, undemanding but willing to explain history and local color as we journeyed to the island's northern tip, seeing bald eagles and orcas, eating well, and generally relaxing. He told us stories in Other Lingo, placated the sullen teenage son who accompanied us, and made light of his own reliance on a wheelchair: "This damned device doesn't work any better than my lovely legs used to. Of course, it isn't pale, white, and skinny." More than anyone I've known, Willie had the capacity to laugh at himself. It was a lesson he taught us through example, and it took.

San Bruno, California, 1987

My uncle wanted no funeral, but friends and family nonetheless assembled at the veterans' cemetery where he would be interred. His stepdaughter, Sharon, asked me to say something, since I was the closest thing to a wordsmith our family had produced, and I immediately contemplated eloquent homilies. My wife and children were there, and so was my dad, along with various distant relatives and friends of Willie's, so I felt as though I had suddenly been put on the spot. Then I heard my uncle whispering through the chill Pacific wind that whipped us, "Keep it short, Gerald, my boy. Just keep it short."

After everyone gathered around the open grave, I cleared my throat and simply stated the truth:

"Willie didn't want a ceremony and I'll respect that, but I just want to say that it was my honor to be his nephew and his friend. I'll miss him, we'll all miss him. He was a damned good guy who didn't need fancy words from me. This world is certainly a lesser place for his passing but a better place for his having lived."

Only when I finished did I realize how near I was to breaking down.

Rogue River National Forest, Oregon, 1988

We are hiking through a cavern of illuminated dogwood and vine maple, sunlit leaves layered like memories as we troop a sandy trail. Occasionally, through clearings to our right, the upper Rogue River appears, slick then tumbling then slick once more. Jan spies two clusters of cadaverous plants beneath ferns on the forest's crowded floor: pale white Indian pipes that are beginning to blacken on their edges. The air is balmy but not hot.

It's a short hike—only a couple of miles—but it's so beautiful that we find ourselves constantly stopping, a little stunned at the lush forest through which we pass. Finally we sense a distant roar. Up a rise, around another bend, then up one more hill and the sound becomes deeper, an ominous shuddering. A few more steps to a rampart, and visual intensity at once surpasses sound: the river's course has dramatically deepened and narrowed—sheer lava walls thrusting far below into a river frenzied by that concentration. A cataract explodes where the canyon veers west, and huge, bleached logs are wedged at painful angles into the cratered walls far beneath us but above that cataclysmic current.

Mist rises from below and, across the cleft, the scarred volcanic surface is sheeted with the brilliant green of young conifers poised at disastrous angles, with patches of darker grass and flowers like vivid mistakes on a painter's palette, with kaleidoscopic slashes of lichen and moss. On a shelf just above the frothing water, a line of bright red roots dangles and sways like disembodied arteries.

This place, Takelema Gorge, is one of the most beautiful that a lifetime of hiking and backpacking has allowed me to see. As is often the case in the presence of such natural grandeur, I can find no words. Jan and I stand around the great lava slash, our arms around one another's waists. Finally I observe, "Willie would love this place."

After a moment she sighs, "Yes."

We are no longer young. We are no longer poor. But we are still in love. And Uncle Willie remains our point of reference.

Very Es-smart

JAN AND I WERE AMAZED at how our toddler grandson seemed able to pick youngsters out of a crowd of equal-sized people. Tara Schaumberg, for example, was about as large as her mother when Loki fixed on her and followed the girl all around our house, walking and even running in that neo-Frankenstein style employed by babies a month after their first steps.

My own mother once told me I'd done the same thing with her younger sister, Marje, who had been a teenager when I was born. "Oh, you were a pest," Mom smiled, clearly tickled at the recollection. "You called her *Narjie* and just wouldn't leave her alone. She always said, *'Aye qué peste,'* but she I think loved having a baby to play with."

I have no memory of that, but by the time I was old enough to hold playing cards, Aunt Marje was skinning me at Steal the Pile or Old Maid. She cheated at everything... visibly, histrionically, so that I wouldn't miss her actions.

When I was older, perhaps twelve, and helping her husband in the summer on the farm where he was foreman, he and I would shower and don clean jeans and fresh shirts every evening for dinner. Afterward, Marje might challenge Uncle Pete to a game of strip poker. He always accepted, so she'd disappear for few minutes, then reappear wearing four layers of clothing and multiple bracelets up her arms, plus a hat or two. For some reason, she always won, and when uncle Pete was down to jeans and undershorts—this was as fore-ordained as the rituals of a bullfight—they'd excuse themselves and turn in. Only years later did the romantic implications of those frolics dawn on me.

For thirteen years, I was the only grandchild in my mother's family, so lots of adults capered with me, but only Aunt Marje seemed then—and now, for that matter—to have been a play-mate as well as a surrogate mother. Perhaps that's because she was the family clown. Mom always laughed when she told a favorite story about how her little sister, not yet in high school, fancied herself a *femme fatale*. Her parents were trying to make a go of a small diner just outside Santa Maria, and all the kids worked with Grandma there, and so did Grandpa when he couldn't find a house-painting job. Occasionally, though, the parents would leave my mother, sixteen at the time, in charge, and immediately, or so she reports, Marje would smear her mouth with lipstick and try to flirt with customers.

"She had a face and a neck so filthy you could plant arti-chokes on it, and her fingernails! Like a mechanic's. But she'd bat her eyes at truck drivers and giggle at their dumb jokes. I'd tell Ton that when she got back, and she'd chase Marje with a dish towel."

"Ton" was my ninety-pound grandmother's nickname; she was the real boss in that family. "Marje was *muy floja*," Grandma would grin when she heard Mom tell that oft-repeated tale. In fact, her younger daughter's mischievousness mirrored her own.

Charlotte Marjorie Johnson was also her father's pet; "spoiled rotten," according to my mother. "She'd *Daddy* this and *Daddy* that, and he'd always give in. Not Ton, though. Marje walked on eggs around her." Mom couldn't help grin-ning then, and adding, "She was sure full of the dickens, pinching and tattling and even a little risqué."

By the time I came along, my young aunt, just out of high school, was working as a telephone operator in her home-town, and I recall being taken into the long room where she and other women plugged and unplugged lines into and out of a vast lighted console. It was a wondrous place to a child, so I still remember it vividly.

About then Marj', who had matured into a dark-haired, olive-skinned beauty with, as my mother said, "the *cutest* figure" (my dad, who often cut to the chase, said, "She was really stacked"), married a handsome young farmer, Peter Epp, Jr., from the German Mennonite community in Shafter. As it turned out, they were unable to have children, and didn't adopt my cousin Melinda until I was a teenager, so Uncle Pete would become a second father to me just as his wife had already become a second mother.

I don't mean that in a casual sense. Uncle Pete, more than my dad, taught me how to work. He took me hunting. He gave me information about sex when I asked. Aunt Marje was an inveterate reader and she encouraged me to do the same. She was, moreover, a singer. By that I mean she sang constantly around the house, or so it seemed; I knew no one else who did that, so when I asked her why, she said people have to "express themselves," and then she broke into another song. William Saroyan could have invented her.

Due to my grandmother's poor health, my own mother had been raised by her maternal grandmother, Esperanza Castillo, a martinet who basically prepared Mom to be a nine-teenth-century Latina. Marje had been raised by her own mixed and very American parents, and she was very much a young woman of her time. Her Spanish wasn't as good as my mother's, but that didn't slow her down; she spoke a dialect of Spanglish unknown in classrooms. She also burlesqued her bilingual kin: "Oh, you're very es-smart."

I became intimately familiar with that when my mother suffered what was called "a nervous breakdown"—almost certainly acute depression. I was almost eight years old, and devastated by the sudden absence of the woman who was the center of my world. Grandma Ton and Aunt Marje stepped in and mothered me with everything from kisses to swats. Their style was lighter than my mother's, so I had to get used to less tension in my life. That was rendered easier because I was used to being part of an extended family, so I settled in, lonely but not alone, until Mom returned. When Marje and Grandma left, I missed them. Later I learned that Marje missed me even more, since she and Pete were childless then.

As a young man, a broken heart sent me into depression, so Marje and Pete invited me to their Utah farm, where I worked my way back to soundness. They were able to do that because, while they were of the older generation, none of my silly rebellion had ever been directed at them. I had worked as a summer employee for Uncle Pete and lived in their house during much of high school. Moreover, both my aunt and uncle seemed far more savvy, or at least more pragmatic, than my parents did about young love and sex and heartbreak. As before, they simply made themselves available: I heard neither sermon nor lecture from them.

Three decades after Uncle Pete's early death had for a time swooped my aunt herself into a terrible depression, I was again in psychological trouble. I was gutted by guilt at having moved my mother and father from their house—the house where I grew up—and having to deposit my mother, sliding into dementia and wracked by obdurate depression, in a nursing home. I felt I had failed her in so many ways. Aunt Marje rode to the rescue. "If Sis could understand what you and Jan've done, she'd be grateful. You can only do what you can do. Were you supposed to quit your job and move back to Oildale to become her nurse? She's ill and you're doing what you have to. She'd understand…"

"Besides, Sis really is a *character*…"and Marje's stories of my mother's boyfriend Rip Ramirez ("He *was* not!" Mom always insisted) or of her bid to become Miss Atascadero Lake ("Dad forced me to," said Mom) lightened that painful time.

After my mother died, Aunt Marje immediately became the surrogate grandmother to my kids—and mother to me—and mother-in-law to Jan, central to our lives. She by then had grandchildren of her own, but she welcomed us to the core of her life.

But now my goofy aunt—voracious reader, singer of love songs, scoundrel at Old Maid, and many-layered maven of strip poker—lies dying in an Oregon hospital. People who see her there likely glimpse only an old lady, but I see the entire edifice. And I recognize that when she goes, my deepest remaining link with that side of my heritage will be gone. As a result, I find myself, well into my sixties, deeply saddened, for with her passing will go not only that sparkling personality, but a generation I so admired and that so shaped me and my own family.

On our recent visit, I observed my wife and my aunt—great and special pals—holding hands and talking about our grandson, Loki, the bright link to the future for all of us, and about the baby our daughter Alexandra now carries—can Marje live long enough to see her or him?

I didn't see an old lady in that bed. I saw, instead, a lovely woman sprinting onto an airport tarmac, far ahead of other family and friends, toward the plane that returned me home from the army in 1960. Her emotions have always been there to be enjoyed or endured...but there. Thank God my kids got to know her. Thank God we all did. Thank God Loki did.

My aunt broke my reverie that day when she asked, "So you have a new book coming out soon, Gerry?"

"Yep."

"Well, you always were a fart smeller...Oh, did I say that?" she grinned. "I meant smart feller, of course. Very es-smart," then she winked at my wife.

Slightly over a month later, my aunt died and this earth lost a special spirit.

Football Lessons

OUR NEIGHBOR'S SON is playing high school football, and she's not entirely comfortable with that. The other day she asked me if I'd ever played. Well...

The long-ago Bakersfield afternoon when my nose was broken for the first time remains as vivid as a lightning strike to me. A running back was trying to veer away but I cut him off, lowered my shoulder, and began to clamp my arms before we collided. I remember only the impact.

When I came to, the middle of my face was numb and my vision was blurred, but I managed to plant first one leg, then the other, then stand. I swayed there between boyhood and manhood—a high school freshman, willow slim, without a whisker on my face—then the coach grabbed my shoulder pads and said for the entire team to hear, "Good hit!"

Tasting my own blood but savoring that intonation— "Good hit!"—a chunk of childhood slipped from me like a loose cocoon. In a society that had lost most of its rites of passage, the controlled violence of football was essential for this young male. As a result, I began then to understand that there were worse fates than physical injury: cowardice, for example, was one, but fear wasn't. I would also learn that losing was by no means the worst possibility, but that not making an honest effort might well be. Life wasn't *supposed* to be easy and on the football fields of Kern County, it wasn't.

I soon perceived some negative aspects of the sport too. It is of course hazardous, but that titillating edge of danger is necessary if you are to test yourself. It is also closely linked to emerging sexuality and often encourages youthful crudity.

Some people—especially ex-players—overvalue football, and that can lead—has lead—to both elitism and arrogance. Does it build character as some coaches claim? As far as I've been able to observe, athletes by no means automatically become better citizens.

My own most important football lesson came when I was a high school junior. After starting on a championship JV squad for two years, I quit the varsity when the coach didn't select me for the first string. The team went on to win the district championship, and I absorbed an important lesson about my own importance.

The following summer I weightlifted, ran, trained harder than I ever had, and apologized to the coach and my erstwhile teammates. I was allowed to rejoin the squad. There were four complete strings of varsity players, but I began as a one-man fifth team, behind kids who couldn't do jumping jacks without falling. They, at least, were not quitters. It was up to me to prove that I deserved to play with young men who didn't fold when things didn't go their way—whether they could do jumping jacks or not. I kept my mouth shut and did everything I was told, then more.

Coming back wasn't easy—nor should it have been—but I finally managed to become a starter, to gain some yards, score some touchdowns, and break my nose once more in those days before face masks. That year, 1954, I absorbed the worst defeat I ever suffered as a player, 0–22 at the hands of Fresno's San Joaquin Memorial.

Ironically, I contributed perhaps my best prep game that night under lights. As the clock wound down, I was still running hard when a future USC starter named Larry Snyder barreled me into his team's bench as I broke a counter play off tackle. I was untangling myself from various Panthers when Snyder grabbed my shoulder pads and jerked me to my feet. He outweighed me by sixty pounds and was an immeasurably more gifted athlete but, thinking he wanted trouble, I thrust my thin chest against his.

"Nice run, guy," he grunted and he slapped my helmet.

Later I would play college football, where I absorbed another lesson: at Sacramento State, I believed that the coach would one day come to his senses and insert me into a game where I would, of course, save the day. Midway through the 1957 season, I had seen only spot duty. Then, in the midst of a close game versus UC Davis, the coach called my name: "Haslam!"

I leaped to my feet, sprinted to him as I fumbled with my helmet, and he said, "Give me your jersey. Leroy tore his and we forgot the extras." Under floodlights in front of ten thousand people, my shirt was stripped and, while my teammates did their best to shield me from view, one more layer of illusion came off with that green-and-gold jersey. I lived through it.

In fact, I was one of the lucky ones able to play after college, but not within the NFL. On the wall of my office today hangs a photograph taken in Wurzburg, West Germany, on Thanksgiving Day in 1959. Still slender as a ballerina, I stand arm in arm with a muscular black man from Mississippi named Richmond Barber, my best friend on the Third Infantry Division's team. We appear exhausted. The front of my jersey and pants are stained with mud, grass, and blood from my much-broken nose; a dazed grin plays across my face. Rich is more somber, his eyes hooded, ominous. We had just completed the final football game of our lives, a 7–0 victory over a better team.

There is a certain defiance in that photograph because racism was rampant among American soldiers in Europe then. At Mainz that year, a black teammate and I were physically attacked by white GIs at a restaurant for the crime of dining together. In a game, though—black, white, or brown—we were as good as our performances: football allowed us more equality than American society at that time encouraged. Rich and I were peers on the field and would forever remain equals off it.

A couple of years after that final game, I married, became a father, and embarked on a career as a writer. It proved more difficult than football, but the discipline and perseverance I had learned as an athlete braced me. Despite what must have been hundreds of rejections, I continued arising at 5:30 a.m. and writing each day. Eventually I produced a successful book.

Thirty years after my last football game, fifteen years after my first book, my father lay dying at our house. Ravaged by strokes and other infirmities, his athletic body had become a trap, but my family and I kept him with us and cared for him as best we could. Those were not easy times, but when Pop finally died, we were comforted by the knowledge that we had not quit. And now, afflicted with cancer myself, I have no plans to give up...I tried that once and it didn't work.

Death of an Athlete

In my dreams I see you as I never saw you, a golden lad of autumn slashing into opponents on the green gridiron of the Los Angeles Coliseum: sweeping around Florida's end, running down Stanford's halfback, slamming Northwestern's quarterback to the turf. Young, swift, and tough, you are Speck Haslam...my dad.

WITH HIS BEST FRIEND, VERDI BOYER, my father was half of UCLA's first outstanding tandem of guards. In 1931, he helped Bruins achieve football respectability. Previously losers to small colleges like Occidental, Cal Tech, and Redlands, losers even to high school squads, that year the Blue and Gold emerged as rivals to USC. They actually upset the nation's number one team, St. Mary's College.

My dad, who weighed only 165 pounds, was the smallest and fastest Bruin, as well as one of the most aggressive and most frequently hurt. "If it weren't for injuries," wrote a *Los Angeles Examiner* reporter at the end of Pop's first UCLA season, "diminutive 'Speck' Haslam would surely be first-team All-American."

That was then. Now he was hurt again.

The gift my wife, Jan, and I gave Pop for what would be his final birthday last December may seem strange: since he was too infirm to appreciate presents, I sent twenty bucks to the Tejon Club, a neighborhood bar he had frequented in Oildale, my hometown, and asked the owner to buy a round of beers for his cronies.

A few days later a birthday card arrived from the club signed by Pop's pals. By then he was in the hospital and only marginally responsive. Nonetheless, when I read the signed names to him, the slightest hint of a smile crossed his face, and his dull eyes opened, focused, and squinted for a moment at the card. It was the last time I would ever see any distinct emotion in his face.

A week earlier, two days before Christmas, Pop had begun aspirating not only liquids but the pureed foods he had previously managed to swallow, and I had rushed him to the local emergency room. He was grunting curses all the way, fighting the forces destroying him, unwilling to surrender.

At the emergency room a team worked quickly. The doctor in charge, a pal of mine, called me into his office, explained the results of various tests: aspiration pneumonia plus an occult infection were the immediate threats. Then he asked, "How aggressive do you want us to be?"

It was a question for which I thought I was prepared. Nevertheless, standing there in that small alcove, my father's gasps echoing through the room, my resolve nearly failed me. Then I replied, "If it was me, I wouldn't want anything exceptional done. Just treat his problems, but no ventilator, no heroic efforts if his heart fails. Let nature take its course."

"Okay, we'll get an IV started and work him up, but we'll no-code him. Listen," my friend added, "hope for the best but expect the worst. He's in rough shape."

"I know." After having watched my father gradually, inexorably come apart, I recognized that death was by no means the worst result. The next morning, however, Pop's breath had quieted and his hands were no longer clenched blue. He had survived, but he remained trapped in the purgatory his body had become.

My father and Verdi had earned All-American honorable mentions in both 1931 and 1933. They had also been champion wrestlers in their weight classes. Professional football had offered them an alluring though by no means financially rewarding career—a chance to extend the joy of competition and attendant celebrity. Verdi accepted an offer from the LA Bulldogs and urged my dad to do the same, but Speck decided he needed a steadier income in order to marry my mother and raise a family, so he took a job in the oil fields near Bakersfield. He later regretted that choice because it closed the most exhilarating segment of his life.

In those loosely regulated times, my father had already played seven years of football after high school—for a junior college, a military academy, and UCLA. He had been, he told me, a kind of football mercenary, part of a group imported by coach Bill Spaulding to turn UCLA's program around.

Pop had previously started at guard for four years at little Santa Maria High School, leading the Saints into the state championship play-offs in 1926 and 1927. Also a state meet–quality sprinter and a basketball standout, he captained that '27 grid squad and was student body president.

Fifty-five years later, subtle clues told us we were losing the man we'd known: forgetfulness, clumsiness, somnolence. He had been the neighborhood's bicycle repairman before his illness, donating time and parts to help kids keep their bikes on the road, but he slowly let it go. Then his driving became erratic. Long a social drinker, he continued imbibing at the Tejon Club or the Oildale Moose Lodge, but now friends had to bring him home because he became disoriented. His coordination began to unravel, his walk slowed to an awkward shuffle.

By the time we moved him in with us, my father's concentration had vacated. He might pull on two or even three pairs of trousers or put his legs into the arms of a sweatshirt. A CAT scan revealed scars in his brain from a number of small strokes: multi-infarct dementia. That same damage had also caused locomotor ataxia—the destruction of his once-superb reflexes—so he could become stuck trying to negotiate a corner or doorway and would have to stand, stiff as stone, calling one of us or cursing the body that was failing him. Soon he was fully incontinent. There was no up for Speck Haslam during those years.

Last spring, Verdi visited and, in the midst of that morning's stories and laughter, Pop's old buddy turned to my wheelchair-bound father and growled, "Hey Speck, wanna wrestle?" A grin immediately lit my father's face and his dull eyes briefly twinkled: he did indeed wanna. His body was skewed, his mind vague, but his spirit remained unbroken. People who didn't know him might have seen only a broken old man, but we— Verdi, Jan, and I—saw the sum of his life.

In a perverse way, this terrible period offered a redemption because we were able to really get to know my dad and to show him our love. We could not significantly improve his condition, of course, but we could see to his needs, protect his dignity, and involve him in our lives as his own withered. If we had a party, Pop was part of it. If he had a problem, we dealt with it discreetly. We saw to it that some family member was always there when he needed us.

A rabbi once observed, "Not to know suffering means not to be a man." My father was certainly a man, worn and battered and unyielding—a man. Afflictions purged him of many things, but not of tenacity or valor. As he had played football fiercely despite injuries, his spirit did not bend when his body was devastated by illnesses. My physician friend observed, "He just might be too damned tough for his own good." My dad had to be destroyed before he could die.

Like my mother, I'm a Roman Catholic, but my dad was not. When I was twelve, Pop encountered a priest he liked so he took instructions in the Faith and came to admire Catholicism as a culture, but the mysterious theology simply didn't make sense to him. I used to kid him, saying I would one day sprinkle him with holy water and make a Catholic of him. He laughed at that suggestion.

Once, when I was grown and raising a family of my own, he asked if I really believed "that stuff." I told him the truth: I consider the human mind to be a distinctly limited instrument and believe life's meaning is beyond rational grasp. I further believe there is a reality dwelling beyond the cusp of the known and the unknowable, and I willingly acquiesce to the supernatural promise of Christianity.

Pop had grunted something, probably more convinced than ever that I'd earned one or two degrees more than necessary at the university.

When I rushed him to the emergency room that fateful night ten years ago, I was told there was a good chance my father would not live to see morning. He and I were alone briefly in an alcove while nurses and doctors prepared to clear his lungs, so I said, "Okay, Pop, I warned you." Then I turned on a tap in the metallic sink behind him, cupped water in one hand, and sprinkled it on his forehead, saying, "I baptize you in the name of the Father, and the Son, and the Holy Ghost."

At worst, I got his forehead wet. At best, I guaranteed that in some fashion I'll be with my dad again. That was my final gift to him, but it was a gift to me as well. When I told my parish priest that I'd baptized my dad, Father Mike said, "Then he's with God now."

Shortly before that hospital visit, Verdi had said to me, "There wasn't any quit in Speck. Knocking him down wasn't enough. You had to *hold* him down."

Ten days later, Speck was held down for the last time. My family and I took solace in the fact that we had seen things through to a natural conclusion. We had done our best to live up to the tenets of the faith that supported us and the heritage that nurtured us.

In my dreams, Pop, the game ends: you and Verdi embrace, slap each other's backs and grin. Then, your blue-and-gold uniform smudged with grass and mud but bright in autumn sunlight, you glance over your shoulder at Jan and me, and a smile crosses your freckled face. You give us thumbs up, a wink, then square your shoulders and jog boldly into that long, dark tunnel at the end of the Los Angeles Coliseum.

Voices of a Place

DAWN AFTER A RAIN in the Great Central Valley of California:
to the east, a veneer of orange rims the crest of the Sierra
Nevada, a thin electric line against nearly starless indigo, then
the sky becomes a cantaloupe slice and sounds rise: a chorale
of birds; far in the distance, roosters are interrupted by the
cough and bawl of a reluctant tractor; at a diner, laughter
accompanies first cups of watery coffee. Finally, the sun pops
free from the Sierra's ragged crest and it is time, it is time...

*Everything smelled good when you got up, and it was cool. I used
to like the way the things smelled in the morning most of all.*

Peter Epp, Jr., farmer, 1952

*If I were to live again, I would want to come to manhood in the
lee of Lassen and Shasta. There it seems to me is the* cor cordium
of California.

Lawrence Clark Powell, writer, 1978

*They drove through Tehachapi in the morning glow, and the sun
came up behind them, and then suddenly they saw the great valley
below them. Al jammed on the brake and stopped in the middle of
the road, and, "Jesus Christ! Look!" he said. The vineyards, the
orchards, the great flat valley, green and beautiful, the trees set in rows,
and the farm houses.*

John Steinbeck, writer, 1939

This vast cleft in the middle of California is one of the world's largest valleys—over four hundred miles long and fifty miles wide. Geologically, it is a trough between the Coast Range and the Sierra Nevada, with the Cascades bordering it above and the Tehachapis marking it below. The only significant break in its generally flat topography is an intrusion of plio-pleistocene volcanic rock in its upper reaches, the Sutter Buttes. It drains two great river systems—the Sacramento flowing from the north, the San Joaquin from the south— which have created paired vales within this vast valley. They constitute the world's richest agricultural region, rice and alfalfa more commonly grown north of the state capital in Sacramento, grapes and cotton typifying the larger and more intensely developed south.

Socially and economically as well as geographically, the valley can—perhaps should—be divided into three subregions: the Sacramento and the San Joaquin Valleys separated by the Sac-Joaquin Delta, an elongated riverine ganglia of streams, marshes, and islands extending roughly from Stockton to the west, connecting interior California with the Bay Area and the sea. In any case, the Great Central Valley—whatever its subregions—defies the state's flashy stereotype: it is a land in which raw, physical labor has attracted people of all colors willing to work those unforgiving fields. Scuffed boots, not Gucci loafers, characterize it.

Today, when natives return, they find cultivated fields where a year ago they hunted rabbits, stucco houses where ten years before almonds were harvested, McDonald's homogeneity replacing the Chat'n'Chew Cafe's intimacy. Amidst the area's considerable wealth, they discover the stumps of antique groves cut and torn from the earth, favorite streams dammed and tamed, old stores boarded and blank, and they die a little.

I still love Chico but...I don't know...it seems so big *anymore.*

Marie Johnson, housewife, 1984

I saw changes all around me and some were good, but I hardly recognized my side of town. They tore down the swinging casing from the cottonwood, and that tree was all that marked familiar ground.

Merle Haggard, balladeer, 1974

Even before there were humans to observe it, the valley was changing. For millions of years it was a shallow sea. After mountains uplifted, "there were extensive lakes formed by flood-season overflow in both the Sacramento and San Joaquin Valleys," reports geologist Gordon B. Oakeshott. A hundred years ago, William Henry Brewer called part of it "a plain of absolute desolation." Despite stretches of what could fairly be described as desert, especially on its west side, it was veined by Sierran rivers and blocked by marshes. During this century, those rivers have been dammed and their waters redirected; most of the marshes are gone.

American settlement has accelerated and directed change, and that settlement has itself been a response to the world's and nation's population explosion: agricultural technology leading to greater and more efficient use of land, so that the valley's apparently inexhaustible larder makes population growth possible which, in turn, creates the demand for more produce. The affluence produced by that cycle then attracts urban dwellers, leading to the paving of farmland as well as both the agricultural conversion of the little remaining virgin soil and chemically intense cultivation of existing farms, what has been described as land being used to convert petroleum into produce.

What the latter leads to is still in question, although evidence of accumulating chemical toxins is becoming undeniable: "In the entire San Joaquin Valley," writes Jane Kay, "more than one quarter of the usable ground water, or thirty million acre feet, is polluted with DBCP." Agricultural runoff, she points out, is now one of the state's major pollution sources. Norman Crow, a prominent grower in Stanislaus County, counters by claiming, "As farmers, we're probably the greatest environmentalists. We see every part of every tree, every acre of land. I'd love it if I didn't have to use these chemicals." Unfortunately, he does have to use them, and evidence of contamination continues mounting.

It is also important to note that the valley not only boasts greater agricultural riches than most nations, but also richer petroleum resources than all but a handful; one county, Kern, which has been called the cradle of California's oil industry, produces considerably more of that commodity than some OPEC nations. This is also a source of both riches and anguish, the industry indicted for various forms of pollution, for economic instability in the face of international competition, and for a history of less-than-enlightened social practices, while at the same time it offers both vital energy resources and an abundance of jobs during good times.

I come here from Texas because there was work, and I been after it ever since. You pull them slips, you dump that mud, and the boss pays you. That's what it's all about.

"Brownie" Brown, driller, 1961

Oil production in Kern County is a technological miracle. Oil around here is heavy, almost like tar, and normal production methods can't pull it out of the ground efficiently. In the sixties, however, scientists came up with an "enhanced" recovery process that injects steam into the deposits to get the oil flowing.

Roger Neal, writer, 1985

How important is this region to the state? Let Irving Stone answer: "Without this central valley, this modern-day Valley of the Nile, California would be a magnificent front, able to support less than half its population, hollow at its economic core."

Still, change is what natives notice, and people are the problem: their technology, their complexity and, most profoundly, their numbers. This greatest agricultural region on earth may stand as a paradigm for the planet...

Except for the lupins and poppies, which covered the valley in the spring, the country was semi-desert and the climate was horrible, with pea-soup fog in the winter, and 110 degrees in the summer. No one ever thought that the valley would be covered with orchards and vineyards as it is today.

Arnold "Jefe" Rojas, vaquero, 1985

No natural landscapes of California have been so altered by man as its bottomlands. The grass-rich stretches of the Great Central Valley are, for the most part, lost to orchards and vineyards, cotton and alfalfa fields. Many miles of curving green ribbon along its water courses have been eradicated, replaced by the sterile concrete of flood control and navigation channels. Most of the tule marshes of the Delta country are now neatly diked rice paddies.

Elna Bakker, ecologist, 1971

It used to be when I was coming off the Grapevine looking out over the southern San Joaquin Valley on a clear night, I could see only scattered lights—the column of white in one lane, red in another—of cars on Highway 99; a glow from Bakersfield thirty miles off in the distance; and only a few lights in the Wheeler Ridge oil field to the left and the Tejon Ranch farmlands to the right. Now there are lights everywhere.

William Rintoul, journalist, 1985

Originally three natural communities characterized the Great Central Valley: riverlands, with dense riparian forests; marshes and shallow lakes; and vast prairies covered principally with perennial bunchgrasses. All have been dramatically altered—maimed, some say. Early travelers found the valley a difficult yet rich environment: to the south, for example, four streams, the Kern, Tule, Kaweah, and Kings Rivers, fed two massive, shallow, almost unnavigable lakes that were surrounded by vegetation and filled with waterfowl. Travelers found the dry prairies blocked by icy rivers with often rampant riverine forests extending parallel to their banks as far as the land retained moisture, sometimes hundreds of yards. But most memorable to those passing through the valley were the prairies themselves.

Evidence of the area's scant rainfall surrounded travelers on the grassland; despite its marshes and rivers, this was essentially a land of low precipitation, with five to twenty inches a year falling, nearly all during the winter, and was periodically drought-stricken.

The Central Valley Project threw a little water and a great deal of electrical power at many consumers to enlist their support, but primarily it was, in design and rationale, a faucet for irrigation farmers.

Donald Worster, historian, 1985

Today irrigation keeps crops green where once grasses browned, but in those increasingly remote and shrinking places where some semblance of the original botanical community can be found, spring brings a kaleidoscopic array of wildflowers, then summer bleaches all to hay and it remains that way until the next spring. It is on just such soil that irrigation has produced riches.

But irrigation may be a mixed blessing. The pumping of groundwater, for example, has caused the valley's floor to sink—land subsidence, geologists call it—so that today many residents of the San Joaquin actually live and work over thirty feet lower than the Indians who preceded them. Another negative result of irrigation is salinity: the occurrence of various salts in soil or water in concentrations that interfere with agricultural growth; more than four hundred thousand acres of farmland are now affected by salts. And these are only two high-profile problems.

California, like many other areas of irrigated agriculture, continues to manage its soil and water systems as if there will be no day of judgment....It is projected that by the turn of the century, in just six-teen years, another million acres could be lost to salinity.

Lowell N. Lewis, director,
Agricultural Experiment Station,
University of California, 1984

Land subsidence in the San Joaquin Valley...represents one of the great changes man has imposed on the environment. About 5,200 square miles of irrigable land, one-half the entire valley, has been affected by subsidence, and maximum subsidence exceeded twenty-eight feet in 1970.

J. F. Poland, B. E. Lofgren, R. L.
Ireland, and R. G. Pugh, geologists,
1972

I believe that introduced annual plants may prevent many perennial grasses from attaining their dominance, that annuals are now a large part of the climax on many sites (if not all of it), and that alien species should be considered as new and permanent members of the grassland rather than as aliens. Their elimination from the California prairie is inconceivable.

Harold F. Heady, botanist, 1977

On the valley's level surface, perennial bunchgrass was the major cover. Across the grasslands, three large ruminants roamed: pronghorn antelope and tule elk were lowland natives, and they were joined by mule deer that grazed down from the foothills. The former are entirely gone from their valley range, while elk roam only small reserves; deer remain common on the valley's edges. The ruminants were prey for an abundance of grizzly bears. More challenging and more conspicuous than beavers or elk, grizzlies were doomed; wrote Henry Henshaw in 1876, "Perhaps few animals have suffered more from persistent and relentless warfare waged by man than this formidable bear." None has been seen in the valley since the last century, leaving humans as the area's most dangerous predators.

Other predators once swam above the valley's floor. Thick marine sediments reveal that an ancient sea covered the region before the mountains rose, and even today sharks' teeth are dug up. "Maximum thickness of [marine] sediments in the Great Valley is more than ten miles," writes Oakeshott. "The present flat floor...has been built up by sediments deposited by streams and shallow lakes during the last million years or so." As a Yokuts creation tale has it, "Once there was a time when there was nothing in the world but water..." Once the water was gone and the Yokuts settled, they did so with an intimacy unknown to the Europeans who would displace them.

My words are tied in one
with the great mountains,
With the great rocks,
with the great trees,
In one with my body
and in my heart...
And you, day,
and you, night!
All of you see me
one with this world.

"A Prayer," Yokuts

The world with which the Yokuts were one was the Great Valley. They captured waterfowl, hunted elk and antelope, harvested grasses and seeds, for they were the most numerous of the region's native dwellers, but there was diversity of human population, with four major tribes—all members of the Penutian language family—dominant: Wintu and Maidu inhabited the north; Yokuts dwelled in the south; Miwoks separated north and south with a relatively small east-central intrusion. Alfred Kroeber called the valley "the Penutian Empire," and the Penutians understood well their relationship to nature:

Thunder and Lightning are two great spirits who try to destroy mankind. But Rainbow is a good spirit who speaks gently to them, and persuades them to let the Indians live a little longer.

"Thunder and Lightning," Maidu

California's heartland boasted one of the densest native populations in North America, nearly 160,000 according to high estimates. "Here were to be found most of her [California's] Indians," writes Theodora Kroeber, "the predominant physical type, and the carriers of the most idiosyncratic culture. Three hundred tribelets of California's five hundred or more belong to this area." Living in an area that, according to their own oral histories, had never suffered a famine, valley Indians were considered wealthy and peaceful.

He-who-is-above planted different acorn trees, different berries, different clovers; he put fish in the rivers, he made all kinds of animals for the Wintu.
All Indian tribes increased all over this island. There were no whites.

"He-Who-Is-Above," Wintu

The figure and form of these Indians is graceful; both men and women are taller than ordinary. The men have the custom of smearing their heads in the form of a cross (the efficacy and mysteries of which are yet unknown to them) with white mud.

Captain Pedro Fages, explorer, 1775

The Europeans who began entering the valley in the late eighteenth century were less wealthy and considerably less peaceful than the Indians they found here. In March 1772, a party that included Captain Pedro Fages and Fray Juan Crespi climbed a spur of Mount Diablo and beheld "a plain as level as the palm of the hand," according to Crespi, "...all level land as far as the eye could see." They had discovered something unusual indeed for, as Bakker explains, "There is

no other flat area of comparable size west of the Rockies."
Moreover, the Spaniards also noted another distinct charac-
teristic of the terrain, a river so wide that Crespi claimed it
was the "largest that has been discovered in New Spain."

*29 the March N 6 Miles and encamp on river. i was obliged to
cross many Slous of the River that were verry miry and passed great
numbers of indians who were engaged in digging Roots. I succeeded
in giving to them some presents. they were small in size and apparently verry poor and miserable. The most of them had little Rbit Skin
Robes. 11 Beaver taken.*

Jedediah Strong Smith, trapper, 1828
(journal entry)

The Spanish did not settle the valley, but Americans did
trickle in—trappers like Jedediah Smith mostly, but some settlers too such as John Bidwell, John Marsh, and John Sutter—
until 1849 and the gold rush made it a place to hurry through
in order to reach the diggings. It also became a larder; commercial hunters decimated waterfowl as well as large mammals:
deer, antelope, elk. In its naturally irrigated regions, produce was
grown; more importantly, an imported, domesticated grass—
wheat—was dry farmed and within fifteen years of the gold
rush, the valley had become one of the nation's great grain-
producing regions. However, it was not until the coming of the
railroad and the development of sophisticated irrigation that the
agriculture burgeoned and farming communities grew.

*The great reapers were drawn by thirty mules, moving like an
army through the square miles of waving wheat. Threshing crews
worked from sunup to dark, their cooks even longer; and the mountains of chaff rose high enough, it seemed, to tower above the Sutter
Buttes. On both the Sacramento and San Joaquin Rivers, barges or
shallow draft, "dew skimming" steamers took the golden grain down
the rivers to the bay, which led to the world beyond.*

W. H. Hutchinson, historian, 1980

Standing at the edge of our city, a man could feel that we had made this place of streets and dwellings in the stillness and loneliness of the desert, and we had done a brave thing. We had come to this dry area that was without history, and we had paused in it and built our houses and we were slowly creating the legend of our life. We were digging for water and we were leading streams through the dry land. We were planting and ploughing and standing in the midst of the garden we were making.

William Saroyan, writer, 1934

It's a countryside created by enterprising landowners who carved fields from ancient lake beds, rearranged the river system of California, and relied increasingly on deadly chemicals.
Sooner or later the water and chemicals would come together.

Lynn Ludlow, reporter, 1985

Today, agriculture and the valley are virtually synonymous. Although two centuries ago most of its land would have been considered semi-desert, it is now the richest agricultural region on earth, producing more than two hundred crops, 25 percent of all table foods consumed in the United States. As Hutchinson points out, "No other economic sector in the state so directly affects every Californian. No other…occupies so much land; uses so many natural resources; involves so many people in the food chain…yet seems so much to be taken for granted."

The next time someone mentions that boring drive along I-5 link-ing the two Californias, just remind them they are crossing a facet of one of the absolute jewels of Western civilization.

Garrison Sposito, environmental scientist, 1985

Fifty or sixty years ago one farmer produced enough food for five or six other people. Now one farmer produces enough food for fifty or sixty people, and you're not going to do that with your hands on a shovel.

Jack Stone, farmer, 1984

The vast natural watershed of the Sierra Nevada makes possible the abundance of valley agriculture for, in combination with the region's rich soil and climate, it has produced even beyond the dreams of its developers. But a fourth ingredient has also been necessary: labor. Hard work and people willing to do it characterize the valley. An anonymous ballad from the 1870s sums up the toil:

> *Don't go, I say, if you've got any brains,*
> *You'll stay far away from the San Joaquin plains.*
> *At four in the morning they're hustling up tools,*
> *Feed, curry and harness ten long-eared old mules.*
> *Plow twenty-four miles through sunshine and rain,*
> *Or your blankets you'll roll on the San Joaquin plain.*

The availability of work has attracted to this area a multi-ethnic cast of tenacious settlers willing to earn their survival with hard physical labor.

Chinese, Japanese, southern European, East Indian, Mexican, Filipino, Okie, black—wave after wave of people providing migrant labor in order to claw their way up the socioeconomic ladder—have migrated to this flat territory; the result is a rigorously heterogenous culture, marred at times by xenophobia and racism, but remarkably free from the sweeps and swoops of coastal trendiness. The ready availability of laborers has, unfortunately, led some growers—especially those with massive corporate holdings that dominate valley farming—to consider it, like cheap water, their due, and that has often resulted in an insensitivity to the needs of migrant workers.

The farm labor problem of California is undoubtedly the worst in the United States. It is bad for the farmers themselves, and worse, if possible, for those whom they employ. In many respects, it is even worse than old-time slavery.

San Francisco Morning Chronicle,
September 5, 1875

No matter how familiar one may be with "rural" California, it is always rather surprising to note the manners and appearance of the gentry who step forward to speak in the name of "the farmers" at legislative hearings in Sacramento. These men are "operators" not "farmers."

Carey McWilliams, historian, 1949

"It's never popular to be poor—only in the Bible," he said. "A man must have invented stoop labor because a snake never would."

Chester Seltzer, writer, 1969

Agriculture is, of course, not the only industry in the Great Central Valley, but it dominates both the image and reality of the region. Despite the fact that, suicidally it seems, the region loses thousands of farm acres each year, despite the fact that it now boasts perhaps the fastest-growing population in the state, despite the fact that many small towns have been engulfed by its growing cities, the valley nonetheless remains a rural area, one that retains cultural values unglossed by the sudden sophistication of urban life. Turn on the radio and you'll hear music not apt to be piped into an elevator—Mexican rancheros or traditional country. Look around and you'll see more dark faces with white foreheads—or dark faces with dark foreheads—than stylish tans. Listen carefully and you'll hear many languages other than English and Spanish: Tagalog, Basque, Sikh, Laotian, and Yokuts among many others. While some residents certainly succumb to passing fashions and gaze longingly at coastal cities, they tend in fact not to be people who work the soil but those who indirectly gain income from it.

*And there's another thing: an excellent labor supply here. People
are steady, hardworking, very little turnover. Something about these
people here, they give a day's work for a day's pay.*

John Somerhalder, division head,
Tenneco West, 1984

*The small owner's landscape is a scattered, localized one, clustering
at the edges of towns, where jobs are available. . . . The landscape of big
ownership stretches all around the small holdings, a sea in which the
waves are arranged in orderly, dirt-brown rows.*

David Rains Wallace, writer, 1984

"Outside the towns," writes James D. Houston, "it is still a
land of pickup trucks and horse trailers and hay bales, a land
of row crops and cattle herds, with vast rice fields in the north
and walking beams that sprout from oil fields in the far
south." And those elements contribute mightily to the particular *sense* of valley life that many natives retain even after education and employment have deposited them elsewhere.
Unless they were part of that tiny, elite caste protected from
tule fog and summer sun by the comforts of wealth, they will
have confronted nature. The area's poets touch a core:

*The fog, that nightlong had lain to the fields,
Earth-loving, lifted at noon, broke to no wind,
Sheeted the sky blue-gray and deadened.
The sun somewhere over the dark height ran steeply down west;
And that hour, silence hanging the wide and naked vineyards,
The fog fell slowly with twilight, masking the land.*

William Everson, Selma

*Late November: a sixty-knot
squall through Carquinez
Strait breaks*

levees, backs salt water miles
inland to preserve
what it kills...

Dennis Schmitz, Sacramento

In our ditch
there are water skaters,
frogs,
tall reeds,
mud bugs,
apple cores and plum seeds,
and little naked children.

Khatchik Minasian, Fresno

In the wild rice fields two rivers meet;
one river from the north bears soil
so fertile that the dead
grow
in their graves.
The other carried the cleaned bones
and empty skin
of animals that once lived
inside the mountain snows...

Gary Thompson, Chico

Winter,
infiltrator of soft linings
perfect tooth of stone,
thief of horses
and children...
When we call, our voices
turn and come meekly
back to us.

Roberta Spear, Hanford

They are varied voices from a varied place where once elk
and antelope roamed, where grizzlies prowled and marshes
hid legions of red-winged blackbirds, where primeval riparian
forests were erogenous zones for lovers intent on secret ren-
dezvous. Today at least some of its land is toxic, a by-product
of scientific farming. Like the rest of California, it is beginning to evidence the ravages of overpopulation. With all its
apparent open space, the valley is vulnerable: it cannot feed
the nation if it is paved; it cannot provide water from contaminated wells; it cannot grow crops in poisoned soil.

Still, in the face of evidence of slow deterioration, the valley retains a stark, sometimes deceptive beauty—here desolate,
there verdant. Concern about human exploitation of the
region is well-founded. But nature is resilient; people may fill
the valley and abuse it, but nature controls the water, the soil,
the weather. How much more human manipulation can this
land endure? People must understand and work within nature's
constraints lest the biological tragedy at Kesterson Reservoir
become but the first visible stage of a downward spiral here in
the Golden State's heartland.

*More recent observations by experts are that the dangerous waste
product is menacing wildlife in the largest expanses of the grasslands
districts in the valley—a far bigger territory than Kesterson. Birds are
being found with selenium levels resembling or exceeding those found
in Kesterson wildlife.*

Editorial, *San Francisco Examiner,*
June 23, 1985

Nonetheless, on summer afternoons when the sun begins
to slip beyond the Coast Range and the frequently polluted
sky hovers dangerously on the cusp of red, irrigators lean
against their shovels and gaze westward across textured crop-
lands, wrinkled rows in soil shadowed by clods, certain that
this their reality is sufficient. But those men and women of
the land tend not to perceive the larger pattern: the place
Sposito identifies as "the most productive agricultural area in

the history of the world" continues to be manipulated, possibly maimed. The old vaquero, Arnold Rojas, who has lived here for three-quarters of a century, sees things clearly: "Some day we will have to plow up the malls to plant something we can eat."

Oildale

To GAZE DEEP WITHIN MYSELF, I walk the streets of Oildale. On December 23, 1985, a frigid tule fog obscuring all but the nearest yards and houses, I wander up McCord Street—no sidewalks here, but many trailer parks in an area where once Dust Bowl migrants built hovels—and I notice two banty roosters scratching and jerking on a patch of brown Bermuda grass, eyeing one another but ignoring, as nearly as I can tell, two wild doves feeding with them. I stop and for a few moments stand motionless, watching while my breath bursts white, then one dove flies with a muffled whir and the other poses warily. Both roosters pause, fighters awaiting the bell.

With a hollow warble, the second dove climbs swiftly into the gray surrounding us, leaving me on the sandy border between lawn and street. I notice then two pickups parked on the far border of the Bermuda, one ancient and huge, the other new, small, and crowned with four yellow fog lights. On the older vehicle's blotched surface someone has painted "Trust Jesus." A bumper sticker on the new one says, "If you love something, set it free. If it returns, it is yours. If it doesn't, hunt it down and kill it." The smaller pickup is metallic red, as are the roosters.

The neighborhood through which I wander is called Riverview because before a dam was constructed in the mountains east of town, you could view the Kern River flowing through your kitchen during wet winters. It was once considered the least prosperous section in this unaffluent and unincorporated community. Today, although new housing developments sprout on Oildale's outskirts, many of the same unpainted shanties I used to see here as a kid in the 1940s remain erect and apparently unchanged—like tribal elders, reminders of our collective past. Two or three rickety lawn chairs—poor people's air conditioners—sit in front of many such residences, as do cars or trucks whose grandeur often contrasts sharply with the setting.

Such older houses are now bracketed by ubiquitous trailer parks and what realtors like to call upgraded houses. The former feature everything from modern mobile homes complete with metallic awnings and metallic porches, to geriatric travel trailers, faded and frayed. Most of the upgraded houses are carefully painted and their yards may be tended by dark-skinned men from other communities; moreover, there seem to be more and more signs announcing security systems, indicating perhaps a siege mentality, the long shadow of hard times past.

Now contiguous with Bakersfield, Oildale grew north of the larger town during the early years of this century. Lawrence Clark Powell worked in the area in the early 1920s and even then, he tells me, "We learned to leave the Oildale guys alone, thank you." It was an enclave of oil-company camps, attracting a disproportionate number of males who did hard, physical labor, and pursued rough, masculine diversions. Except that agriculture and not petroleum was the principal lure, this was also the pattern for much of the San Joaquin Valley, where waves of migrants have been attracted since the 1870s not by gold nuggets or movie careers but by the availability of what can only be called toil: Chinese, Japanese, East Indians, Mexicans, Filipinos, blacks, plus many varieties of whites.

Despite their resulting heterogeneity, most agricultural towns have by no means been racially integrated but have at least hosted residents of varied colors, whereas the oil industry, unofficially but actually, did not welcome nonwhites. So towns like Taft, Coalinga, and Oildale developed racist reputations. In my youth there was even said to have been a sign—which no one ever saw but everyone talked about—on the outskirts of town: "Nigger, don't let the sun set on you here."

In any case, my hometown's renown as a rough section intensified following the so-called Dust Bowl migration of the 1930s when large numbers of Southwesterners settled here. This is Merle Haggard's home town; Buck Owens Enterprises is a major local business. Today, fifty years after that migration began in earnest, and now boasting its own hospital, its own high school, its own civic organizations, Oildale is nonetheless spoken of by local liberals as a redneck enclave.

A close friend of mine—a Bakersfield boy who understands well what my hometown *means* locally—mentioned the other night that his therapist had suggested that Oildale is a crucible for fascism, which might simply mean that people here voted for Ronald Reagan, hyperbole being what it is. But my friend guessed that the three Rs—racism and rowdiness and the right to bear arms—were troubling her, so he rattled the therapist's cage, telling her about the night a group of us, all high school pals, had driven to my house from Bakersfield. In our exaggerated sense of adventure, we had suggested that the one black among us duck as we entered Oildale—he'd laughingly complied—then we had dashed from the car into my place where we'd spent the night.

While our dramatics were unnecessary, they symbolize an aspect of Oildale's lingering reputation among those who do not live here: it is said to be an environment unconducive to notions as diverse as affirmative action, gun control, cigarette warnings, and seat belts. More to the point, Oildale has been to Bakersfield as Bakersfield has been to California, a scapegoat; "You're from *Oildale?*" I've heard at genteel parties, tone saying it all.

It is also what thin-wristed experts like to call a working-class area, and it remains predominantly white. Because so many of Oildale's citizens over the years have been fair-skinned Southwesterners, lovers of country music and the self-serving version of patriotism it posits, the community has been assigned a gothic Southern stereotype. This has been aided by the more important fact that many white migrants were poorly educated, products of generations of yeomanry, so they had to compete with nonwhites for jobs on nearby farms or work in the now-integrated oil fields. More than a little local pontification on matters racial has been in fact an expression of economic fear.

Racism, as well as other narrowness, hangs on most desperately among the desperate, but in this state it cannot be easily separated from issues of social class, for the latter, usually unspoken but as real and as certain as the surging of sex, often triggers racist regression. Here in California some non-whites—the number need not be large, only visible—have been able to take advantage of the state's educational system to escape chronic destitution and assumed inferiority. While the society as a whole benefits from such a development, to whites stranded on that same desperate level, the underclass, even the slightest gain for nonwhites is clear evidence that something is wrong with America: *This is white country but a damn Mescan's bossin' me. Shee-it!* This is one reason why racist organizations tend to contain so many marginal members rather than men and women of accomplishment; the former are the threatened ones.

In the court of $225-a-month houses across the street from my folks' place, I see fair-skinned young men with long unkempt hair, bearded, disheveled, angry after three beers at a world that does not offer them well-paid jobs or much prestige but does provide drug dealers to rip them off and does provide candy bar and soda pop lunches. They carry home-made tattoos on their knuckles, and their shoulders are splendid with murals of nude women on horses, but few high school diplomas grace their mantels: school sucks, man. If asked, they will often reveal that they are about to tell someone off or to kick someone's ass.

Christmas Eve, 1984, I walked out of my mother and father's small house and heard howls and screams from the courts: one young man was beating another in the street while two women shrieked and a third man yelled encouragement. The puncher was shouting over and over at the punchee something like "Take my fuckin' money!" It was not a new scene to me, but that night it struck me: those cries should have echoed through the halls of Congress, or through that therapist's office, because they were battling each other in lieu of opponents they could neither see nor understand. And I, raised on this street, having seen my father fight here and having bled here myself, fresh from a comfortable Christmas celebration with my family, I knew exactly what was going on, and was swept by imprecise guilt along with enormous gratitude for my own good fortune. But I did not allow myself to say, "There but for the grace of God go I," for I did indeed go there, or at least some part of me did. A moment later, a sheriff's cruiser pulled up and I returned to the warmth of family within my parents' house, reminded as my hometown frequently reminds me of the proximity and the possibility of poverty, and of its consequences.

Not only young men dwell in those $225-a-month units. My own grandmother lived in one—$50 a month then—and those small houses have long been refuges for the impecunious old. Many young women reside there too, more all the time it seems, often single mothers, also poorly educated and often tattooed—a small butterfly on a shoulder, a rose on one breast. In their too-young, too-fleeting primes they may combine bad teeth with bodies that make men gnaw chrome, but their boyfriends gnaw something else and soon babies ride on each hip; with them come food stamps, hours watching daytime television and, usually, revolving males who cannot support themselves, let alone families; and with them may come the unfocused outrage that accompanies an erosion of hope.

As is true of people floundering at the bottom, these young and old, women and men, tend not to see over the rim to reality, so they remain frustrated by and angry at a world that offers them only blue-light specials. And when things go wrong, as they so persistently do, someone must be blamed: mother dies and the damned doctors are responsible; the car doesn't run and the dirty Japs are guilty; I don't get the job because that other bastard has suck. Niggers cause this, and Jews, and slopes, but mostly niggers because blaming blacks has long been an acceptable way for lower-class whites to vent general grievances. Anyway, Rambo or Jimmy Swaggart or the Klan will save us—white men banded together. And no niggers better move into Oildale because this is white people's territory; at least we're better than niggers. It is an irrational, probably unavoidable stance, one held with the desperate, uncritical grip of divine revelation: it *must* be true.

My own parents, for reasons I've never fully understood—his better education, probably, and her Latin attitudes—but for which I remain constantly grateful, did not indulge in such delusion. Instead, they taught me to accept people as individuals; my dad's dictum, for example, was "Is he a good guy?" not "Is he colored?" Thus Quincy Williams and Freddie Dominguez and John Takeuchi slept and ate at our house, just as did Raymie Meyer and Ernie Antongiovanni and Tommy Alexander. If my folks had given me only that I would have been well served.

Poverty and race and class churn a bitter stew: history dictates that a much larger proportion of blacks than whites inhabits the dungeon of unabating want, so race has been and remains an effective camouflage for our system's inability to reach many endemic poor. Because it is convenient to keep the hungry fighting one another, racism is frequently *part* of poverty, just as idealized egalitarianism is *part* of liberalism: default assumptions.

I must challenge my pal's therapist: Oildale is not a breeding ground for fascism, but poverty certainly is, poverty and ignorance and hopelessness so deep that education and government programs cannot deflect it. My hometown is a place where low-rent housing and the rumor of jobs for the unskilled have traditionally attracted whites on the bottom hoping to struggle toward the middle.

Those who do make that transition may carry lower-class fears and prejudices longer than is conscionable, but the real problem is that others never make it. In Oildale you cannot be unaware of this nation's class system because this is a cusp where hopelessness and hope, or at least the *hope* of hope, abut. When even that slimmest of threads frays, despair engulfs and violence erupts, in Oildale as elsewhere.

Therein lies the rub. Without this community and its unpretentious styles, many people would be utterly abandoned by a society that fears fascism or attacks socialism but dreads and distrusts losers most of all, would be ignored by an elite often willing to love the poor only as it imagines them, not as they are: hopeless as well as hopeful. Since the poor exist, they must exist somewhere, and Oildale predictably harbors a proportionate number of losers: *Who's got the dope, man?*

But the losers constitute a small if visible minority here. I stride past the Assembly of God on Wilson Street, and from within I hear voices raised to a God who can accept, and I hear people—some of them from the courts, grown broad-hipped and repentant—praying for me, their brother burdened by sins unknown to them, but burdened, surely burdened, because that is the human condition and with God's help it can be endured. In that congregation now as in the neighborhood, one might find a sprinkling of dark faces reflecting the slow erosion of stereotypes as well as the enduring truth that class profoundly influences the acceptance of nonwhites—too rich or too poor excluded. Unfortunately, the continued lack of blacks also illustrates the persistence of America's most heinous racist illusion.

What fearers of fascism forget is that most of Oildale is populated by folks who have established themselves in the middle class by dint of hard work, survivors whose daughters now aim for honor roll and university, whose sons play football and fight wars. Oildale's citizens pay their taxes, frequently resent welfare, and shake their heads at punk rock, at "Fit 'n' Forty" medallions, at sprout sandwiches, but accept the churning present anyway. When I stroll through town, nearly everyone I meet says hello, often with a Southwestern drawl. Folks I've never seen before discuss the weather—"This *dern* fog…"—while waiting for traffic to pass. Their children have no drawls at all.

I notice other things on my visits home, little glimpses I no longer take for granted. On North Chester Avenue, aging men and women who struggled here from Oklahoma now drink coffee in a McDonald's that is identical with several in Tulsa. There seems to be an inordinate number of "Beware of Dog" signs, especially on those blocks populated by folks who have edged into the middle class. And on winter mornings if fog doesn't obscure the world, steam plumes rise from the hills north where, on the leases that lured so many here, leases where my father and I worked, heavy oil is liquefied by the hot vapor, then pumped to the surface.

It seems to me now that older women always boast hair care comparable to matrons in Palm Springs, their tresses freshly dyed, curled, piled, and sprayed. Coiffures are taken seriously even if bodies are not. The other morning, at about 9 a.m., I passed a gal unlocking the front door of a beer bar, her hair deep red and elaborately swirled high above a leathery face imprinted "Texas, 1914." A cigarette dangled from her crimson lips when she smiled at me. I smiled back.

And there is an aggressive angle at which many men wear hats—billed caps, straw Stetsons, but no plaid snapbrims or berets—that advises you not to let your mouth overload your ass. Short sleeves may be rolled up, biceps bulging, and beer drinking after work seems sacramental. Cars and guns are icons taken seriously, offering reasons for taking oneself seriously.

It is finally the mix of people hereabouts that most compels: friendly, plainspoken, conservative, protestant in work ethic if not religion, scarred but not embittered by hard times, they constitute what I like to call a "front porch" society. In the days before air conditioners tamed the long, scorching summers, it was common for neighbors to gather on porches, drink iced tea, perhaps play cards or checkers, occasionally sing to the accompaniment of a guitar or banjo, but usually just talk. Many older folks still do these things, such gatherings livening balmy summer evenings, while kids clatter up and down sidewalks on skateboards now rather than skates.

Oildale is changing as the rest of California is, but its reputation is not altering apace. There is a sidewalk in front of my parents' place, built by the WPA in 1941, or so says the inscription on the corner. There is also a small parking strip there with a tree that has been so brutally trimmed that scar tissue knots it like tumors—a peculiar local style of arboreal coiffure that seems more ritual maiming than practical necessity. Below it, on summer mornings, runoff water from lawn irrigation settles in the gutter to make a small pond, and every morning if I arise early I can sip coffee with my dad and watch doves drinking out there—an unchanging reality—dipping their fawn heads, bobbing their white-splashed tails. They rise with a whir when a truck bounces past on its way to the oil fields. Then the birds return, drink again, and occasionally call—a haunting, hollow sound that says "Home."

Permissions

Special thanks go to Clark Sturges and Devil Mountain Books for their helpfulness and generosity.

"The Doll," "Sally Let Her Bangs Hang Down," "She's My Rock," and "Ace Low" are reprinted from *Okies*, published by Peregrine Smith, Inc. © 1973, 1975 by Gerald Haslam.

"Walls," "Happily Ever After," and "The Great Kern County Gator Hunt" are reprinted from *The Wages of Sin*, published by Duck Down © 1980 by Gerald Haslam.

"The Call of the Great Frog King" and "Hey Okie!" are reprinted from *Hawk Flights: Visions of the West*, published by Seven Buffaloes Press © 1983 by Gerald Haslam.

"That Constant Coyote," from *That Constant Coyote: California Stories*, by Gerald Haslam. © 1985 by Gerald Haslam. Reprinted with the permission of the University of Nevada Press.

"Growing Up at Babe's" is reprinted from *Voices of a Place*, published by Devil Mountain Books © 1987 by Gerald Haslam.

"Death of a Star-Nosed Mole" is reprinted from *The Man Who Cultivated Fire & Other Stories*, published by Capra Press © 1987 by Gerald Haslam.

"Oildale," from *The Other California: The Great Central Valley in Life and Letters*, by Gerald Haslam. © 1988 by Gerald Haslam. Reprinted with the permission of the University of Nevada Press.

"The Cusp of the Future" is reprinted with permission from *Great Central Valley: California's Heartland*, published by the University of California Press © 1993.

"Mal de Ojo," from *Condor Dreams and Other Fictions*, by Gerald Haslam. © 1994 by the University of Nevada Press. Reprinted with the permission of the University of Nevada Press.

"The Great Xmas Controversy" and "The Great Vast-ectomy Escapade" are reprinted from *The Great Tejon Club Jubilee*, published by Devil Mountain Books © 1996 by Gerald Haslam.

"Reflections from an Irrigation Ditch" and "Homage to Uncle Willie" are reprinted from *Coming of Age in California*, published by Devil Mountain Books © 2000 by Gerald Haslam.

About the Author

Gerald Haslam, the product of a California mother and a Texas father, is a blue-collar native of Oildale, in the southern end of the Golden State's Great Central Valley. He has published six volumes of nonfiction, seven collections of short fiction, and three novels, and he has edited eight anthologies. His most recent novel, *Straight White Male* (2000), won the Western States Book Award, and his latest nonfiction, *Workin' Man Blues: Country Music in California* won the Ralph J. Gleason Award from *Rolling Stone*, New York University, and BMI. He was a professor of English at Sonoma State University for thirty years prior to retirement in 1997. He now lives in rural Penngrove, where he has one wife (plenty), two dogs (plenty), five children (plenty), and six grandchildren (not nearly enough).

Great Valley Books is an imprint of Heyday Books, Berkeley, California. Created in 2002 with a grant from The James Irvine Foundation and with the support of the Great Valley Center (Modesto, California), it strives to promote the rich literary, artistic, and cultural resources of California's Central Valley by publishing books of the highest merit and broadest interest.

GREAT VALLEY

Great Valley Books and other Central Valley titles published by Heyday Books:

Workin' Man Blues: Country Music in California, by Gerald Haslam, with Alexandra Haslam Russell and Richard Chon

Peace Is a Four-Letter Word, by Janet Nichols Lynch

Magpies and Mayflies: An Introduction to Plants and Animals of the Central Valley and Sierra Foothills, by Derek Madden, Ken Charters, and Cathy Snyder

Lion Singer, by Sylvia Ross

Dream Songs and Ceremony: Reflections on Traditional California Indian Dance, by Frank LaPena

Walking the Flatlands: The Rural Landscape of the Lower Sacramento Valley, by Mike Madison

Two-Hearted Oak: The Photography of Roman Loranc, with text by Lillian Vallee

Bloodvine, by Aris Janigian

Structures of Utility, by David Stark Wilson

Highway 99: A Literary Journey through California's Great Central Valley, edited by Stan Yogi

How Much Earth: The Fresno Poets, edited by Christopher Buckley, David Oliveira, and M. L. Williams

Picturing California's Other Landscape, edited by Heath Schenker

Indian Summer: Traditional Life among the Choinumne Indians, by Thomas Jefferson Mayfield

Henry Sugimoto: Painting an American Experience, by Kristine Kim

Bitter Melon: Inside America's Last Rural Chinese Town, by Jeff Gillenkirk and James Motlow